Paul: Libertine or Legalist?

PAUL LIBERTINE OR LEGALIST?

A Study in the Theology of the Major Pauline Epistles

JOHN W. DRANE

LONDON
SPCK

First published in 1975
by SPCK
Holy Trinity Church
Marylebone Road
London NW1 4DU

Printed in Great Britain by
The Camelot Press Ltd, Southampton

SBN 281 02864 8

To Olive

Contents

Contents

Acknowledgements

Thanks are due to the following for permission to quote from copyright sources:

Wm B. Eerdmans Publishing Co., Grand Rapids, Michigan: *Theological Dictionary of the New Testament*, vols. I and II, ed. G. Kittel and G. Friedrich; and *Galatians*, by H. N. Ridderbos.

Harper and Row, Publishers, New York: *Paul, Apostle of Liberty*, by R. N. Longenecker.

Harvard University Press, Cambridge, Massachusetts: *The Singular Problem of the Epistle to the Galatians*, by J. H. Ropes.

Hodder and Stoughton Ltd: *Galatians*, by G. S. Duncan.

Longman Group Ltd: *Paul*, by M. Dibelius and W. G. Kümmel.

Marshall, Morgan and Scott Ltd: *Galatians*, by D. Guthrie.

The Paternoster Press: *Apostolic History and the Gospel*, ed. W. W. Gasque and R. P. Martin.

Rivingtons (Publishers) Ltd: *The Earlier Epistles of St Paul*, by Kirsopp Lake.

S.C.M. Press: *Essays on New Testament Themes*, by E. Käsemann.

Preface

Much of this book is based on research done in the course of preparing a doctoral dissertation accepted by the University of Manchester in 1972. It is essentially a study of the development of Pauline thought in the four major epistles (Galatians, 1 and 2 Corinthians, Romans) and the relationship between the theology of the apostle and that of his opponents.

I am indebted to Professor F. F. Bruce, Rylands Professor of Biblical Criticism and Exegesis at Manchester, who guided my original research. His personal interest in the reconstruction of Pauline thought set out here has been a great encouragement.

In the course of my research I soon realized that I was discovering far more about Paul in the context of the living church than in the study, and I wish to express my appreciation to the members of the Manchester Chinese Christian Fellowship, whose invitation to expound the book of Acts at their weekly Bible Study in 1971 first sparked off my interest in this particular approach to my subject. I must also express my thanks to the members of Glenbrook Chapel, Higher Blackley, Manchester, during the years 1969–73. Though they can hardly have realized it at the time, I probably learned more about Paul from them as we tried to see how his teaching applied to our own situation in the local church than I learned from all the literature I had previously read on the subject.

No doubt that is how Paul himself would have wished it to be. It is therefore my hope that this study will be of value not only to the academic student of theology, but also to those who are involved in the ongoing work of the church of God.

The University of Stirling,
Easter Day, 1975

JOHN W. DRANE

Abbreviations

Bauer	W. Bauer, *A Greek-English Lexicon of the New Testament*, Eng. trans. edited by W. F. Arndt and F. W. Gingrich (Chicago, 1957)
Beginnings	F. J. Foakes-Jackson and K. Lake (eds.), *The Beginnings of Christianity, Part I, The Acts of the Apostles* (London, 1920–33) (5 vols.)
BJRL	*Bulletin of the John Rylands Library*
BNTC	*Black's New Testament Commentaries*
CBQ	*Catholic Biblical Quarterly*
ENTT	E. Käsemann, *Essays on New Testament Themes*, Eng. trans. (London, 1963) (Studies in Biblical Theology 41)
EQ	*The Evangelical Quarterly*
Evan. Theol.	*Evangelische Theologie*
ExpT	*The Expository Times*
FRLANT (NF)	Forschungen zur Religion und Literatur des Alten und Neuen Testaments (Neuen Folge)
ICC	*The International Critical Commentary*
JBL	*Journal of Biblical Literature*
JTS	*Journal of Theological Studies*
KEK	*Kritisch-exegetischer Kommentar über das Neue Testament*, founded by H. A. W. Meyer
MC	*Moffatt New Testament Commentary*
NCB	*New Century Bible*
NIC	*New International Commentary*
Nov. Test.	*Novum Testamentum*
NTA	E. Hennecke/W. Schneemelcher, *New Testament Apocrypha*, Eng. trans. ed. R. McL. Wilson (London, 1963) (Vol. I) and 1965 (Vol. II)

NTQ	E. Käsemann, *New Testament Questions of Today*, Eng. trans. (London, 1969)
NTS	*New Testament Studies*
RGG[3]	*Die Religion in Geschichte und Gegenwart* (Tübingen, 1957ff.) (3rd edn), in 7 vols.
S-B	H. L. Strack and P. Billerbeck, *Kommentar zum Neuen Testament aus Talmud und Midrasch* (München, 1922–28) (Vols. I–IV), 1956–61 (Vols. V–VI)
SJT	*Scottish Journal of Theology*
TDNT	G. Kittel/G. Friedrich (eds.), *Theological Dictionary of the New Testament*, Eng. trans. ed. G. W. Bromiley (Grand Rapids, 1964 on)
THNT	*Theologischer Handkommentar zum Neuen Testament*
TU	*Texte und Untersuchungen zur Geschichte der altchristlichen Literatur*
WC	*Westminster Commentaries*
WMANT	Wissenschaftliche Monographien zum Alten und Neuen Testament
ZNW	*Zeitschrift für die Neutestamentliche Wissenschaft*

Biblical books and other ancient writings are abbreviated according to the current conventions, and are not listed here.

Commentaries on biblical books are cited in full at the first reference, but subsequently with only the author's name and the title of the biblical book in question.

Other books frequently mentioned are cited (after the first reference) with the author's name and the most important words of the title, e.g. W. Schmithals, *The Office of Apostle in the Early Church*, Eng. trans. (London, 1971), becomes Schmithals, *The Office of Apostle*.

1

The Man and his Mind

There have been just a few great men in history who, by writing a relatively small volume of literature, have managed to provoke a great avalanche of books, all written in the effort to understand their thought with greater clarity from one particular angle or another. Of no genius is this more true than of the Christian apostle, Paul. All of his writings put together would scarcely equal in length even one of the great classics of English literature, and with the possible exception of Romans, none of his books was intended to be read and studied. Most of them were hastily conceived in a mind that was under siege by one kind of enemy or another, only to be brought to birth in historical circumstances that have been and still are an enigma even to the most sympathetic observer. This is supremely true of three out of the four major Pauline writings. Though Romans appears to be a cool and calculated exposition of Paul's theology in certain of its aspects, Galatians, 1 Corinthians, and 2 Corinthians present the exegete with a plethora of unsolved mysteries, many of which seem no nearer to final solution now than they were when the Church Fathers first pitted their wits against them.

In modern times, scholars have found the key which is said to unlock the mind of the great apostle in any number of different places. F. C. Baur found that he could understand Paul best when he was placed in the context of a violent struggle in the early church between Gentile and Jewish elements of Christianity, with Paul being the main protagonist on the side of the Gentiles.[1] Not many followed in his train, if only because his theory required such a radical rewriting of most of the evidence that it was almost self-evidently doomed to failure from the start. But many scholars, perhaps even a majority, have claimed that a full appreciation of the person and teaching of Paul can only be gained through a proper understanding of his relationship to contemporary Judaism. In 1913, H. A. A. Kennedy, in his book *St. Paul and the Mystery Religions*, argued that almost everything in Paul's theology that could conceivably have had a Hellenistic background of some kind was actually to be accounted for by the fact that he had been a leading Pharisee before his conversion. More recently, W. D. Davies and R. N. Longenecker have amassed a mountain of evidence to show that Paul was so deeply indebted to his Jewish understanding of the Old Testament and of life in general that on no other basis can we hope to understand the exact nuances of his theology.[2] Jewish scholars like H. J. Schoeps have also been quick to draw attention to its similarities with the best in Judaism.[3] Yet, though it is possible to formulate a comprehensive, even a convincing, exposition of Pauline theology on these lines, we need only to glance at what is often taken to be the starting-point of that theology in the epistle to the Galatians to realize that this theory is not without its difficulties. J. C. O'Neill is far from overstating the case when he says in a recent book that 'the great difficulty about accepting all Galatians as written by Paul is that Paul can scarcely have adopted the attitude towards Judaism that sometimes appears in Galatians'.[4] If we regard Paul as a Pharisee-cum-Christian, that is certainly true. But this is precisely the thing we cannot assume. We know that Paul was a zealous Pharisee before his conversion, both from his own evidence and from that of Acts, but this does not justify us in laying down norms which he should be expected to follow as a Christian in his attitude to the Old Testament and Judaism. Even less does it provide a firm enough foundation for us to excise parts of his epistles as the later additions of interpolators and editors.

Other scholars have sought the key to Pauline theology elsewhere, in the Hellenistic and Oriental milieu that was the birthplace of the Gentile churches. This was the view of the *Religionsgeschichtliche Schule*, especially associated with the names of W. Bousset and R. Reitzenstein, whose most vigorous exponent at the present day is the German, Walter Schmithals, in his three books *Gnosticism in Corinth*, *Paul and the Gnostics*, and *The Office of Apostle in the Early Church*. According to him, the answer to every problem in Pauline theology is to be found in a proper understanding of the nature of Paul's opponents, whom he claims to have been Jewish Christian Gnostics in every case—though the distinction between apostle and opponent was one of degree only and not of substance, for Paul himself was at heart some sort of Gnostic. This approach certainly has its attraction as a single thoroughgoing explanation of Paul and his message. But it can only be upheld by a disregard for the date and origin of the Gnostic documents with which Pauline theology and that of his opponents is often compared, and those who follow such an interpretation all too often seem to have a peculiar blind spot for the fact that Gnostic theology and biblical theology are so completely different that it is hard to find anything significant that is common to both.[5]

Again, the key to Paul's mind has been sought in some process of development, whereby he was either more Jewish to start with and gradually changed his mind so that his outlook became Hellenistic;[6] or he was at first Hellenistic or Gnostic in his thought, only to change at a later date to a more legalistic Jewish attitude.[7]

In the study which is presented here, we begin by taking as objective a view as possible of Paul's theology as it is expounded in Galatians. On the basis of this we can make certain observations on the opposition Paul was dealing with in Galatia. Our observations in this regard provide a secure foundation for an analysis of the other major epistles, 1 and 2 Corinthians and Romans. Since it is clear that, whatever view we take, we cannot understand Paul without also taking some account of the nature of his opponents in each situation, the consideration of this matter will naturally be a large part of this work. In what follows here, it is argued that Paul's letter to the Galatians is a true, though extreme, representation of his thought at a time when he was facing Judaizing opposition in an especially vehement form. By using the exegetical clues provided in the Galatian epistle, it is then argued that the situation behind 1 Corinthians was quite different, involving Paul with Gnosticizing opponents. This also necessitated an about-turn in his own theological expression so that whereas in Galatians he often appears to be a libertine of the worst sort, in 1 Corinthians he operates under a cloak of pseudo-legalism. Part of the reason why Paul needed to adopt such a position was that his own earlier teaching, of a Galatians type, had combined with other elements in the historical situation to produce a Gnosticizing movement in the church at Corinth, and so Paul was not only opposing what he considered to be false teaching, but was also setting out his own teaching in a new form that would be less liable to misinterpretation. 2 Corinthians, however, presents a slightly different picture, with a new combination of a Galatians type of teaching and a 1 Corinthians type of teaching—a process of synthesis which came to final fruition in Romans, where we have a more or less balanced and neutral expression of Paul's theology, neither libertine nor legalist.

The arguments set forth here will not convince every reader. In some cases I am not fully convinced myself by every detailed part of the evidence. The mind of Paul was so complex that no one theory can ever hope to comprehend it in all its facets. This study will throw light into many a dark corner; it will inevitably leave other corners in the gloom of theological uncertainty. But perhaps this is what we might expect of a man who claimed to be no ordinary religious teacher but 'an apostle of Christ Jesus by the will of God' (2 Cor. 1.1).

2

The Letter to the Galatian Churches

The letter to the Galatians has always held a central place for interpreters of Pauline theology. There can be no possible doubt about the character of this letter as an authentic statement of Paul's convictions, and in its teaching we come close to the heart of this Pharisee-turned-Christian, as we listen first to his explanation of his own conversion and position as a Christian apostle, and then hear his repeatedly devastating denunciations of the Old Testament Law and all that it stood for, as he sets forth a new way of life, not now under the scourge of the Law, but in the freedom given by Christ. It is perhaps just these very things that sometimes make it difficult for the modern interpreter to appreciate the full impact of what Paul was saying in Galatians. We are fortunate to have in Romans a fuller treatment of many of the same themes, and there Paul explains in greater detail his attitude to the Law and to the Christian life in general. As we read Galatians, we find ourselves unconsciously linking it up with other statements made in Romans, and too often the result is that we end up with a body of thought which we call 'Pauline theology', rather than an exposition of Galatians in its own right. The aim of this chapter is to examine Galatians, and to try to understand it in its own terms. We shall see that when we do this the result is not quite what we sometimes imagine it to be. It is therefore important that we should beware of introducing teaching from other epistles to interpret or to amend Paul's clear statements in Galatians. In some cases, of course, it is only in the light of his teaching elsewhere that particular passages can be fully understood, but we should nevertheless avoid the unconscious introduction of ideas and concepts from other epistles into contexts in Galatians from which they are conspicuously absent.

Whatever view one adopts on the date and destination of the

epistle, it was obviously written in the heat of a great controversy. This point comes out clearly in the opening verses, where we find (1.1–5) a salutation which, by comparison with the general pattern followed in the other Pauline epistles, is quite unusual. It is a commonplace of exegesis to point out the significant omission of any thanksgiving for the readers' faith here, and also to notice that a more abrupt mode of expression is adopted. In writing this letter, Paul had no time for platitudes: his was the more urgent task of opposing false doctrine which was not only unacceptable to him but which, in his view, could well lead to complete disaster for the Galatian churches. At the same time Paul was eager to emphasize that what he wrote was not his own opinion, for his apostleship was 'not from men nor through man, but through Jesus Christ and God the Father' (v. 1). In view of the clearly polemical nature of the letter, we cannot expect to find here any comprehensive and balanced exposition of Paul's views on the matters discussed, and even less of those of his opponents. But since our first aim is to place Galatians in its historical context in the early church and in the development of Paul's own thought, we are obviously justified in treating its teaching in isolation, though of course we can never forget that it was by no means Paul's final word on the various matters raised.

re the Law

It is particularly important to bear this in mind as we consider some of the statements Paul makes in Galatians about the relevance of the Torah of the Old Testament. Here in Galatians Paul displays a strangely equivocal approach to the Old Testament Law. On the one hand he obviously regarded it as inspired Scripture, for he repeatedly quotes its teaching in order to support his own arguments. On the other hand, however, he can go so far as to suggest that it was not divinely originated in a direct way (3.19), though in the same context he implies that the cross of Christ was an affirmation of the Law's relevance, since its sentence of condemnation had to be carried out (3.13). When we read the rest of Paul's correspondence, especially Romans, it soon becomes clear that this apparent dichotomy can be resolved for Paul by a proper understanding of the significance of the work of Christ: the rejection of the Law is an essential consequence of the cross, though the principles it enshrines can still be regarded highly (cf. Rom. 1.2; 4.3; 3.1–2; 15.4).

But in dealing with the problems of the Galatian churches, Paul found it necessary to give not the balanced exposition which we find in Romans, but what we can only regard as a rather one-sided view of the matter. It is because of this that C. E. B. Cranfield has argued that it is 'extremely unwise to take what Paul says in Galatians as one's starting-point in trying to understand Paul's teaching on the law' ('St. Paul and the Law', in *SJT* 17 (1964), p. 62). But this is undoubtedly going too far, for Galatians is after all the starting-point made by Paul himself in his teaching on the Torah: whatever date may be given to Galatians, it is usually thought to be earlier than Romans, the other main epistle in which Paul deals with the question of Christ and the Law.

The problem with which Paul was concerned is made clear in the first section of the epistle after the salutation (1.6–9): the Galatian Christians, much to his surprise (*thaumazō*, v. 6) had, at the instigation of false teachers who had infiltrated the churches after his departure, forsaken the true gospel which Paul had declared to them, in favour of a so-called *heteron euangelion* (v. 6). In the rest of the letter Paul deals, now systematically, now in haphazard fashion, with the main elements of this false teaching, and, though the argument of the epistle is interrupted by two personal appeals to the Galatians (3.1–5; 4.8–20) and is rounded off by a final sarcastic note of triumph (6.11–18), these elements are dealt with more or less consistently. A complete outline of Paul's arguments in Galatians is given in Appendix A, where it is suggested that Paul deals in turn with three main tenets of this false teaching:

1. 1.10—2.21 shows that an important aspect of the false gospel was a denial, or at least a disparagement, of Paul's claim to divine appointment as an apostle of Jesus Christ. What he knew of the gospel was merely something he had learned by rote, employing his previous Pharisaic methods, and he had neither a direct commission as an apostle nor did he have the stamp of the authority of the foundation apostles in Jerusalem.

2. 3.6—4.7 suggests very strongly that a second major element in the false teaching concerned the person of Abraham and the promises made to him and his descendants. The false teachers were probably suggesting that, since the promise of the messianic kingdom had originally been given to Abraham and his descendants

(cf. Gen. 12.3; 18.18; 28.14 and 22.18; 26.4), anyone wishing to have a part in that kingdom ought to become a member of his family by circumcision and continued obedience to the Torah.

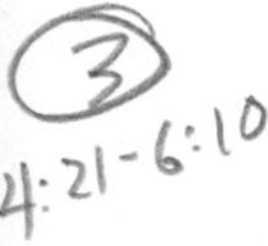

3. The third, and most widely recognized, teaching of the heretics was that Christians, even Gentiles, ought to keep the Torah and to be circumcised. This question is the subject of the long section of the epistle from 4.21 to 6.10, where Paul deals in turn with three separate questions in relation to the legalism of the false teachers: the question of the Torah (4.21—5.1); the question of circumcision (5.2–12); and the question of Christian social ethics (5.13—6.10).

In dividing up the epistle in this fashion, and suggesting that Paul was directly countering certain elements that formed a part of the false teaching, we are following the generally accepted, traditional lines of interpretation of Galatians. Our definition of the issues involved and our division of the epistle into these three sections is somewhat different from that commonly proposed by New Testament scholars. It is more usual to separate the section 5.1—6.10 from what precedes, and to view it as a general paraenetical section. But it seems better to regard it as an integral part of Paul's refutation of his opponents' arguments on the Torah and circumcision, for it was just at this point of social morality that the Jews claimed their Torah gave them a superior code of conduct in comparison with their Gentile neighbours, and if Paul was to abolish the Torah for Christians he had to show that this would not have disastrous ethical consequences.

In any event, the basic presuppositions of our approach can be found in most of the standard commentaries on the epistle. From time to time, however, the validity of this kind of approach has been questioned, and it will be a good thing to pause here and consider this fundamental matter before proceeding to an exegesis of the epistle on the basis of the scheme outlined above. We shall do so by examining an article by A. E. Harvey in *Studia Evangelica* IV, which sets out the problems involved in a most succinct and persuasive manner.[1]

Harvey begins his paper by suggesting that two possible types of opposition to Paul's teaching could have arisen in the churches. The first would be of a strictly theological nature, in which the other side was taking issue with Paul on rationally argued grounds;

and in such a case, it is legitimate for us to infer their arguments from Paul's reply to them. The question of the resurrection and its meaning, dealt with in 1 Corinthians 15, is an example of this kind of opposition. The second type, however, which according to Harvey was far more widespread, and is the type described in Galatians, concerned a situation in which Paul's addressees were behaving in ways contrary to Pauline teaching, but not on any theological grounds. Thus, for instance, the difficulties over the Eucharist dealt with in 1 Corinthians 11 can be explained as follows:

> The Corinthians have not paused to consider the implications of what they are doing; and Paul's theological treatment of the question is provoked, not by the arguments of the Corinthians, but by the fact that they clearly have not given it any serious thought at all (art. cit., p. 320).

In the light of this distinction, Harvey goes on to consider the Galatian situation, key to which he finds in the use of the verb *ioudaizein* in 2.14 (a *hapax legomenon* in the New Testament). Parallels are adduced from Greek literature and from Josephus to show that the word means not 'to hold Jewish beliefs' but 'to adopt Jewish behaviour'.[2] It is doubtful, however, whether this single occurrence of the exact word 'to judaize' can carry so much weight, even supposing that Harvey is correct in his etymological explanation of the term. Though Bauer gives as the meaning of the verb *ioudaizein*, 'to live as a Jew, according to Jewish customs', even a passing acquaintance with the Judaism of the day suggests that 'to follow the Jewish way of life' was synonymous with obedience to the Torah, which for the Jew was the norm by which life was to be regulated. The context in which the same verb is used in Ignatius' epistle to the Magnesians (10.3) suggests that it could mean more than simply following Jewish practices for their own sake. But in the context where Paul uses the word, he was far more concerned with the equivocation of Peter in regard to eating with the Gentiles than with giving a full exposition of the various ways in which the Galatian Christians could be made into Jews. What he says in the rest of the epistle can hardly leave us in any doubt that acceptance of the Jewish Law as both a religious system and a way of life played a prominent part in it.

Harvey recognizes, however, that the heart of the matter lies not here, but in Galatians 3 which, on what he called the 'traditional approach', is usually held to show that there was some theological debate involved in the opposition to Paul in Galatia. He outlines three points arising out of this chapter, with which he claims the traditional approach is unable to deal; and, having thus demolished the case of other scholars, he is able to proceed with his own reconstruction, on the basis of 6.12. The argument, however, is quite unconvincing. Harvey assumes that the issues involved in 3.6—4.7 must be circumcision and the Law (art. cit., pp. 323ff.), but we hope to show in our exegesis that this is not the *main* subject of this section at all. Rather is Paul arguing that now 'through God you are no longer a slave but a son, and if a son then an heir' (4.7). The question of the Law and circumcision is not formally introduced until 4.21—6.10. This being the case, Harvey's reconstruction of the evidence falls to the ground. The capital which he makes out of the statement in 6.12, that by accepting circumcision one could escape persecution, can readily be understood, for the Christian who was prepared to compromise on a matter of principle would obviously not scruple over avoiding the persecution that would otherwise follow his association with the church of Jesus Christ.

In addition to this, however, three major criticisms can be made of Harvey's argument here. First of all, it is clear from what Paul says in 1.6ff. that some form of doctrinal teaching is involved. He could never have spoken of practical aberrations isolated from theological beliefs as *heteron euangelion*. Again, what now follows in 1.10—2.21 on Paul's apostolic authority, becomes almost inexplicable if Harvey's view is to be accepted; for why would Paul have gone to such great lengths to establish his own position if the only issue involved was the casual, almost unconscious observance of a few Jewish practices? Finally, and perhaps most important of all, in the matter of belief and morality Paul's basic approach was almost the same as that of the Judaism of the period. Both Judaism and Christianity stood in sharp contrast to the Greek world of ideas, in which religion and ethics were quite distinct and separate. For Paul, both as a Pharisee and as a Christian, the two were inseparable: right conduct could only be the outcome of right belief.

We can only conclude that the view which sees Paul countering specific theological teachings of his opponents here is the more likely one. Yet Harvey is perhaps correct in drawing attention to one aspect of the problem which is often ignored, for it was almost certainly the case that there would be those in the Galatian churches who were following the false teaching in its practical expressions without ever having given serious consideration to the theological basis on which it was established. Those of us with any experience in the Christian ministry know all too well that even today there are always many willing to be swept along by whatever current of opinion may be flowing, without ever having any regard for the basic principles that may be involved. But this does not justify us in supposing that the problem faced by Paul was in essence practical rather than theological: it was probably both. We can accordingly now proceed to an investigation of each of the three strands of debate around which the false teaching in Galatia was centred.

I

The Question of Paul's own Position (1.10—2.21)

The first aspect of the false teaching which Paul needed to take up and refute was obviously the question of his own authority as an apostle, for unless he could establish that he had himself experienced a direct call to this office, in virtue of which he had been given divine authority to instruct the congregation, he would be wasting his time in attempting to answer the other problems raised by his opponents, for his replies would carry no conviction. The exact form in which Paul chose to refute the suggestion that he was in some way inferior to those apostles who were serving the Jewish community is, unfortunately, at the centre of one of the most complex historical problems in the whole of the Pauline corpus. For in dealing with the accusations made against him, Paul gives an extended and detailed account of his meetings with the original Jerusalem apostles, and the question of how Paul's statements here are to be fitted into the Acts account of his life and ministry is one that has been a burning issue for as far back as we care to look in the history of biblical interpretation, and will probably continue to be so. It is not our intention here to make a detailed study of the issues raised by this problem; rather must we concentrate our attention on the theological issues involved.

Theologically, the main issues here are concerned with the section 1.11–17, in which Paul discusses 'his gospel', its relation to that of the Jerusalem apostles, and the origin and authority of his own apostolic office. Three main questions confront us, and we shall deal with each of these in turn.

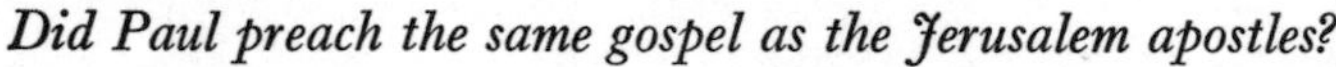

Did Paul preach the same gospel as the Jerusalem apostles?

Paul begins here by making a very firm and clear statement on the gospel which he proclaimed: 'The gospel which was preached by me is not *kata anthrōpon*' (v. 11). At least one scholar has no doubt that, on the basis of a statement of this kind, 'it becomes immediately apparent that the Galatian Gospel is not the traditional gospel as taught by the church in Jerusalem, and by its leaders'.[3] But this is not an adequate answer to the problem, for four main reasons:

1. We have already seen that in expressing his surprise at the unexpected turning of the Galatians, *eis heteron euangelion* (v. 6), Paul at once goes on to qualify his remark by emphasizing that, though he speaks of 'another gospel', in fact there is no such thing: there can be only *one* gospel (v. 7). There is no suggestion here that the Jerusalem apostles held to any different gospel from that of Paul. 'For him there is only one Gospel . . . , the Gospel of Christ, and he shares this with the original apostles.'[4]

2. The fact that Paul says here that his gospel was not *kata anthrōpon* (v. 11) cannot be held to imply that it had no connection with the Jerusalem apostles, for they are not envisaged here at all. Lightfoot long ago translated this phrase, 'after any human fashion or standard',[5] and it is clear that Paul is speaking here of 'man' in a generic sense, as a species, as distinct from Christ (v. 12), and with the main emphasis laid on the sinfulness and weakness of human nature and its inability to produce such a gospel, in contrast to the perfection of Christ and the character of his *apokalupsis*.[6]

3. In the account in 2.1–10 of his visit to Jerusalem fourteen years after his conversion, Paul seems to imply quite clearly that the message he had received, and which he had preached to the Galatians, was precisely the same as that of the Jerusalem apostles. He tells us that 'I laid before them . . . the gospel which I preach among the Gentiles' (v. 2), and the result of this was that the 'pillar apostles' immediately recognized 'the grace that was given to me' (2.9). The mention of *to euangelion tēs akrobustias* over against *to euangelion tēs peritomēs* in 2.7 does not contradict our argument here, for they are both the same. The parenthetical statement made immediately following this (2.8) shows beyond any reasonable doubt that in characterizing the work of Peter and himself in this way, Paul had in mind not so much the content of the preaching as the character of its recipients.[7]

4. In these chapters, Paul is evidently answering the charge that he was a spiritual nobody precisely because he had received his gospel as an academic tradition from the 'pillar apostles', and therefore, in every sense of the term, at secondhand. It ought to be clear that such a charge would have been completely meaningless

if Paul's gospel had *not* had the same doctrinal content as that of the Jerusalem leaders.

What was the source of Paul's authority as an apostle?

This conclusion leads us on to a far more complex issue, for if Paul's gospel was of essentially the same character and content as that of the Jerusalem apostles, how can we explain the statement of v. 12, that 'I did not receive it from man, nor was I taught it, but it came through an *apokalupsis* of Jesus Christ'? Is Paul here contradicting what he has just said, by claiming that the authority of his apostolate is different from that of the Jerusalem apostles in both source and character? Or are we to assume that his argument here is incomplete, emphasizing only one element in view of the opponents whom he faces—in which case, we cannot regard this passage as in any way a comprehensive exposition of his thought on the matter? It cannot be denied that Paul lays great emphasis on his direct encounter with the risen Lord (*apokalupsis Iēsou Christou*) over against the possibility of his having received the gospel by the usual channels of tradition (*paralambanō*) or formal instruction (*didaskō*), and in view of the life-shattering nature of this experience we need not be surprised that it came to assume a central place in Paul's understanding of his vocation. But is there perhaps a different, more theological explanation for the emphasis that Paul makes here? Can we go along with one recent German writer, Professor Walter Schmithals, and claim that 'this argument is genuinely Gnostic', on the ground that 'the Gnostic apostle is not identified by means of a chain of tradition, or by the apostolic succession, but by direct pneumatic vocation'? (*Paul and the Gnostics*, p. 29).

Schmithals bases his case on what is known of the history of the concept of the apostleship, as it emerged towards the end of the first century A.D. and on into the second.[8] In the face of the growing Gnostic threat, with its promise of secret 'knowledge' revealed to accredited divine messengers, the only way out of the problems which it faced was for the catholic church to suppose that originally, in the apostolic age, Christianity had been a uniform faith whose origins could be traced in a direct line from Jesus himself to the teachings and beliefs current in the catholic church.[9] On this basis, the true Word of God could be taken to be the message proclaimed by the church and its leaders, and any deviation from that message was to be seen as a corrupting element. At first, in the period of so-called *Frükatholizismus*, it was still admissible to refer to the oral traditions of the church by which the words and teachings of the apostles had been handed on, since there were many who could recall the disciples of apostles, and the 'elders' who had allegedly been the associates of the apostles and their pupils. Thus, for instance, Papias, bishop of Hierapolis, in a fragment of his *Logiōn Kuriakōn Exēgēseis*, probably to be dated *c.* A.D. 130–140, and preserved by Eusebius (*H.E.* III.39.4) could still say, 'I did not think that what was taken from books would profit me so much as what came from the living and abiding voice.' But with the passage of time, this kind of approach became impossible and, in addition, the Gnostics could also lay claim to oral tradition of their own, as when we find in the *Epistle of Ptolemy to Flora* mention of 'the apostolic tradition which we too have received by succession'.[10]

The apostles or, more often, individual apostles, had a large following in Gnostic circles, as is evidenced by the titles of so many of the Gnostic works found at Nag Hammadi, which serve only to substantiate the similar evidence of the Church Fathers on this score. Irenaeus tells us how secret revelations were given by the risen Christ to selected disciples (*Adv. Haer.* II.27.2), information which, in turn, according to Tertullian's *de Praescr.* 25, could be revealed only to a small spiritual élite who were endued with the pneumatic capacity for the reception of such *gnōsis*. Clement of Alexandria, who himself laid claim to apostolic authority for the esoteric *gnōsis* which he taught, emphasizes the oral character of such secret revelations, all of them delivered in a direct *apokalupsis* of the risen Christ to certain selected individuals, who were then entrusted with passing on the message to suitable recipients (*Strom.* VI.61.3). By virtue of the very nature of such revelations, it is often difficult to find traces or reflexions of the transmission of this secret *gnōsis*, though even in the literature which we have we can trace something of the popularity of the various apostles. In the *Pistis Sophia* and the two *Books of Jêu*, the disciples as a body are highly esteemed.[11] Of individual apostles, Peter often plays an important role, though not so important as he came to assume in the catholic church.[12] According to Clement of Alexandria, Basilides was keen to establish a connection with him through a certain Glaucias, who was alleged to have had some association with the apostle.[13] In the *Apocryphon of John*, one of the disciples in the 'inner circle' became the recipient of secret revelations. James also had secret revelations, according to Clement of Alexandria (*Strom.* I.11), and the Nag Hammadi texts provide examples of three different Apocalypses (or Apocrypha?) of James (one in codex I, and two in codex V), though it is not always clear which James is intended. Of the other apostles, Thomas, Philip and Paul[14] feature in the Nag Hammadi texts. Finally, Judas Iscariot, the traitor, was held in esteem by the Cainites, who regarded him as an instrument of Sophia, and so as an object of hatred to the Demiurge. As such, he was the only one of the Twelve to see the truth, and this led to the betrayal (cf. Irenaeus, *Adv. Haer.* I.31.1). There is also extant a *Gospel of Judas*, preserved in a few fragments (cf. *NTA* I, pp. 313ff.).

Though this summary is by no means exhaustive, yet it is illustrative of the essential elements in the Gnostic understanding of the function of the apostles: they received direct from the risen Christ Himself secret revelations, by virtue of which they themselves were given the task of passing on the substance of this *gnōsis* to those capable of receiving it because of their predetermined pneumatic character.[15] By way of reaction to all this, and in the effort to counteract it and thereby to stem the tide of Gnostic ideas that was flooding into the congregations, the catholic church developed two ways of proving the apostolic authority which *it* claimed to have received in a direct line from the earliest times:

1. The statement of Acts 1.21ff. was taken up as proof that the true apostles had always been with the Lord, and had therefore known everything he said and did (cf. Irenaeus, *Adv. Haer.* II.22.5). The *Gospel of the Ebionites* goes so far as to make the call of the disciples precede the baptism of Jesus in order to conform with this qualification (cf. *NTA* I, pp. 156ff.). A further stage is seen in the Clementine *Recognitions* IV.35, where Peter advises the Tripolitans to trust no teacher who has not been attested by James, the Lord's brother, for apart from such authorization there can be no genuine prophets or apostles (cf. also Clementine *Homilies* XI.35). The ultimate outcome of this kind of thinking was the establishment of the apostolic succession of bishops, who represented the legitimate line of authority going back to Christ Himself.

2. The written traditions that were claimed to be of apostolic origin also came to bear greater importance, the more so in view of the Gnostic emphasis on oral tradition. In the New Testament itself, 2 Peter shows clear signs of this (cf. 1.20ff.), and at least in the circles from which this writing came Paul's epistles were by this time considered to be sacred Scripture (3.15ff.). 2 Clement (*c*. A.D. 120–140) also shows evidence of a written tradition being considered as Scripture (cf. ch. 2). This process ultimately produced the canon of the New Testament, one of the other weapons used by the catholic church in their fight with Gnostics and other groups of heretics.

We can now return to Galatians 1. According to Schmithals, Paul's ideas of apostolic office as expounded especially in 1.12, reflect the Gnostic concept outlined above as opposed to the concept allegedly held by the Jerusalem apostles, which would correspond to that of the later catholic church, laying emphasis on proper succession and the handing-on of traditions—but which, on that account, Schmithals would see as the invention of 'early catholic' writers in the New Testament, such as Luke, whose writings he wants to date as late as A.D. 120–130.[16] On this theory, the Christian apostolate as it actually existed in the lifetime of Paul, in contrast to the idealization of it by later writers, was derived from a Gnostic concept of apostleship which antedated the emergence of the Christian church and which was taken over *in toto* by Paul, albeit in a Christianized form.

Can this interpretation be substantiated from Paul's description of his call as an apostle in Galatians 1? Before coming to the text itself, we must confess that, even on general considerations, this hypothesis can hardly be sustained. The whole of Schmithals's argument here (and, indeed, throughout the whole of his work) is based on the assumption that Gnosticism as a system was of pre-Christian origin, and therefore if we find a Gnostic concept of apostleship in the extant literature (all of it dating from the second century onwards), we can automatically transfer it *en bloc* to the first century and apply our findings to the interpretation of the New Testament. Though this belief can be traced through a noble scholastic ancestry, centring mainly on Bousset, Reitzenstein and Bultmann, it simply cannot be substantiated on the basis of any known evidence; and even so sympathetic a scholar as J. M.

Robinson has had to admit that this is a weak point in Schmithals's thesis.[17]

Again, it is surely no coincidence that the very core of what most scholars understand by truly Gnostic teaching (i.e. a radical cosmological dualism) is explicitly denied by what Paul says in this very context, when in vv. 13ff. he makes it quite plain that the God whom he served as a Pharisee and persecutor of the church was the same one whom he now served as a Christian.

> The idea . . . that the Christian God was a new and strange god, was worlds away from Paul. . . . The God whom he had served as a Pharisee and as a persecutor of the Christians was the one who had made his Son Jesus appear to him in heavenly glory.[18]

It has also been shown in recent studies that, though visions and direct confrontations of men with the divine were undoubtedly more common in Hellenistic religions generally, including Gnosticism, 'a sense of immediacy between God and man was possible in the Hebraic Pharisaism of Paul's day',[19] which at least suggests that Gnosticism is not the only direction in which we can look to find this kind of experience. Indeed if, as seems probable, Paul is here drawing a parallel between his own experience and that of the Old Testament prophet Jeremiah,[20] we ought probably to see in this a hint that we are to interpret it in the light of the Old Testament rather than against a background of any kind of Hellenistic belief, whether Gnostic or any other. An interesting account has also come to light in the Coptic Gnostic texts discovered at Nag Hammadi, which shows that at least some Gnostics did not think Paul was giving an account of 'Gnostic apostleship' in Galatians 1. In the *Apocalypse of Paul* (Nag Hammadi codex V) there is an account of Paul's encounter on the way to Jericho with a small boy who asks his name. But, in true Gnostic fashion, this little one already knows that Paul is blessed from the womb (cf. Gal. 1.15), and he calls on him to awaken his understanding and know the Hidden One in the Revealed. The existence of such an edited version of Paul's conversion experience certainly suggests that it was open to Gnostic misrepresentation. But by the same logic, it can hardly have been 'Gnostic' in its original form.[21]

Such considerations as these already give us good reason to doubt the validity of Schmithals's suggestion that here Paul emerges as a 'Gnostic apostle'. But the strongest support for our position comes from the text itself, and to this we now direct our attention.

The crux of the matter lies in the meaning of the clause, 'I did not receive it from man, nor was I taught it' (v. 12), and particularly in the meaning of the verbs *paralambanō* and *didaskō*. The key to a correct understanding of the passage is to be found, we suggest, in a comparison with the quite similar passage in 1 Corinthians 15.3–8 where, also in a polemical situation, Paul was making a pronouncement on precisely this same question: the origin and content of 'his' gospel. The language which introduces the subject in each case almost suggests that in the Corinthians passage he was consciously alluding to his statements in Galatians, for exactly the same terminology is found in Galatians 1.11 and 1 Corinthians 15.1. In the Corinthian context, Paul goes on to declare that in his communication of the gospel to the Corinthians, 'I delivered to you as of first importance what I also received' (15.3), a statement which would appear to be quite contradictory to that of Galatians 1.12, especially since it has been conclusively demonstrated that the statement in 1 Corinthians 15.3–8 is almost akin to the repetition of some traditional creedal formula of the early church.[22] The language he uses to describe the origin of this information contains at least two technical terms for the receiving and transmitting of tradition (*paralambanō* and *paradidōmi*), one of which (*paralambanō*) he uses in Galatians ostensibly for the purpose of saying exactly the opposite. There are two possible lines of approach to the solution of this difficult question. One is to assume that Paul is contradicting himself, and therefore we ought tacitly to ignore one or other account. This has been the approach adopted by several scholars, including such notables as C. H. Dodd and Rudolf Bultmann. Dodd, in his otherwise admirable exposition of *The Apostolic Preaching*, lays all the emphasis on 1 Corinthians 15 and, though he mentions Galatians 1.11–18, he interprets it in the light of the Corinthians passage.[23] This is a natural outcome of his theory that the apostolic kerygma consisted of a set of facts and figures, leaving no room for the kind of existential demand which Bultmann has seen at the heart of the evangelical proclamation. In consequence of this, Bultmann and those who have followed him lay all the emphasis on Galatians 1 to the detriment of 1 Corinthians 15.[24] Is there then a *via media* in this debate, or are we to conclude that Paul was simply being inconsistent with

c. take both

himself? The best solution is probably to allow both Galatians 1 and 1 Corinthians 15 to have equal emphasis in Paul's thought, and then for us to try to explain the difference between them in some other way. We will suggest later that such an explanation lies ready to hand in a proper understanding of the different background circumstances of Galatians and 1 Corinthians, and that Paul's explanation of his own calling is directly affected by the different kinds of opponents he was facing.

It is the singular merit of an article entitled 'What is the Kerygma?', written some years ago by William Baird,[25] that it reaches to the heart of the problem exegetically, though failing to take account of the historical situations that lay behind this diversity of Pauline expression and thought. Baird concludes that:

> the two texts make different emphases: 1 Cor. 15:3–8 stresses the form by which Paul proclaimed his gospel, while Gal. 1:11–17 refers to its essential dynamic character. . . . Thus *in its form* his kerygma was essentially the same as the tradition of the Jerusalem church—a tradition which he could have readily received from his persecuted victims, Cephas, or the Jerusalem Council. Yet *in its essential dynamic nature*, his gospel could not be transmitted by men, but was communicated by divine revelation (art. cit., p. 190).

In a more recent study, G. E. Ladd makes a broadly similar observation:

> There exists a dynamic unity between the event and the proclamation of the event, for the proclamation is itself a part of the event. It is impossible to place primary emphasis upon events as past history, or as present proclamation; the two are inseparably bound together. . . .[26]

It is, however, one thing to propose a simple solution to a complex problem, but quite another to prove that it is the correct solution. Three points may be urged in favour of an acceptance of this particular interpretation here:

1. This is the interpretation of Galatians 1.12 which best fits in with what we have seen to be the most likely meaning of v. 11. If we were correct to conclude that Paul preached the same gospel as the original apostles in Jerusalem, we must also assume that in

v. 12 he was not meaning to imply that the content of his *apokalupsis* of Christ imparted to him any different understanding of the gospel than had been imparted by God to the others.

2. This is also the simplest explanation of the passage *vis-à-vis* Paul's statements in 1 Corinthians 15.3–8, for it involves neither rejection nor emendation of either text. Since it is *a priori* unlikely that Paul would intend to contradict himself, any theory which implies this must be rejected. Though perhaps neither Dodd nor Bultmann would go so far as to reject completely one or other of these passages, by placing all the emphasis on one to the detriment of the other, this is the practical outcome of their method. Even in the context of Galatians, however, 6.6 shows that Paul reckoned his gospel to be something that could be passed on and learned within the context of the church fellowship.

3. The use of *paralambanō* both in the Pauline corpus and elsewhere is not always consistent. G. Delling (*TDNT* IV, p. 14) has convincingly shown that we should discern two different uses of the term in the Pauline epistles, one corresponding to the Jewish usage with reference to the handing-on of a tradition, and represented in 1 Corinthians 15.1, 3, and the other coming closer to the original Greek usage, implying 'to receive the intellectual *and ethical* content of religious life', which is the usage attested in Galatians 1.12. So

> Paul emphasises very strongly that the life which he passes on is not in any sense inherited by him from human bearers of revelation, . . . but that he has received it directly from the Author of this revelation on the Damascus road. . . . It must be an inward and living faith which gives religious certainty to a historical narrative which is not wholly immune from questioning. For this reason *paralambanein* cannot be . . . the reception of purely intellectual material. It is acceptance into the essential core of personality, which is more than the intellect alone.

Other examples of the Pauline usage of the term can be cited to support this meaning (e.g. 2 Thess. 3.6; Phil. 4.9).

We may, therefore, confidently conclude that what Paul says in Galatians 1 does not preclude his having inherited the historical facts about Jesus' life and ministry from his predecessors in the Jerusalem apostolate. Even so, the reader may yet complain that, if this is the case, he has still expressed himself in a very odd manner—an observation which leads us to our third and final question in regard to the problem of Paul's apostolic authority.

C

Why does Paul express himself as he does in this situation?

The key to a proper understanding of Paul's mode of expression here is to be found in the contrast which the apostle is intending to draw between the events recorded in vv. 11–12 and what he goes on to say in vv. 13–15. This is nothing less than the contrast between his way of life as a Jew and his new experience as a Christian. More exactly, we can agree with a recent commentator in declaring that: 'There is a strong contrast here with Jewish methods of transmission.'[27] Though the commentary in question does scant justice to the full implications of this statement, we cannot doubt that Paul is contrasting the way in which as a Jewish rabbi of the Pharisaical school he had read, learned and analysed the minutiae of the Torah, and the traditions of the Fathers which had accumulated over the centuries. Paul had been brought up as a Pharisee, and so zealous was he in the pursuit of the religious knowledge purveyed by that sect that he even overtook others of his own age, who had been given the same opportunities as he to absorb the Pharisaic traditions (v. 14). Because of what we may call Paul's 'Pharisaic mentality', one can easily imagine that any critics of his Christian message would be quick to accuse him of having learned it by rote, as a purely intellectual exercise. It is some such accusation as this which seems to lie behind this whole question of Paul's authority as an apostle in the Galatian churches.[28] His opponents were not accusing him simply of being dependent in some vague way on the Jerusalem apostles. Rather were they setting him in the same relationship to Jerusalem as existed in the teacher/pupil relationship of the Pharisaic schools. Paul, they argued, had received his message secondhand, not because he learned the facts of Jesus' life, death and resurrection from the other apostles, but because this was *all* he had learned. Unlike them, his knowledge of the gospel was a mere intellectual knowledge, such as he had formerly possessed as a Pharisee. The original disciples had been with Jesus for some considerable time during his ministry, and Paul had not. Though they had all scattered and left him at his crucial hour, yet the appearances of the risen Christ and their reception of the Holy Spirit had confirmed that vital revelation of his true character, and had led in turn to their full commitment to the cause of the gospel of Jesus Christ.

Such a view of Paul's argument here explains the odd terminology of v. 12. As we have noted, *paralambanō* can in certain cases refer to the handing-on of tradition, but even more than this, Paul's use of *didaskō* in the same verse seems to confirm beyond any reasonable doubt that it was only formal, academic instruction that he had in mind here. Paul was denying that his knowledge of Christ was of that strictly intellectual stamp that had characterized his religious experience as a Pharisee.[29] Despite some of the outdated observations made by Rengstorf in his article on *apostolos* in *TDNT* I, he did surely perceive the truth on this particular issue, and we can do no better than end this section by concurring with his judgement that, while the other apostles 'came to full dedication to Jesus only after much vacillation and a long course of instruction by him', in Paul's experience we

> find no evidence of either vacillation or instruction. On the contrary there is a sudden and yet no less resolute committal to the Messiah Jesus whom he hitherto had passionately persecuted. The reason for this is that the concept of God had from the very first determined the thinking and action of Paul, and yet only outside Damascus did it attain to an absolutely dominating position. *Only in this light can we understand the distinctive nature of his self-awareness and assurance of apostolic mission* (*TDNT* I, p. 438).

II

The Promise to Abraham and his Descendants (3.6—4.7)

After the brief interlude of 3.1–5, in which Paul made a direct and personal appeal to the Galatians' own experience, which itself showed that they had become Christians not 'by works of the law' but 'by hearing with faith' (3.5), he then came to the second main question which had arisen as a result of the false teaching in the Galatian churches, and which seems to have centred around the promise to Abraham. The conclusion that Paul draws from his arguments here, twice stated, shows that the basic issue in question was not the Law and circumcision, but sonship to Abraham, and through him to God Himself (cf. 3.29; 4.7). In some ways it is difficult to separate this question from that which follows in 4.21—6.10 (the Law and circumcision), since Paul's argument here necessitates a mention of the Law and its relevance to the Christian. Yet the distinction that we have drawn, and whose full implications we are about to show, is by no means an artificial one. The section which lies before us is concerned with the major question of the relationship of the church of the New Testament to the People of God, Israel, in the Old Testament. The relationship of Gentile Christians to Jews under the old covenant is dealt with here as a theological principle, rather than the practical issue that it certainly was in the Galatian churches. In the next and final section of Galatians, on the other hand (4.21—6.10), Paul investigates the practical outworking of what he here concludes on the theological level.

On any account of the history of the earliest church, one of the most difficult questions for the Christians of the first generation was to decide whether the Christian faith was to be just a sect of Judaism, and whether therefore their preaching should be restricted to Jews, or whether the message was intended for Gentiles also. It is striking that, whatever explanation we may offer for it, the early disciples could find no direct indication in the traditions of Jesus' teaching as to what considerations should decide their own practice. On the one hand, Jesus had reputedly made such statements as: 'Go nowhere among the Gentiles, and enter no town of the Samaritans, but go rather to the lost sheep of the house of Israel' (Matt. 10.5ff.); yet on the other hand, he himself had spoken to Gentiles and commended their faith,[30] and according to two separate gospel traditions, the Samaritans and their faithful response had played a significant part in his ministry (John 4.7–43; Luke 10.29–37). As they looked to their Master for guidance the disciples must have found at least a paradox, if not an outright contradiction, between his words and his actions. Nor did their own experience in the early days of the church give them any clearer guidance, for the events of the Day of Pentecost had largely been restricted to people who were already Jews by religious persuasion; and yet, at the same time, according to Acts, the prophecy that Peter said was fulfilled had declared that 'I will pour out my Spirit upon all flesh' (Acts 2.17, quoting Joel 2.28, *Heb.* 3.1). According to the account in Acts, the question really came to a head with the appointment of the seven deacons (6.1–6), and more especially was its climax at this stage represented in the speech Stephen is reputed to have made before the Jewish leaders. Whether this speech is a more or less accurate account of what was actually said, or whether it was Luke's idea of what ought to have been said, or even material brought in from some other source, does not matter for our purpose here: at least it suggests that this was the kind of problem that was troubling the church at this particular point in its experience. Even if Acts is not an authentically historical account of the life of the early church, the fact that this problem was so important right from the outset of Paul's ministry certainly shows that its roots must be traced back to the very beginning of the church's existence.[31]

Whatever may have been its origin in history, it is clear that the New Testament writers had a conscious awareness of being a part of that covenant community to which the promises had been given in the Old Testament through Abraham, Isaac, Jacob, and Moses. In so far as the old nation of Israel had been faithless to the trust that God had given her, she had rejected her part in the divine plan. The condition of the promise made to Abraham had been his willingness to 'go from your own country' (Gen. 12.1), and walk before Yahweh in faith, the basic requirements of which had been spelled out more fully in the terms of the Sinai covenant (cf. Exod. 20). Israel had lost that faith, and had thereby abrogated the covenant. But through the remnant, and thence through Christ, men of all races were enabled to enter into that same covenant relationship with God, and so we find, for instance, in 1 Peter 2.9–10 and in Romans 9.25ff., two very clear indications that the Christian church considered itself to be the true spiritual successor to this ancient People of God. There is a definite insistence almost throughout the New Testament that the church is not so much the 'new Israel' of God, but the heir of the promises made to the People of God in all ages, and so Christians have become a part of the spiritual offspring of Abraham himself. There can be no doubt at all that this question was always close to the heart of Paul himself. Chapters 9–11 of Romans bear eloquent testimony to the way Paul was torn between the Israel after the flesh and the spiritual Israel.[32] He saw the salvation of both Gentiles and Jews to be closely bound up with each other, and in Galatians he specifically and directly applied the name 'Israel' to the Christians whom he was addressing, thus reminding his readers that, whatever others may claim or disclaim, they were themselves God's own people (6.16). Again, in 1 Corinthians 10.1–10 Paul regards the patriarchs of Israel as the ancestors of the Christian church, a claim that clearly could not signify racial descent, for of all the churches addressed in the New Testament, that at Corinth was one of the most cosmopolitan (cf. also Rom. 4.16). Even on the hotly disputed issue of circumcision, Paul was not prepared to allow the misuse of the idea by others to stop him making a spiritual application of it, and so he could insist in Philippians 3.3 that 'we are the true circumcision', though he then went on to redefine the terms of reference, for he was speaking of those who 'worship God in Spirit, and glory in Christ Jesus, and put no confidence in the flesh' (cf. also Rom. 2.29). Moreover, so important was this principle for Paul that it could even be regarded as the foundation principle and binding force of the church itself (Col. 2.11ff.). By a redefinition of circumcision, Paul was able to apply the term to the church, and by being thus 'circumcised', Christians, whatever their racial pedigree, could also become true sons of Abraham (Gal. 3.29; Rom. 4.12). For Paul, to be a son of Abraham meant to share the faith of Abraham (Rom. 9.8) and, as a consequence of that, to do the same works as he did, willing to rest on God's promises alone (cf. also John 8.38ff.; Heb. 11.17ff.). When the Jews denied the significance of the intervention of God in Christ, they were denying the faith of Abraham and so were no longer his sons, even though their physical descent was beyond question. But those who were willing to accept God's actions by faith were indeed the 'true Israel', and the real descendants of Abraham.

It is against a background of this kind of thought that we should interpret the section of Galatians which concerns us here, and when we take this into account it is obvious why Paul must go to such unusual lengths in dealing with Abraham's spiritual career. It is also clear why his thought in this section began, perhaps even unconsciously, to overlap what was to be his main argument in the next section of the epistle. Paul's argument here, designed to show that Christians are a part of the 'true Israel' of God by virtue of their possession of the Holy Spirit, falls naturally into three sections.

THE THEOLOGY OF THE PEOPLE OF GOD

In this section of his argument (3.6–14), Paul approaches the question from a theological angle, and seeks to show, using the usual means of rabbinical exegesis, that though indeed the Old Testament may be taken to suggest that in order to share in the blessings of God one needed to become a Jew in the full sense of the term (i.e. by accepting circumcision and the burden of the Law), this was not its real meaning. Rather, since Abraham had *pistis*, it is only *hoi ek pisteōs* (v. 9) who can inherit the blessings promised to Abraham. At the same time, 'all who rely on works of the law are under a curse' (v. 10). Paul therefore begins (vv. 6–7), in response to his own rhetorical questions in the preceding verses, by declaring the basis on which Abraham (and, therefore, the Galatians) had found acceptance before God, and he finds this in the words of the Old Testament itself: Abraham 'believed God, and it was reckoned to him as righteousness' (v. 6, cf. Gen. 15.6). Doubtless Paul here had in mind the fact that in the Old Testament 'faith' was essentially faithfulness to the experienced acts of God in history, coupled with a confidence in his future activity in the same sphere of operation. In the aftermath of the Babylonian exile, and then in later Judaism, the traditions of the Old Testament had gradually become canonized, if not formally at least by usage, so that by the time Paul was writing, 'obedient faithfulness acquires the character of obedience to the Law' (R. Bultmann, *TDNT* VI, p. 201). This change of emphasis in Judaism had led to the production of all kinds of sacred legends to show that Abraham had in fact kept the Law. Even more than this, it was held that the merits his righteousness had built up could be of representative character for the whole of Israel, for all those who were *hoi huioi tou Abraam*. Even proselytes, though they might be circumcised and accept the Torah, could not have this sacred title applied to them in the Judaism of the day (cf. S-B I, pp. 117–21). But of course Paul was working from different presuppositions, as he went on to explain: 'The scripture [foresaw] that God would justify the Gentiles by faith . . .' (v. 8). Though there were those within Judaism who saw that the divine plan included a place for Gentiles, none would have gone so far as Paul did.[33] If we approach the question with complete impartiality and objectivity, there can be no doubt that Paul was here, and in what follows, deliberately denying the plain statements of the Old Testament, for it is clear from the Genesis account that circumcision and the keeping of the Law were an essential part of the covenant, and without them one could have no part in the blessings promised to Abraham (Gen. 17.14). At the same time, however, as a good Jew, and indeed as a Christian, it was impossible for Paul to conclude that somehow Scripture was wrong or outmoded, and so in what follows here he proceeds to apply the normal exegetical methods of his day in order to extract the 'true' meaning from the text.

In doing so, Paul uses three specific arguments in vv. 10–14. The first, in vv. 10–11a, is introduced to show that no one is able to fulfil the requirements of the Law, so that even if in theory it was possible to gain a righteous standing before God by this means, it would in fact be a practical impossibility. The argument of vv. 11–12 and v. 14 is then brought in, to show that the Law actually cancels itself, and Paul adopts a standard canon of Jewish exegesis to prove this and then to find a way out of the difficulty. The third strand in Paul's argument is found in v. 13, where the *katara* of v. 10 is taken up again and, with the aid of another Old Testament verse, is expounded in the light of the work of Christ. For convenience, we shall deal with each of these strands separately, though of course recognizing that they are all intimately connected.[34]

Could the Law ever be fulfilled? (*vv. 10–11a*)

What Paul says here is meant to imply that no one was capable of fulfilling the whole Law (cf. also v. 3).[35] In making this claim he was going beyond his earlier convictions as a Pharisee, though his basic insistence that in order to obtain the benefits of the Law one must obey the whole of it, is in accordance with Jewish thought. Longenecker draws attention to the fact that an '*am haaretz* who had assumed the obligations of a *haber*, and a proselyte who had imposed on himself the obligations of the Law were not to be accepted unless they performed all the Law without exception' (*Paul, Apostle of Liberty*, p. 120, n. 46). But while the rabbis shared Paul's concern over the difficulty of actually doing this in practice, they did not reach his conclusions. They laid a rather more positive emphasis on the Law as the will of God, and therefore as the basic foundation for life as a whole. Yet while it is natural to compare Paul's thought with that of contemporary Judaism, ultimately we will fail to understand the apostle if we regard him as still a Pharisee at heart. As a Pharisee, it was quite likely that he could have imagined a situation in which he was capable of keeping the Law,[36] a situation in which also he probably imagined God to be more tolerant of sin than he now saw him to be in the light of Christ. But in dealing with what Paul is now saying, we do well to heed the reminder of Longenecker, that 'his statements in Galatians . . . are not supposed to represent the accepted theology of the best of Judaism, but his Christian understanding'.[37] This being the case, we cannot treat too seriously the argument of Schoeps, when he suggests that Paul can spiritualize circumcision as the sign of the covenant and abolish the Law 'because . . . he sees the reality of the covenant only as an abstraction, and he misunderstands its symbolism as a covenant pointing to the law of holiness' (*Paul*, p. 198). On the contrary, it was precisely because Paul saw the character of the covenant as the requirement of a holy God, and because he saw that in Christ this holiness had found both its fulfilment and its source, that he was able to argue as he does. The particular question raised by Schoeps really amounts to one of authority and inspiration. No Jew would accept the exegesis that Paul gives of the Old Testament here, for it was not Paul's rabbinical training that led his thought along these lines. It was the fact that he now recognized as the Messiah of Israel one whom the leaders of his people had put to death but whom, in his opinion, God had now raised from the dead. *This* was why he could say that 'no man is justified before God by the law' (v. 11).

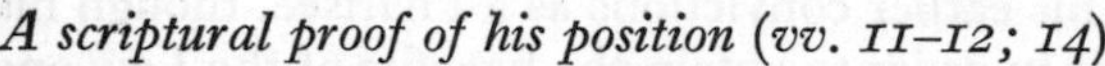

A scriptural proof of his position (*vv. 11–12; 14*)

Though in many ways Schoeps has missed the point of Paul's convictions, we must accept the general lines of his exegesis at this point. It seems best here to regard vv. 11–12 and v. 14 as a proof from Scripture, argued in the rabbinic fashion, of the truth of what Paul has just said, and then to treat v. 13 as a kind of parenthesis brought in because of a LXX word association, viz. the occurrence of *katara* in each case. By this means Paul takes up the *katara* of the Law mentioned in v. 10 (Deut. 27.26) and connects it with the person of Christ Himself, in whose death he sees a connection with the *katara* of Deuteronomy 21.23. According to Schoeps, Paul was here utilizing the same principle that lies behind the thirteenth *midda* of the second-century rabbi Ishmael ben Elisha, that 'two verses contradict one another until a third verse reconciles them' (*Sifra*, intro. 5). Here, Paul set up the antithesis of Habakkuk 2.4, with its emphasis on life through faith-righteousness, and Leviticus 18.5, which appears to emphasize law-righteousness.[38] To provide the solution to this apparent contradiction he brought in another text, already alluded to in v. 6 (Gen. 15.6), and recalled here by the mention of *hē eulogia tou Abraam* (v. 14).[39]

Thus, having argued that the Law could never be fulfilled in practice, even though such may be desirable in theory, and having expounded the Old Testament Scriptures to show that the faith principle is of crucial importance over against the *erga tou nomou*, Paul now goes on in the parenthetical statement of v. 13 to show the Christian answer to the dilemma.

Christ the Curse (*v. 13*)

Though Schoeps is right in suggesting that this verse is interposed here because of the LXX word association between Deuteronomy 27.26 and 21.23, there is no reason to suppose that the essence of what Paul is saying should be treated as an aside for the purpose of dispelling the scandal which, in Jewish eyes, attached to the method of Jesus' death.[40] Having recognized the association of Deuteronomy 21.23 and 27.26, it is quite gratuitous to try to distinguish between the curse which Jesus became in his death and the curse which Paul earlier said that the Law made on those who transgress it.

Paul's thought here is dominated by the quotation already made from Deuteronomy 27.26, and the mention of Deuteronomy 21.23 in v. 13 is introduced almost as an afterthought, and only as a further proof of what has already been said, that 'Christ redeemed us from the curse of the law, having become a curse for us'.[41] We should therefore beware of reading too much into the mention of the curse attaching to one whose body was hung up after death. When W. L. Knox, for example, finds the clue to an understanding of the verse in the Philonic interpretation of Deuteronomy 21.23 as 'cursed is the man who clings to corruptible matter instead of to God', and then seeks to understand this in the light of the later mention of the Law's delivery (3.19ff.) and purpose (4.3ff.), he introduces an unnecessary and misleading line of thought, though he is right to insist that Paul was here emphasizing the centrality of Christ in the whole redemptive process, replacing the centrality of the Torah in the Jewish religion.[42] Büchsel perceives the more natural understanding of the passage when he writes: 'The one who is hanged is thus regarded as accursed in the sense that as "a publicly exposed example of the pitiless severity of the Law", he stands under the very curse which the Law brings on those who transgress it.'[43]

THE HISTORY OF THE PEOPLE OF GOD

In the second part of his argument, Paul goes on to deal with the question of *hoi huioi tou Abraam*, not now so much from a theological angle as from a historical viewpoint (3.15–24). He argues that since, as a matter of historical fact, the Torah came long after Abraham's time, it could not possibly have affected a direct promise made to him by God. The *klēronomia* cannot be by both Law and promise (v. 18). But nevertheless, the Law did have a function: (i) to reveal sin as a transgression against God (v. 19, cf. Rom. 4.15, 5.13); and (ii) to be man's *paidagōgos* until Christ came (v. 24). As they tried to gain salvation through their own efforts at keeping the Law, men came to realize that it was an impossible task, and so the way was prepared for God's act of grace in Jesus Christ.

In showing the historically secondary character of the Law as opposed to the promise of God, Paul again takes up the figure of Abraham (vv. 15–18), though not this time from any theological standpoint. He paints a picture familiar to his readers, of a will (*diathēkē*, v. 15) which, once it has been executed, cannot be altered. On this analogy, he argues, the covenant promise made by God to Abraham cannot be overridden by a Law which came 430 years afterwards.[44] This understanding of what Paul is saying here is preferable to the more theological emphasis of Lightfoot, who argues that since in v. 17 *diathēkē* clearly refers in a technical sense to the divine covenant, that must also be its meaning here.[45] Nor can we accept the view of Whiteley that 'it makes no difference to St. Paul's argument whether *diathēkē* means "will" or "covenant" . . .'[46] In view of Paul's love of legal terminology and his use of such allusions to elucidate theological truths, it seems best to take this as a conscious picture of Hellenistic legal usage, with the emphasis being on the absolute inviolability of the will of a dead person. If this can apply in the human sphere, argues Paul, how much more is it true of the covenant promise of God!

Paul now continues, still arguing on historical lines, to show further the inferiority of the Law, and also to show something of its positive value. In describing its overall inferiority he elicits three facts, two drawn from the history of Israel and one from the common experience of the human race:

The Law was inferior by virtue of its character (*v. 18*)

This, for Paul, clearly followed from what he had just said about the distinction between the Law and the promise. Since the Law was not the same as the promise, and since the latter was determinative of man's divine inheritance, then the Law was self-evidently to be rejected.[47]

The Law was inferior because of its origin (*v. 19b*)

What Paul says here has caused many a headache to interpreters, for by suggesting that the Law 'was ordained by angels through an intermediary', Paul is apparently denying the direct divine origin of the Torah, something that would be quite unthinkable to Jews, and that is difficult to reconcile with Paul's own teaching elsewhere. Whiteley asserts that since 'the excellence of the Law is fundamental to St. Paul's thought', this statement must be balanced by others, like Romans 7.12ff. (*Theology of St. Paul*, p. 79); while Cranfield, in his valuable study 'St. Paul and the Law', makes the following points about understanding this passage:

1. We must beware of exaggerating the depreciatory tendency. Paul's intention, according to Cranfield, 'is probably simply to suggest a certain superiority of the promise, as given directly by God, over the Law, as given by means of angels' (art. cit., p. 62).

2. In evaluating the way Paul depreciates the Law here, we must remember the polemical character of Galatians. 'It is not that Paul desires, absolutely, in any way to disparage the Law, but that, in relation to this false exaggeration of the Law, he is forced in some manner to depreciate it.'[48]

3. Paul here regards the Law in a narrow sense. He distinguishes the Law from the promise, though both are contained in the Pentateuch! What Paul is really disparaging here is 'not the Law in the fulness and wholeness of its true character, but the Law as seen apart from Christ' (p. 63).

This is an admirable statement of Paul's view of the Law when Galatians is examined in the light of other Pauline passages. But for our purposes, at least for the present, we must regard it as special pleading. In respect of Paul's statements in Galatians, Schoeps's comment is undoubtedly nearer the mark: 'In the last analysis this [Gal. 3.19] means that the law springs not from God but from the angels'; though even he goes on to admit that 'in the heat of the contest Paul had allowed himself to be drawn to make assertions which on calmer reflection he could hardly have maintained seriously . . .' (*Paul*, p. 183).

What did Paul mean by saying that the Law came through angels? The first mention of angels in connection with the Law is in Deuteronomy 33.2 (LXX), *ek dexiōn autou angeloi met' autou.* Speculation on the precise meaning of such statements seems to have been widespread among Jewish writers of many traditions (cf. S-B III, pp. 554ff.), and indeed we find the same idea elsewhere in the New Testament (Acts 7.53; Heb. 2.2). According to Josephus, *Ants.* 15.5.3, however, the angels were brought in by the rabbis to glorify the Law, which is also the intention in Acts 7.53.[49] Professor A. T. Hanson has argued that both here and in Acts 7.53 the purpose of this allusion to angels was the same. Both Paul and Stephen were meaning to draw a contrast between 'direct grace and indirect Law, and the angels are brought in to underline the indirectness, not to suggest that the Law was not from God'.[50] Thus he can conclude that 'Paul does not represent the Law as given by angels: they only carried it down or delivered it. According to Paul it was given by God, or, even more probably, by Christ. . . .' This may well be an accurate assessment of Paul's overall theological position, but again it can be objected that such a view can only be reached on the basis of a combination of the evidence of Galatians with Paul's teaching in Romans. We have already pointed out that in Galatians there is a definite tension between Paul's view of the Old Testament as inspired Scripture and some of the statements he makes about it; and nowhere does this tension come out more strongly than in the present context. If we interpret Galatians in total independence of Romans (as its original readers had to do), it appears more likely that Paul intended the mention of angels to disparage the Law, and on the basis of this particular passage we can only conclude that here he was meaning to issue a categorical denial of the divine origin of the Torah.[51]

The Law was inferior because of its moral weakness (*v. 21*)

Though Paul expresses himself in a slightly more positive fashion here ('if a law had been given which could make alive'), he is clearly implying that the Law that *was* given was utterly unable to give a man life in God's sight. The ultimate test was that of practical performance, and in this the principle of law was a failure. 'It had brought no life because it had never been intended for that purpose. If law could have brought life, it would have no longer been inferior to promise.'[52]

Yet even here, Paul could still see *some* value in the existence of the Law, albeit of a very transitory nature:

The Law has value as a revealer of sin (*v. 19a*)

What Paul suggests here is the same kind of thing as he speaks of in Romans 5.20ff., viz. that until the Law came to show up sin as a transgression against God's holy will and character, there was no possibility of God dealing with it because its true nature was unknown. But there is a great difference here from what Paul says in Romans. Here he simply makes a bare, factual statement about the Law's function, whereas in Romans he goes on to draw out the positive implications of this function in terms of the ultimate saving purpose of God. There he makes it plain that, since God's purpose was to overcome sin, and since the Law was the means by which unconscious wrongdoing could be shown up as defiance of God's will, the introduction of the Law was a gracious and benevolent action on God's part. But here in Galatians, the same thought is applied to show almost the very opposite! What follows in the rest of the verse almost cancels out what Paul has said of the Law's positive function. Not only was the Law not the direct gift of God Himself, but it was only valid *achris an elthē to sperma hō epēngeltai*, an expression which picks up *to sperma* of v. 16, referring to Christ. Since Christ has already come, even this limited value of the Law has now ceased to be of any benefit![53]

The Law was man's paidagogos *until Christ came* (*v. 24*)

Here Paul takes a slightly more positive line towards the Law, for the final goal to which it pointed forward was none other than Christ, and its intention in pointing to him was 'that we might be justified by faith'. Yet even here it seems unlikely that Paul is suggesting that the *individual's* experience of the Law and its imperative somehow prepares him to receive Christ: '. . . the context makes it clear that the apostle is speaking, rather, of the historic succession of one period of revelation upon another, and the displacement of the law by Christ'.[54]

THE CHARACTER OF THE PEOPLE OF GOD

In the final section of his argument on Christians as the true Israel and as *hoi huioi tou Abraam*, Paul now goes on to conclude and summarize his own position on the matter (3.25—4.6). He does so by making a further brief allusion to both the theological and the historical arguments which he has put forward in the preceding sections, and draws the same broad conclusions on each premise: 'If you are Christ's, then you are Abraham's offspring, heirs according to promise' (3.29); and 'So through God you are no longer a slave but a son, and if a son then an heir' (4.7). First of all, in 3.25–9, Paul makes two assertions, centred on vv. 27 and 29. Those who have been baptized as Christians *Christon enedusasthe* (v. 27), i.e. they have received the same standing before God as Christ had. In the light of what follows (4.6ff.), this must clearly refer to Christ's position as the divine Son, and we cannot therefore agree with Bousset that this is an allusion to the Hellenistic Mystery-cults, in which the rite of putting on a garment was part of a mystical deification of the subject.[55] Any such allusion here is secondary. The background to this language is more probably to be found in Old Testament exhortations to put on strength, righteousness, etc. (cf. Duncan, *Galatians*, p. 123), and its implication here is that when a person is baptized, so clearly does he become identified with Christ that he himself lives no longer, but Christ lives within him (2.19ff., cf. Schlier *Galaterbrief*, pp. 173ff.). Because of this, all Christians are *heis . . . en Christō Iēsou* (v. 28). Paul goes on to draw a further implication from this by taking up again one aspect of what he had said in vv. 15–24, through the word association of *sperma* in vv. 16 and 19. There, he had pointed out in rabbinical fashion that, since the Old Testament had the singular in Genesis 12.7 and its parallels, this must point to the Christ as the (singular) fulfilment of the promise.[56] The idea that the Christ when he came would be the true seed of Abraham, and so in a sense both the ideal representative and the embodiment of his race, was not alien even to the rabbis. What Paul says here in v. 29 shows that he was speaking with the insight given to him by the risen Christ: while Christ Himself was the singular fulfilment of the promise to Abraham's descendants, in him Christians become a part of the true and spiritual Israel. 'Without Christ the Christian people have no existence. He is the source of their spiritual life. They are one in Him.'[57]

Then finally, in this part of the epistle, Paul draws the same conclusion once again on historical grounds (4.1–7). Again he resorts to legal terminology and practice to provide an analogy for his spiritual lessons. An heir, while he was still a child, would normally be subject to guardians and trustees. But this was only a temporary measure until he came of age, at which point he entered into his inheritance and assumed the full status of a son and heir.[58] Similarly, in the spiritual realm, mankind had hitherto been under the guardianship of *ta stoicheia tou kosmou* (v. 3). But with the coming of Christ the time had arrived for God to bring mankind to full growth, and thereby to set them free from this bondage in order that they might assume their true position as sons and heirs of God Himself. The main point of difficulty here is in the use of the term *ta stoicheia tou kosmou* (v. 3, cf. vv. 9ff.). Two possible implications have been found here:

1. The phrase may be taken to indicate the physical elements of the cosmos, the stars, heavenly bodies, etc., and so it would have a basic cosmological reference. This interpretation was the almost universal view of the Fathers, who explained it in the light of v. 10 to indicate the observance of days and seasons which, after all, were regulated by the heavenly bodies.

2. Another possible approach is to take the phrase to indicate 'elementary teaching', in which case the reference would be directly to the prescriptions of the Torah, with its food laws and its emphasis on the proper observance of days and seasons (cf. v. 10). This interpretation is preferred by Lightfoot and Burton, and among the Fathers it was held by Tertullian and Jerome. In favour of this view of the matter is the apparent parallel between v. 3 and v. 5, for in v. 3 Paul says that we were *hupo ta stoicheia tou kosmou*, while in v. 5 he goes on to say that we were also *hupo nomon*.

This distinction, however, though perfectly valid, need not necessarily apply here, and it is possible that Paul was using the term rather more loosely, to include both implications. Several points may be urged in favour of this understanding of the text:

1. The use of the genitive *tou kosmou* here tends to speak against a simple identification of *ta stoicheia* with the Jewish Torah. There is much evidence elsewhere in Paul's writings that he did consider the spiritual forces of the universe to be a potential threat to both Christian and non-Christian alike (cf. Rom. 7.38ff.; Col. 2.8, etc.).

2. The fact that Paul speaks of *hēmeis* in v. 3 cannot be held to show that he was thinking only of Jews in this context. Nor can the effort to separate Jews (*tous hupo nomon*) from mankind as a whole (*hina tēn huiothesian apolabōmen*) in v. 5. Schlier (*Galaterbrief*, p. 197) has demonstrated that the two-purpose clauses here are simply repeating each other, and so both refer to the same set of people. Nor can we separate vv. 3ff. from vv. 8ff., with the former speaking of Jews and the latter of Gentiles, for Paul was speaking of all those who had become Christians, whatever their racial pedigree. The fact that elsewhere Paul mentions a law of the

Gentiles, corresponding in some way to the Jewish Torah, suggests that the implication here is that Gentile service of *ta stoicheia* was in reality service of the Torah, and vice versa (cf. Rom. 2.14ff.).[59]

3. Though astrology and magic were officially forbidden to Jews, the evidence shows that, as was so often the case, the forbidden fruit was simply grafted on to another tree rather than left alone. W. L. Knox has adduced evidence which suggests that Paul could have been the heir of a Jewish tradition which united the place of the Torah as one of the foundational elements of existence with the widespread popular interest in astrology. According to *Genesis Rabba* 45.12, Israel herself was free from the power of the stars and heavenly aeons, though this was not to deny the existence of such powers, for the other nations were said to be subject to them. R. Meir (Tosefta *Sukkah* 2.6) suggested that Israel's freedom from the stars was tied up with the central place of the Torah, and so it is possible to conclude that Paul

> had been brought up to boast that the Torah delivered mankind from the power of the stars which rule the natural world; he was perfectly ready to hold that, while the Pharisees were wrong in attributing this salvation to the Torah, their error lay not in their conception of salvation, but in their ascribing to the Torah what could only be found in Jesus (*St. Paul and the Church of the Gentiles*, p. 104).

This certainly provides an important guideline for our understanding of the Law over against *ta stoicheia tou kosmou*. That Paul included the Torah in the *stoicheia* is clear, but we should not suppose that this is all he included. In speaking of *hēmeis* he was doubtless speaking subjectively, as a member of the human race rather than as a Jew, and his conception of those things which could enslave a man would be correspondingly wide.[60] *Anything* that can prevent a man from coming to the full maturity which God intends him to have in Christ is to be regarded as a stumbling-block, and as one of the *stoicheia tou kosmou* which Christ has done away with so that all men may become sons and heirs of God Himself.

III

The Law and Circumcision (4.21—6.10)

Finally, Paul comes to a formal consideration of the question of the Torah and circumcision, though in each case he finds that since he has already needed to say so much about these two problems in dealing with the true Israel, nothing more than a summary statement is called for here before he goes on to explain the ethical consequences of his teaching.

THE LAW

On the question of the Law (4.21—5.1) Paul makes yet another appeal to the Abraham saga, this time using the story of the free woman, Sarah, driving out the slave woman, Hagar, as an allegory of the superior position of the good news in Christ over against the legalism of the Jewish Torah. According to Burton (*Galatians*, p. 251) this entire passage is introduced by Paul as an afterthought, and therefore has little relevance to his main message. But in view of the peculiar nature of the passage, it is unlikely that Paul would have brought it in for no other reason than that it happened to come into his mind as he was writing. Duncan (*Galatians*, p. 144) sees a more positive function for this section, and one that fits in well with other factors we have already noted in Galatians. The story of Hagar and Sarah would probably be especially familiar to Jews because of its contrast between the legitimate son, Isaac, and the illegitimate son, Ishmael, and because of this it would be 'one to which Jewish preachers and controversialists must often have turned as a divine proof of the superiority of their nation to lesser breeds who were outside the covenant'. In contrast to the lessons drawn by his Jewish counterparts, Paul declares that even the Old Testament shows that there were two types of 'children of Abraham', only one of which had any moral and spiritual claim to be Abraham's descendants.

The main point of what Paul intended to say by using this picture is therefore clear. It is simply a recapitulation of what had already been implied about the Law and the Christian life: 'For freedom Christ has set us free; stand fast, therefore, and do not submit again to a yoke of slavery' (5.1). There are, however, many

uncertainties in the text itself. Most of these we cannot consider here, and in any case they are not of fundamental importance to our purpose. But one question we can hardly avoid is the way in which Paul handles the Old Testament Scripture here, for it is quite unlike most of the rest of Galatians, and some have found its origin in the kind of exegesis practised in Alexandria, whose most eloquent exponent was Philo. If Paul was here consciously adopting the kind of interpretation of the Old Testament taken up by Philo, this fact would have important consequences for our understanding of the teaching of Galatians. In particular, it would have an important bearing on the validity of Schmithals's claims that Paul was dealing with some sort of Gnostics here, for it is generally recognized that the teaching of the Alexandrian Jew has some, as yet undefined, importance in the development of Gnostic thought.[61] Before drawing conclusions, however, we must establish the facts of the matter by exegetical means. Two main points should be considered here:

Is this an allegory?

Paul specifically says in 4.24 *hatina estin allēgoroumena*, and so it is certain that he himself regarded it as such, though in what sense is not immediately obvious, since the word had no precise and well-defined meaning (cf. Burton, *Galatians*, pp. 254ff.). Chrysostom had no doubt that Paul could call this an allegory only 'by a misuse of language . . . What he means is this: the history itself not only has the apparent meaning but also proclaims other matters; therefore it is called allegory. But what did it proclaim? Nothing other than everything that now is' (*Commentary on Galatians*, ad loc.).

In so far as this passage has been compared with the allegories of Philo of Alexandria, it must be admitted that there are striking differences between the two writers.[62] The most obvious difference is that for Paul, the fact that the story which he took up could be given some other, 'spiritual', meaning, did not necessitate the conclusion that it was of no historical value, as was so often the case with Philo. Though indeed instances can be cited in which Philo interpreted passages allegorically while also accepting their historical, literal sense as meaningful (cf. *Mut. nom.* 81), these are more in the nature of exceptions which prove the rule that Philo normally rejected the literal meaning of a passage as absurd and ridiculous (cf. *Somn.* I.102). In his treatment of the same Old Testament passage which Paul takes up here, Philo adopts precisely this kind of attitude, arguing that the story shows Abraham as a learner of wisdom, with Hagar being his preliminary instruction, and Sarah representing the chief good of all learning, true virtue (cf. *de Congress. Erud. Grat.* 11–24; *Quaest. in Gen.* III.21). Paul, however, admits the historicity of the actual events which he takes as an illustration of spiritual lessons, and it is precisely because of this that he can use the story to such good effect.[63] In fact, the lessons which Paul brings out in his 'allegorical' interpretation are directly based on the historical nature of the story which he allegorizes. When Duncan characterizes this kind of argument as a claim that 'a shadow from the eternal world [is] cast upon the sands of time', he has not appreciated the main point of Paul's method here,[64] for the story of Sarah and Hagar does not *conceal* the reality of the divine will as it exists in some other, ethereal, world: it shows in its historical comprehension the operation of the divine will, for the experiences of Sarah and Hagar in this world manifest the principles according to which God will always operate. So Paul can see the whole story as a foreshadowing of the principles according to which God could be expected to work in the messianic community of the true Israel: 'Sarah and Hagar in their experiences foreshadow and manifest the principles seen in full flower in the Messianic Community versus legalistic Judaism' (Ellis, *Paul's Use of the Old Testament*, p. 130).

This kind of approach to the Old Testament is more what we would call 'typological' than 'allegorical', at least if we use the latter term as it has come to be associated with the methods of Philo and, later, Origen. At the same time, however, we should not lose sight of the important fact emphasized by Schlier: 'The fact is that this is not pure typology, since Hagar does not represent another person, but another covenant (*diathēkē*) and then corresponds to the present Jerusalem, just as Sarah does to the Jerusalem above' (*Galaterbrief*, p. 219). Perhaps we ought rather to adopt some such view as that put forward by A. T. Hanson (*Jesus Christ in the Old Testament*), and speak not even of typology, but of 'the real presence of the pre-existent Christ in OT history' (p. 7). Whatever is the precise definition we give to Paul's thought here, we must conclude that, while he uses an allegorical *form of expression*, the content which he puts into the form belies its true nature, which is more like the typological. Whereas for Philo the Old Testament was often a completely meaningless book in its literal and historical sense, requiring the enlightenment of *gnōsis* to bring out its true 'spiritual' meaning, for Paul the Old Testament was a book containing an account of the spiritual pilgrimage of man. It revealed the character of both man and God, showed the dealings of God with men of old (and therefore also his dealings with contemporary men), and revealed that those who would have an experiential understanding of the spiritual realities of biblical religion needed not *gnōsis* but *pistis*, whereby they could share in those same experiences whose validity was vouched for by historical record.

Is there onomatology here?

This device again is said to be of Alexandrian origin, but in the case of the alleged use of it here ('Now Hagar is Mount Sinai in Arabia . . .', 4.25) not only the interpretation but the text itself is in some confusion. Having asserted in the previous verses that Hagar's part in the story represented the conditions of the Sinai covenant, Paul now goes even further and actually identifies Hagar with Sinai itself. The difficulty of understanding precisely what this means is doubtless the *raison d'être* of the variant readings in those MSS. which omit mention of Hagar, preferring instead to read a geographical description of Mount Sinai. According to Chrysostom, however, the explanation of the verse is to be found in the fact that, in the language of the natives of the area, Sinai was spoken of as 'Hagar', though he gives no indication of how this information had reached him, still less how it would have been known to Paul or why the apostle should have introduced it here. Others have traced various linguistic parallels, while Burton (*Galatians*, p. 259) would like to treat the verse as a later gloss, an explanation which raises more problems than it solves. It is even more difficult to understand why a later editor should have wanted to insert such an odd statement than it is to see why Paul wrote it in the first instance.[65] For our purposes, two things need to be noted:

1. If there is a case of onomatology here, this in itself does not stamp Paul's method as being either Alexandrian or anything else. Word play on the significance of names was common enough in

the Old Testament, and there are significant examples of it in the very context to which Paul is here alluding (Gen. 17.5; 21.3–6). It can also be found in the Talmud (cf. *Berakoth* 7b) as easily as in Philo (cf. *Leg. alleg.* III.244).

2. According to C. H. Dodd, the key to the understanding of the problem is to be found in the use of *sunstoichein* in verse 25, which he argues was a technical term used to denote a regular practice of arranging the elements of such a narrative in a series of columns.[66] So, in the case of this narrative, the following parallels can be discerned:

1	2	3	4
Hagar Sinai covenant	Ishmael	Sarah New covenant	Isaac
Present Jerusalem	Children of the present Jerusalem	New Jerusalem above	Children of the new Jerusalem above

In view of the many divergent views of Paul's argument and methodology here, probably the most we can say with certainty is that, while he is 'not quite in line with what we know of Hebraic thought at this point, Paul is not quite Philonic either' (Longenecker, *Paul, Apostle of Liberty*, p. 61). But a more pressing problem arises, for can we assume that Paul, in fighting opponents who were posing a grave threat to his churches, would have brought in such a patched-up argument as we seem to have here?[67] In the context of Paul's writings as a whole, this passage is unique.[68] Nor is it the only passage in Galatians where we have noticed that Paul uses a strange form of argumentation to prove something that in other contexts he could prove far more effectively by more conventional means (e.g. 3.6–14). The conclusion to be drawn from such observations is surely that Paul is here using the kind of argumentation put forward by the false teachers whom he was opposing; and if his method appears to be confused, it is only because it is a reflection of the confusion in the Galatian churches. In contrast with what Paul says on the Law in Romans, reaching the same broad conclusions but by more forceful and, one may add, more logical arguments, it seems best to suppose that this peculiar section of Galatians was directly conditioned by some special circumstances in the churches to which he was writing. Even today, experience often shows that the best way to deal with false teaching is to refute it on the basis of its own presuppositions. Christians who have attempted to dispute the claims of British Israelites, Jehovah's Witnesses, and the like, usually discover that it cannot be done in a manner that will even gain a hearing from the adherents of such sects unless they accept many forms of argument that they would otherwise be unhappy to employ. We surely have no right to deny to Paul expedients which we often use ourselves. Perhaps this was the only way Paul could even draw the attention of those whom he was seeking to oppose.

This conclusion is reinforced by what follows, for Paul now goes on in 5.1 to give us an admirable summary of his own convictions, showing that while others may be confused about what they believe, he himself is quite clear on the matter. There are many textual difficulties in the MSS. at this point (cf. Burton, *Galatians*, pp. 270ff.), but it is probably best to take the verse as a new sentence, not grammatically linked to 4.31. Taken thus, it seems to draw out the practical conclusion from the 'allegory' of Sarah and Hagar which Paul has just used. What Paul is saying is: 'Because we have been born free (cf. 1.31), we as Christians ought to live in the freedom which Christ has secured for us.' Paul's thought here is clear and concise, as well it might be if in fact this statement comprises 'an epitome of the contention of the whole letter' (Burton, *Galatians*, p. 270).

Just one question needs further clarification here: the background of Paul's use of the term *eleutheros*. Parallels have often been sought in the Old Testament, on the one hand, and in Cynic/Stoic, or even Gnostic, philosophy, on the other. As with so many things in the interpretation of this epistle, however, the advocates of each viewpoint tend to overstate their case. Longenecker can regard Paul's thought on freedom as almost purely Jewish only by subordinating the distinctively Christian content of Paul's convictions to their Jewish forerunners.[69] Similarly, the attempt to base Paul's thought here on either Stoic or Gnostic thought, both of which were essentially anthropomorphic, fails just because in some ways Paul's concept was similar to the Jewish view, though his is quite definitely Christocentric. The key to what Paul is saying here lies in the active form of the first part of the verse, with especial emphasis laid on the subject of the verb: 'For freedom *Christ* has set us free.' When we look back in the context of Galatians to find out from what Christ has set us free, we discover that he has released us from *ta stoicheia tou kosmou* (4.3),[70] which he accomplished by taking upon himself the curse of the Law (3.10ff.). Since the only positive purpose served by the Law was to show up wrongdoing as a transgression against God (3.19), then Paul obviously assumes that we have also been set free ultimately from the power of sin—something which he takes up at a deeper level later in the epistle (5.13—6.10). From what we have seen of Paul's intentions in the contexts just cited, it is plain that he would have rejected the idea that his concept of freedom was either Jewish, Stoic, or Gnostic: it was simply his *Christian* idea, which saw the abrogation of all legal devices in the person of Jesus Christ, and found the secret of true personal liberty in self-surrender to him.[71]

CIRCUMCISION

We shall return shortly to the problem of Christian freedom in connection with 5.13—6.10. Meanwhile, we turn to the next section of Paul's argument, 5.2–12, where he goes on to deal, again in summary fashion, with the matter of circumcision. The heart of this section is, of course, v. 6: 'In Christ Jesus neither circumcision nor uncircumcision is of any avail, but faith working through love.' This is the basis for Paul's teaching elsewhere that Christians are to be regarded as the 'true circumcision', but it is important to notice that he does not say this here. In writing to the Galatians, Paul was utterly convinced that the rite of circumcision and all that it represented was completely opposed to the freedom in Christ which he himself enjoyed. On the basis of his own experience, and of what he had seen amongst Gentile Christians, Paul had no doubt that the work of Christ in the life of the believer had nothing to do with external things like keeping the Torah or being circumcised. So strong was his conviction that the natural implication of what he says here seems to be that people who would insist on such things were not merely introducing unnecessary complications into the Christian faith: they were actually opposing the very basis of that faith by suggesting, perhaps unconsciously, that circumcision was of greater importance and of more lasting spiritual efficacy than the work of Christ himself. Kümmel's comment on the situation is worth quoting at length:

> It was not a question of two different possibilities of Christian faith in opposition to each other, but of taking up once more, at another stage, the struggle between Jesus and the Pharisees. As the one who brought and proclaimed God's final act of divine salvation and his decisive and unconditional claim, Jesus had roused the hostility of the representatives of official Judaism, to whom the Jews' salvation seemed to be based on the fulfilment of the law within the framework of the Jewish religious community; and now this Jewish moral religion was asserting itself once more, with its reliance on the works of man, and against the gospel of God's saving work in Christ for all men and of his unique act of salvation as the basis of human action . . . and so what was really at stake in this struggle was not Paul's influence or success, but his Lord's cause (Dibelius/Kümmel, *Paul*, pp. 134ff.).

There are, however, two particular problems in this section of the epistle. The first, which is also the most important, concerns the interpretation of v. 3; and the second, simpler, problem is the odd statement in v. 11, 'if I . . . still preach circumcision'.

In connection with v. 3 Schmithals, in his valuable and provocative study already referred to at some length, makes two assertions:

1. The way in which Paul has to point out to his opponents the necessity of keeping the Law if they are also circumcised shows beyond any doubt that they were not Judaizers, but Jewish Gnostics (*Paul and the Gnostics*, pp. 33ff.).

2. The occurrence of the rite of circumcision in the Galatian heresy likewise does not prove that the heretics were Judaizers, since Gnostics also used the rite of circumcision, though in their case it was as a symbol of spiritual release from the flesh and its inhibiting powers (op. cit., pp. 35ff.).

These two assertions are closely connected with one another, and so we will take them both together in our discussion here. The first point to be noted is that it is by no means certain that Paul was here revealing some new truth to his opponents when he suggested (5.3) that if circumcision was to be of any value to them they must also keep the Law in its entirety.[72] In spite of Schmithals's protests (op. cit., p. 33, n. 49), Kümmel still seems to have more concrete evidence on his side in concluding that 'no one can deny that the Galatian intruders demanded the acceptance of the Law' (*Introduction*, p. 194), in support of which he draws attention to 2.16; 3.21b; 4.21; and 5.4. Of these verses, 5.4 is better left out of account, since it is in the disputed context, and our understanding of it will largely depend on our view of the preceding verses. Verses 2.16 and 3.21b likewise are slightly equivocal, and could be made to fit in with whatever overall pattern of interpretation may appeal to the individual exegete. But 4.21, both grammatically and logically, seems to prove beyond the slightest possibility of doubt that the Galatian herctics were promoting the observance of the Law as well as circumcision. Though the use of the present participle *thelontes* possibly indicates that the majority of the Galatian Christians had not actually taken upon themselves the burden of the Law, we can hardly doubt that it is meant to imply that this was precisely what they were about to do (cf. Burton, *Galatians*, p. 252). The use of *thelō* here recalls 4.9, where Paul had associated the Law with the *stoicheia tou kosmou*, and again had stated the Galatians' desire to be in bondage to these *stoicheia*—a fact which speaks strongly against the suggestion that in the context of 4.21 he was telling them something they did not already know. Unless they were actively seeking to place themselves under the Law, his argument here would be emptied of meaning, for the irony of what he says depends for its effect on this one simple fact: 'Since you want to be under the Law, why do you pay no attention to what the Law actually says?' The fact that they were unable to live up to their aspirations by actually keeping the Law is another matter altogether, but it can hardly be used as an argument to suggest that the Law had no place in their thinking. If in the light of 4.21 we now turn to 5.3 we can see the significance of what Paul says. It is reasonable to suppose that here Paul is drawing to the attention of his readers either a fact of which they were ignorant, or one which they had not taken sufficiently into consideration. But we must not pose a false dichotomy between these two possibilities. By far the simplest solution is to suppose that 4.21 and 5.3 were each directed to a different sector of the Christian communities which Paul was addressing—not in the sense that some were Judaizers while others held to other beliefs, but simply according to the practical distinction which will always appear in such a situation. We have already taken note of the principle that in any potentially 'heretical' situation, two groups will naturally emerge: the leaders, who have worked everything out on a theological basis, and others who, for various reasons, are willing to follow the leaders in a practical way, without taking upon themselves the burden of formulating any precise intellectual foundation for their actions (see above, pp. 10ff.). In 4.21 Paul is probably addressing the better educated members of the Galatian churches, who had worked out the full implications of the step that was being urged upon them by the 'heretics', while in 5.3 he is making the same appeal to those who had neither the inclination nor the capacity to take account of the theological implications of the practice of circumcision. In view of 6.12, where one of the 'advantages' of circumcision is said to be escape from persecution, it becomes quite likely that those Galatians who were pragmatists before they were theologians would as a matter of expediency accept the one thing without even thinking of the other. Burton (*Galatians*, p. 274) goes too far when he says that 'the judaisers had not proposed to them to keep the whole law'. Being wise strategists, Paul's opponents would know that it was easier to persuade the Galatians to do something that was 'external', such as circumcision, than it was to persuade them to keep the Law which, in spite of Paul's depreciation of it, was still in some sense an 'internal' exercise. If it was circumcision rather than the keeping of the Law that could result in escape from persecution, this would obviously satisfy the unthinking members of the churches. Those who wanted to have a more theological insight, on the other hand, seem not to have been circumcised as yet (cf. also 4.21). Paul's opponents, whoever they were, only wanted something to prove that the Galatians were following them and not Paul; and on any score, it was easier to prove that a man was circumcised than it was to prove that he had kept the Law.

Schmithals's interpretation at this point must, therefore, be rejected, for four main reasons:

1. By any canon of exegesis, Schmithals's theory grossly complicates the situation in Galatia. On the assumption that, in general,

the simplest explanation is likely to be the more correct, we may claim greater historical probability for the reconstruction of events set out here.

2. There can be no doubt that 4.21 does prove that the Law had a part in the Galatian heresy, and Schmithals has taken insufficient account of this and similar verses, while over-emphasizing 5.3. The difficulty could be overcome by adopting some such theory as Ropes, for example, has put forward, and attributing 4.21 to a Judaizing heresy, and 5.3 to alleged Gnostic elements.[73] But since Schmithals sees only one sort of opponent (Jewish Gnostics), this must be regarded as an inconsistency in his argument.

3. Schmithals seems to assume too readily that if it can be proved that Paul's opponents were not Judaizers, this automatically shows that they must have been Gnostics. But we can assume no such thing. Both the Law and circumcision were differently estimated in the different Gnostic systems of which we know, not to mention scores of others of which we have lamentably little knowledge. To base any theory on such flimsy evidence as we have is to court disaster.

4. The internal evidence of the epistle itself suggests that the Law as well as circumcision played an important part in the Galatian heresy. Our exegesis so far has shown that the epistle can be intelligently understood on this assumption and, though there is a danger here of arguing in a circle, this is something that must be taken into account, if only as corroborating evidence.

But Schmithals also argues that the circumcision mentioned here, whatever connection it may have had with the Law, was not Jewish circumcision but a 'Gnostic circumcision' symbolizing release from the flesh and its powers. As proof of this, he refers to three main types of so-called Jewish Gnostic groups, all of whom laid emphasis on circumcision: the Ebionites, the Elchasaites, and Cerinthus (*Paul and the Gnostics*, pp. 36ff.). That they all stressed the need for circumcision is clear. Unfortunately, it is by no means equally clear that they can all be called 'Gnostic'. The Ebionites had a great hostility to Paul, as can be seen from the Clementine *Homilies* and *Recognitions*. But it is far from certain that they could be described as 'Gnostic'. Indeed, in the Pseudo-Clementines they often characterize Paul as Simon Magus, reputedly the first Gnostic, so at least they can have had little interest in the kind of Gnosticism represented by Simon. The Ebionites had certain Gnostic traits, holding an adoptionist view of the person of Christ which, according to Irenaeus, *Adv. Haer.* I.26.2, was not so very different from the Christology of Cerinthus and Carpocrates. But their main distinguishing mark was their belief that Jesus came as a 'new Moses', not to abolish the Law but to reform and reinforce it. This stands in striking contrast to the belief of many Gnostics, that the Old Testament Law was itself a powerful weapon in the arsenal of the demonic Demiurge, often used in the fight against the divine *pneuma* imprisoned in man. It was in *this* context that the Ebionites practised circumcision, and not in the Gnostic context that Schmithals supposes.[74] In any case, Schoeps has put forward a powerful argument for seeing them as nothing more than a deviant group of Jewish Christians.[75] We are probably better to admit that we know too little of them to reach any firm conclusions at all about their relationship, if any, to other religious groups.

The same can be said of the Elchasaites, of whom, if anything, we know even less. Most of what we know of them comes from the so-called *Book of Elchasai*, found in a number of fragments in the works of Hippolytus and Epiphanius, conveniently collected together in *NTA* II, pp. 745ff. The Elchasaites practised circumcision, though they rejected, or at least devalued, the Old Testament, while keeping the sabbath and praying towards Jerusalem! Gnostic ideas seem to have been entertained about Christ and the Holy Spirit. Elchasai himself evidently emerged as a prophet of some kind in the third year of Trajan's reign (A.D. 101), though there is some doubt as to whether the name 'Elchasai' was the name of an actual person. The fragments of the *Book of Elchasai* certainly give this impression, though Epiphanius (*Pan.* 19.2.10) realized that the origin of the name lay in the Aramaic *ḥayil kasayh*, meaning 'hidden power'. Working from this, Schmithals is of the opinion that the name 'originally certainly does not have reference to any individual person, but rather the power which is concealed in all Gnostics, which redeems itself in the *stas*' (*Gnosticism in Corinth*, p. 37, n. 34). It could also denote 'that "Dynamis" also called Christ, which is found on earth in all

Pneumatics and can be active as redeemer in each of its parts' (op. cit., p. 50). Unfortunately, in making these associations Schmithals is taking as his basic presupposition just the very thing that we cannot be sure of, viz. whether the Elchasaites really were Gnostics. The few fragments of evidence that we have suggest that we are rather foolish to draw any very sweeping conclusions in the present state of our knowledge.

Of Cerinthus we have more information. He also held a strange mixture of Jewish and Gnostic ideas. On the Old Testament, his view approximated more to the classical Gnostic dualistic view, for he argued that the 'Supreme Father' was unknown, while the God of the Old Testament, who had created the world and given the Law, was simply an angel. He combined with this a Docetic view of the person of Jesus, uniting the whole lot with a strongly Jewish eschatological outlook, partly based on the New Testament Apocalypse, of which at least one ancient writer accused Cerinthus of being the author! (Cf. Eusebius, *H.E.* III.28.2.)

Schmithals has undoubtedly drawn out some intriguing parallels here, but the central problem still remains as unsolved as ever. For there is no evidence at all to suggest that the Ebionites, the Elchasaites, or the Cerinthians existed as early as the time of Paul's ministry. Even if we suppose (as we must) that these sects had their historical roots in the soil of the first century, it is foolhardy to assume that the peculiar combination of doctrines which we find in our sources had any existence in precisely that combination prior to the time at which we have specific evidence of it.[76] Moreover, in speaking of a 'Gnostic circumcision', Schmithals has not taken account of other Gnostic traditions with different estimates of circumcision. We need look no further than two of the more important finds at Nag Hammadi, the *Gospel of Philip* and the *Gospel of Thomas*. *Philip* has a statement which makes circumcision a symbol of release from the flesh (log. 123), but the *Gospel of Thomas* rejects it altogether.[77] It must be obvious that the parallels adduced by Schmithals can prove absolutely nothing at all about the situation in Galatia. On the contrary, as we shall shortly see, the situation in Galatia, and Paul's statements in the epistle, can shed considerable light on the development of such Gnostic ideas.

We now come on to 5.11, which can be dealt with much more briefly. It is clear that Paul himself still observed the Jewish Law, and apparently expected Jewish Christians to do the same, despite his strong conviction that Gentiles should never be placed under the burden of the Torah. But was he also 'preaching circumcision'? If we can believe that Paul was here fighting a battle on two fronts, against Judaizers and against Gentile antinomians or Gnostics, it is possible to take this verse to be a reply against the latter group, who had accused Paul of not having quite overcome his Jewish background himself (cf. Ropes, *Singular Problem*, pp. 39ff.). According to the account of Acts 16.3, Paul did on one occasion circumcise Timothy, and it is conceivable that something of that kind lies behind this verse, though Acts makes it clear that this was an act of expediency and not one of principle. But if Galatians is to be dated earlier than the incident with Timothy, this cannot have been in mind; and the mention of Titus in 2.3 is so equivocal that it can provide no exegetical basis for supposing either that he was circumcised or that he was not. Probably the best explanation of this verse is therefore to take it as an elaboration of what Paul said in 1.13ff., and so it would refer to his former life as a Pharisee.[78] Before his conversion he had no doubt been a powerful advocate of circumcision, and the whole point of his statement here would be the contrast between his days as a Jewish missionary and his new task as an apostle of Jesus Christ. Though his opponents may try to make out that the apostle himself was an advocate of circumcision, the fact that he was persecuted for his work showed clearly that it had no part in his message.[79] If on occasion he found it expedient for the sake of his mission to circumcise a Timothy, or possibly a Titus, then that was a proof not of his bondage to legalism but of his liberty in Christ, for the liberty under which he operated included the freedom to circumcise as well as the freedom to refrain from doing so. In any case, the indisputable fact that the persecutor had become the victim must prove that some basic change had overtaken him.

CHRISTIAN SOCIAL ETHICS

So we come on to the last section of this epistle with which we shall deal in any detail: the question of Christian social ethics, in 5.13—6.10. Having dismissed the relevance of the Law and the rite of initiation into the Law-orientated community, Paul now feels himself constrained to demonstrate that this does not, in his view, lead to lawlessness. To the Jew, the Torah of the Old Testament was the main bulwark against the morality of the pagan world, and there can be no doubt at all that because of the eminent place occupied by the Torah in Judaism, the Jews enjoyed a considerably higher moral standard than any of the peoples among whom they lived in the ancient world. If Christians rejected the Law, were they not also rejecting the morality which it represented? On the contrary, argued Paul, those who reject the Law out of Christian convictions have rejected only the outward form of morality, which could never ultimately make a man completely righteous anyway. The Christian has the Spirit of Christ within him, which is a 'law' in the sense that it is a principle of action, and also a source of moral strength and ability. What Paul says here makes it clear that the Jewish Law, with its specific precepts, has gone for ever, and he proposes to put in its place as the spring of moral action not a new set of rules, but Christ Himself. It is noteworthy that hardly anything Paul says here can be taken as a specific instruction to be applied in a particular set of circumstances: rather does the main emphasis now rest on the conviction that Christians live on a new level of existence, and so their actions will automatically follow from this new kind of existence which they enjoy. Paul draws a strong antithesis between the two possible modes of existence, spiritual existence and fleshly existence. The freedom which we have in Christ is not to become an occasion for *hē sarx* to come in, since 'those who belong to Christ Jesus have crucified the *sarx* with its passions and desires' (v. 24). As a result of this, the Christian's moral imperatives are formulated by the fruit of the Spirit, which manifests itself in his life. Because of his own recognized weakness, the Christian should beware of judging others. Instead, his duty is to 'fulfil the law of Christ' in everything (6.2), for in order to reap the harvest of eternal life, one must sow not to the flesh, but to the Spirit (6.3–10).

Two main points deserve further discussion here: the antithesis of flesh and spirit (*sarx* and *pneuma*), and 'the law of Christ' (*ho nomos tou Christou*).

Sarx and pneuma

Schmithals has again seen Gnostic influences at work here, and suggests that the kind of libertinism envisaged in 5.13 is of a

Gnostic stamp, since the *sarx* played a great part in Gnosticism as the evil principle in which the divine *pneuma* was imprisoned (*Paul and the Gnostics*, pp. 51ff.). But the grammatical form of 5.13 is against Schmithals here. The absence of a verb in the phrase *monon mē tēn eleutherian eis aphormēn tē sarki* suggests that Paul's thought has had an abrupt change of direction, and what he says is almost an afterthought as he realizes that there was the possibility of his emphasis on Christian freedom being taken as an antinomian licence. If such an antinomian libertinism was already operative in the Galatian churches, Paul would probably have introduced it earlier in the epistle and made more of it. But what he says here suggests that at that time it was simply a theoretical possibility in his own mind.

The same general criticisms of Schmithals's position that we have already noted can also be made here. The idea of the *sarx* is not prominent in the earlier Gnostic systems and, in addition, for Paul it was something entirely different.[80] Whereas the Gnostic would have seen the flesh as a part of the evil world, which was ready to confine man's spiritual nature, Paul regarded the flesh as something essentially inward and human. It was not some external force impinging on man's spiritual well-being from the outside: it was an integral part of man's own personality. Thus when Paul spoke of putting to death 'the flesh' (5.24), he meant that Christians were to put to death *themselves* (cf. 2.19ff.). This is much closer to the Qumran equation of flesh with sin than it is to anything in Gnosticism.[81] The question of the life principle according to which a man lives is decisive in the ordering of all his thoughts and actions: '. . . orientation to the *sarx* or the *pneuma* and hence life in the power of the *sarx* or the *pneuma* is a total attitude which determines everything' (E. Schweizer, *TDNT* VII, p. 135). The question is not one of substance but one of nature and principle. For Paul, this also means that one's standard of morality is determined not by reference to fixed rules and regulations, but according to the life principle under which one operates. Thus, the believer in Christ quite simply does not do the works of the flesh (5.19ff.), but in all his activity produces the fruit of the Spirit (5.22ff.), which is both the foundation and the principle of action in the Christian sphere of existence.[82] For a man to be righteous before God by the work of the Spirit through Christ naturally and inevitably leads to the production of a life that is Christlike, and any other standard is for Paul a contradiction in terms (5.25). This leads us on to the second main point here:

'The law of Christ' (*ho nomos tou Christou*, *6.2*)

The question that now arises is whether, having stated that Christian morality finds its source not in an ethical code but in a living relationship to Jesus Christ, Paul goes back on what he has said, and introduces some form of embryonic church law. Both Davies and Longenecker, in their respective works on the relationship of Paul to his Jewish background, answer this question in the affirmative. Davies goes so far as to say that 'Paul the Apostle of the freedom of the Christian man from the bondage of legalism has turned out to be a catechist after the manner of a rabbi.'[83] Thus the church,

> despite its freedom in the Spirit . . . had to know moral order also, it had to regulate its life. The Church, like every new sect within Judaism, had to draw up rules for the moral guidance of its members and had to define its position. Moreover, there is solid evidence that in doing this Paul and the other Christian leaders drew upon certain Jewish codes or regulations (op. cit., p. 130).

This is a more extreme position than Longenecker's, and Davies himself realizes the uncertain nature of much of what he says, for when he tries to find evidence to support himself, he confesses: 'We are in difficulty. It is impossible to give a cut-and-dried answer.'[84] Perhaps, we may suggest, because he is looking in the wrong direction. Longenecker sees the inconsistency of Davies's position, though his own is no better. He argues that in order to reconcile the legal and pneumatic aspects of Paul's theology, it is necessary to distinguish between the directing principles of the 'law of Christ' and the pneumatic guidance of the 'mind of Christ' (*Paul, Apostle of Liberty*, pp. 191ff.). But he still believes that the teaching of Jesus and the example of his earthly ministry were 'an external and authoritative norm and pattern for the outworking of Christian liberty' (op. cit., p. 190). According to O'Neill (*Recovery of Paul's Letter to the Galatians*, p. 70), this phrase is the work of a later interpolator. But to suggest that Paul could not have used it here is simply begging the question and solves nothing. Several points must be considered:

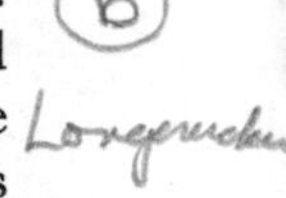

1. In so far as Jewish parallels are concerned, both Davies and Longenecker have shown conclusively that the idea of a new Torah in the messianic age was firmly established at least within a major sector of Judaism (cf. also S-B III, p. 577). But this in itself is no reason to suppose that Paul, as a Christian now and no longer a Jew, would have held precisely this view.

2. Both Davies and Longenecker lay great emphasis on the fact that Paul either quotes from, or alludes to, the ethical teaching of Jesus. This is a well-established fact, though there are no indisputable examples of it in Galatians.[85] But again, even this cannot prove that Paul thought of Christ as a 'new Torah' in the sense of a purveyor of a new set of external moral rules. The very suggestion that Paul may be doing this is absurd, for it is now widely recognized that in no sense could the moral teaching of Jesus Himself be described as a rule book of life. When A. M. Hunter called his exposition of the Sermon on the Mount, *Design for Life*, he saw more clearly than Davies and Longenecker, for this is just the very point of all Jesus' teachings: he gives broad spiritual principles only and leaves the detailed working out of them to the individual. Paul would add that this process is the work of the Holy Spirit in the believer's life, which in many cases is just another way of saying that Christ himself must live in the believer in order that the Christian ethic may be fully worked out.

3. Leading on from this, it seems to us that the weakness of the approach of Davies and Longenecker lies in the fact that, though both of them have sought to dig up material hidden beneath the surface of Paul's epistles, in the shape of quotations from, or allusions to, Jesus' words, they have in many ways, like the Pharisees, strained out a gnat and swallowed a camel (Matt. 23.24). In trying to understand Paul's attitude to the example of Christ as a viable pattern for the life of Christians we are better to start from plain, unequivocal statements, and then in the light of these to seek to understand the allusions and quotations. It is of no small significance that in only two places does Paul specifically set forth Christ as a viable example for Christians to follow; and it is even more significant that in both of them (Phil. 2.5–8; 2 Cor. 8.9), he draws attention not to the details of our Lord's life and ministry, but to the central act involved in the whole mystery of

the incarnation, Christ's emptying himself of his divine glory, and his coming among men to die for them. This points us back not to the gospel traditions but to what Paul says in Galatians 5.13–26, and can only serve to reinforce our conclusions on that passage.  For Paul, the *basis* of Christian morality was not in a tradition of the words and teachings of Jesus, nor even in an account of his deeds, but in the person of the Lord whom he served. This was central to all Paul's thought, and if we miss this we shall never fully understand him.  There is more than a little truth in John Oman's claim that, supposing one was able to model his life according to the pattern of activity which Jesus Himself followed in his ministry, even 'the exactest imitation would only be lifeless unedifying mimicry. . . . Though echoed to the letter . . . the soul of it would still be wanting, and would be no more His example than a death-mask a living face.'[86] The conclusion to be drawn from all this seems to be that, if we really must describe Christ as a 'new Torah' (and Paul himself gives us no grounds for doing so),[87] it can only be done by a redefinition of the terms of reference. In so far as the Torah was the centre of the Jews' life, establishing, guiding, and controlling all that they were, then Christ can be likened to it. For He was indeed the centre of Paul's life; but not so much in his teaching as in his person.[88] When Paul wrote at a later stage in his ministry, 'to me to live is Christ' (Phil. 1.21), he was expressing not only the basis of his existence, but the heart and source of his ethical theory.

4. Before leaving the subject we must make one important observation on the methodology of Davies and Longenecker. It seems to us that where their approach has failed is in its assumption that the ethical teaching of Galatians and 1 Corinthians can be used interchangeably.[89] The 'law of Christ' can be found in 1 Corinthians 9.21 only on one interpretation of the evidence, but the phrase used there, 'under law to Christ' (*ennomos Christou*), is so similar to expressions used elsewhere by Paul to refer to being 'under the rule of Torah', that it is clear Paul is referring in that context to some new, Christian moral code. In Galatians, however, 'The law of Christ deals with what a man is, not, like other laws, with what a man does.'[90] Wilfred Knox appreciated the distinction between the two epistles, though he did not draw out its full implications: in 1 Corinthians, because of the situation in

that church, Paul 'is forced to introduce an elementary form of a Christian moral code, but it is certainly inconsistent with his theology in . . . Galatians'.[91] One of the things that is immediately obvious as we compare the ethical teaching of Galatians with 1 Corinthians is that here in Galatians there is no mention at all of the principle of limiting one's Christian liberty for the sake of a weaker brother. Though Paul mentions love of one's neighbour (5.14), though he gives very general advice on personal relationships (5.27), and though he speaks of Christians serving one another in love (5.13; 6.1), this is not the same as the explicit advice given in both 1 Corinthians 8 and Romans 14. We shall consider the reasons for this later. But in Galatians, the main emphasis is on the person of Jesus Christ, his significance in the plan of God, and his indwelling in the life of the believer. Heinrich Schlier has admirably summarized Paul's thought at this point, and we can do no better than refer to his judgement:

> As the Spirit applies the act of God in Jesus Christ, who has overcome us, there is fulfilled in us that which the Law as the will of God demands for our life. . . . If we open our lives to this incursion of the Spirit of the act of God in Jesus Christ, there takes place in them the grounding of our lives in the realised love of Jesus Christ. By the Spirit and power of the life of Jesus Christ radically offered up in love, there is brought into being in our lives an existence which is unselfish and self-forgetting because it is dynamically hidden in love and can no longer be self-seeking and self-willed. In the Spirit of the freedom of Jesus Christ, there arises our freedom (*TDNT* II, p. 499).

IV

A Last Triumphant Appeal (6.11–18)

Paul's argument is at an end, but he once again emphasizes it with a final appeal to his readers in his own handwriting (6.11–18). He does so first by scoring two points against his opponents, and then, as a foil to these, he makes two positive statements about his own beliefs and practice. He points the finger of accusation first at the spiritual bankruptcy of those who were corrupting the Galatian Christians: they 'want to make a good showing in the flesh' (v. 12), the very thing that Paul had denounced in the previous section, since 'he who sows to his own flesh will from the flesh reap corruption' (v. 8). Then he turns upon their inconsistency (v. 13): they may emphasize the outward, fleshly sign, but they are not willing to accept even such spiritual discipline as would be involved in keeping the Torah!

In contrast to this, however, Paul can make two very positive statements about himself. Though his opponents want to glory in the flesh (v. 13), he realizes that the only legitimate cause of glorying before God is that the Christian has been crucified to the world, through the cross of Christ. This kind of 'new creation' (v. 15) is the only thing of any value in the sight of God, and the sole qualifying mark of 'the Israel of God' (v. 16). Then finally, in v. 17, Paul emphasizes that, though he may well be criticized as being some kind of renegade Jew, yet he does possess the mark of true spirituality before God: 'I bear on my body the marks of Jesus.' To the very end of the epistle, Paul continues the battle against his opponents, confident that in the end he must win, because Christ has already won the victory for him.

3

Paul's Corinthian Correspondence

In the Corinthian epistles, we are presented with one of the most complex historical problems of New Testament interpretation. In the effort to simplify our own approach to the problem and also in the hope of introducing some sort of order into what at times seems to have been an aimless debate, we shall divide our own consideration of the matter into only two sections. In this chapter, we shall draw attention to certain features of both Corinthian epistles which appear to be significant for a correct understanding of their teaching when seen in the light of our exegesis of Galatians. Then, in our next chapter, we shall briefly survey some other studies of the Corinthian situation, considering the conclusions reached on different premises by other scholars, and showing how our own approach can bring fresh evidence to bear on the solution of some of the most pressing historical and theological problems.

1 Corinthians

In dealing, first of all, with 1 Corinthians, two main topics deserve special consideration. These are the place of tradition within the Pauline congregations, and the problems of Christian ethics.

We have already seen in dealing with Galatians that one of the differences between Paul's apostolic claims in Galatians and 1 Corinthians is centred on the place of tradition. Though we have argued that the two statements of Galatians 1.11ff. and 1 Corinthians 15.3ff. are not necessarily contradictory when viewed in the light of Paul's overall theological position, nevertheless there is a distinct difference of emphasis which we should not ignore, and which is very real. In fighting his opponents in the Galatian churches Paul had found it necessary to emphasize that what he knew of the gospel of Christ was not something he had learned from others, but something which was the result of a moral and spiritual change of a quite fundamental nature in his own experience. Now, in dealing with a different situation in the Corinthian church, he made a different approach, not indeed for the purpose of contradicting what he had said in Galatians, but in order to draw out another aspect of his Christian experience: 'Both senses were equally true to his experience, but the apologetic or polemic requirements of the moment might lead him at times to emphasize the one to the seeming exclusion of the other.'[1] We can therefore have little reason to doubt that what Paul says here, and the way in which he says it, is directly conditioned not by some new experience but by the historical conditions of the moment. The fact that he uses precisely the same language in 1 Corinthians 15.3 as he had earlier used in Galatians 1.11ff. makes the distinction even more marked, and at least opens the possibility that Paul's opponents in Corinth had actually quoted his statements in Galatians to prove their own point of view. This can, of course, never be proved one way or the other. But since it is clear that the Galatian congregations were known to the Corinthians (cf. 1 Cor. 16.1), and in view of what we know of Paul's desire for his letters to be exchanged among the churches (cf. Col. 4.16), it must at least be a possibility that some of the Corinthian Christians could have been familiar with Paul's teaching in Galatians.

It is also significant that elsewhere in 1 Corinthians Paul speaks of 'traditions' which had been handed down by him to the Corinthian Christians, an emphasis which appears to represent a definite attempt by the apostle to place himself within the mainstream of church tradition as it existed at that time. 1 Corinthians 11.23ff. is the other passage which readily springs to mind here, because of its importance not only in the Corinthian correspondence, but also in the understanding of early Christian history and theology in general, for it is the earliest account of the institution of the Eucharist. But it is not the only place in 1 Corinthians where Paul emphasizes a 'tradition' in the sense of something that had been handed down to the Corinthians by an apostolic authority, and which therefore was binding on them and also on the other congregations of Christians with which they were linked. In 11.2, the Corinthians are commended because they have maintained 'the traditions' which Paul gave to them, either during his ministry among them or in the problematical 'previous letter' —a statement which at least one commentary takes to refer to 'some rudimentary creed which was given to missionaries and catechists',[2] and which presumably Paul had received from someone else before passing it on to his converts.[3] Even when the term itself is not used, the authoritative character of such 'tradition' is emphasized over and over again in 1 Corinthians, as Paul introduces a new moral motive: that Christians should act in accordance with the 'rule in all the churches' (4.17), something we shall consider shortly.

The different attitude which Paul displays here to the question of tradition over against his teaching in Galatians is clear enough. But when we look to Paul's ethical teaching in 1 Corinthians, we move in what at times seems to be a different world from that of Galatians. We can conveniently consider Paul's ethical teaching in 1 Corinthians under three main headings, in each of which we find significant tensions with his earlier teaching in Galatians: on the nature of ethical principles, ethical motives, and ethical behaviour.

ETHICAL PRINCIPLES

Two main passages require consideration here in connection with the ethical principles enunciated by Paul in 1 Corinthians 4.16ff.

and 7.19. In 4.16ff., we find that Paul is represented as an accredited, authorized example of Christ himself, and so he can instruct his readers to 'imitate me' (v. 16). Just as in normal secular life one's father was to be the subject of imitation, or as in the philosophical schools the pupil imitated the teacher (Xenophon, *Mem.* I.6.3), so in the spiritual realm one ought to follow the example set by the apostle. Though it is doubtless true to say, as one writer points out, that 'the Lord is the great example, but it is the lives of the saints that bring home His life to men',[4] this cannot be a complete explanation of Paul's moral exhortations here. In the light of the preceding verses (vv. 6–13), it is clear that one lesson Paul was hoping to teach his converts by his own example was the ideal of humility and self-sacrifice. But it is surely notable that in other situations where Paul wished to teach his readers exactly these same lessons, he drew a direct parallel not with himself as an accredited apostolic example, but with the person of Christ (cf. Phil. 2.4–11; 2 Cor. 8.9).[5] In Galatians, the whole emphasis of his moral teaching was that Christians should turn away from the rules and regulations imposed by the behavioural patterns of mere men who, after all, are basically sinful. They should, rather, be guided exclusively by the Holy Spirit, whose fruit produced in the life of the believer would bring forth that purity of character which was found supremely in Christ Himself (cf. Gal. 5.16ff.). Yet here, in 1 Corinthians, Paul even goes on to speak of 'my ways in Christ' (v. 17), moral principles comparable with the *Halacha* of the Jewish rabbis.[6] Moreover, as C. K. Barrett has pointed out, this can be taken to indicate 'moral standards, expressed to some extent in recognised patterns of behaviour . . . *which can be taught*'.[7] In Galatians, on the other hand, Paul had emphatically spoken against the possibility that morality could be the subject of education, even of a religious education of the kind provided by the Old Testament Law. Rather was a Christian morality the natural and almost inevitable outcome of one's association with Christ Himself. The believer who had 'put on Christ' (Gal. 3.27) would have no problem with moral principles, since his sinful nature had been 'crucified' (Gal. 5.24), and he was now living the life of freedom in the power of the Spirit. From our own standpoint, we may well think that Paul was being somewhat overoptimistic in supposing that moral problems could be solved quite so easily, even in the Christian community, but we should not on that account ignore the important difference which comes out here between Galatians and 1 Corinthians. The way Paul reinforces his exhortation here is also significant. His 'ways in Christ' have even greater importance because 'I teach them everywhere in every church' (v. 17), a statement which presupposes the existence of some form of moral law in the Pauline congregations.

Two important points need to be noted here:

1. Paul begins this moral exhortation, at least implicitly (cf. vv. 6–13), by an appeal to a broad ethical principle, based on the known characteristics of Christ himself, viz. the principles of humility and self-sacrifice, which in other contexts he considers to be the supreme moral attributes of his Lord. At this level, therefore, Paul is still holding to the same basic moral principles as he had outlined in Galatians.

2. Having done so, however, a significant distinction emerges, for Paul now proceeds to apply the basic moral principle in a way that, in the light of Galatians, is quite unexpected. There, he had referred to the work of the Spirit producing the perfect Christian character. Here, he goes on to define in very precise terms the ways in which the principle of Christian ethics should be applied, and by bringing in himself as an authorized example, and his own teaching as a kind of universal moral code, he moves a considerable distance in the direction of the 'law ethics' which he had so much deplored in the Galatian situation. The way Paul quotes a ruling of Christ, e.g. in 1 Corinthians 7.10ff., also tends to move in a 'law direction'. Though Paul also retains his emphasis on the indwelling of Christ in the believer as the very basis of Christian morality, he still introduces a 'thou shalt not', which is altogether absent from Galatians. Not that he goes back to a legalistic basis for salvation, of course. We should rather follow Longenecker, when he observes that the

> Christian ethic is *motivated by love* and not impelled by a desire to gain righteousness . . . [it] has not the character of works which establish the relation of man to the beyond, but it *takes the form of obedience* to the One who has already established that relation for the believer (*Paul, Apostle of Liberty*, p. 179).

We find precisely the same pattern in 1 Corinthians 7.19, where Paul actually takes up in the first half of the verse a statement out of which he had made great spiritual capital against his opponents in Galatia, but quite unexpectedly he now modifies it in such a way that he appears to be saying exactly the opposite of what he had said in Galatians! Again, Paul first states the principle: 'Neither circumcision counts for anything, nor uncircumcision', a statement found also in Galatians 5.6 and 6.15. We have already seen that in dispensing with circumcision Paul was by implication abandoning the absolute authority of the Old Testament, a position which was quite consistent with his other arguments in Galatians. But here in 1 Corinthians 7.19, Paul goes on to make a statement which, on the face of it, is totally incompatible with his position on circumcision: 'Keeping the commandments of God *is everything*' (the translation of Robertson and Plummer, *I Corinthians*, p. 147). To try to combine the Galatians statements and this statement into one comprehensive view, as some commentators do, is of little value in understanding Paul's thought in either context.[8] The exact phrase which he uses, 'keeping the commandments', was in certain contexts almost a *terminus technicus* for keeping the Mosaic Law of the Old Testament (Ecclus. 32.23; Wisd. 6.18; Matt. 19.17; cf. Gal. 5.14).[9] We need not suppose, of course, that it was necessarily the Old Testament commandments that Paul had in view here. But the least we can do is to observe that whereas in Galatians Paul was able to reject legalism in all its forms, here in 1 Corinthians he reintroduces the *form* of legal language, which in turn leads him into an ethical position in 1 Corinthians not so very much different from the legalism he had so much deprecated in Galatians.

ETHICAL MOTIVES

When Paul seeks to apply his moral principles by laying down particular reasons for which one ought to follow the course he advocates, rather than some other course, he again does so in two quite different ways in Galatians and 1 Corinthians. In Galatians, Paul considers that the mere desire to enjoy the freedom which Christ brings and thereby to allow the Holy Spirit to work out the principles of Christian morality within one's life is a sufficient motive for allowing one's activity to be directly controlled by

Christ himself. In 1 Corinthians, however, a new element is introduced: the desire for conformity to the universal practice of other Christian congregations. We have already seen this in 4.17, where Paul reinforces his moral directives with an appeal to what he teaches other congregations to observe, and the same ultimate appeal is made elsewhere. This is particularly obvious in 11.16 and 14.34ff., where Paul is dealing with the subject of the relative position of the sexes within Christian worship and witness. This was a subject on which Paul had made a specific pronouncement in his Galatian epistle. He was convinced that 'there is neither male nor female; for you are all one in Christ Jesus' (Gal. 3.28). Presumably this is also what the apostle had taught the Corinthians when he founded their congregation; and there is good reason to suppose that the Corinthians had taken Paul at his word, and that believers of both sexes played a more or less equal part in the service of the church.[10] The situation had evidently arisen, however, in which such a prominent part was being played by certain women in the congregation that not only the social ideas of the time but even Paul's own sense of propriety was being offended. In this situation he wished to assert, first, that the women should be veiled when taking a public part in the worship of the church (11.2–16), and then also that in certain (unspecified) situations the women should keep quiet altogether (14.33ff.). Paul himself was clearly torn between two opinions on the matter, for these two passages are, essentially, mutually contradictory, though countless explanations have been put forward in the effort to reconcile the two. On the one hand, Paul realized that if his principles of Christian liberty set out in Galatians were to be sustained, this meant the full and free participation of both sexes in the church's corporate worship; on the other hand, there was some particular reason why he did not wish this to be the case in the church at Corinth.[11] It is unnecessary for us to sort out the tangle of Paul's views on the place of women in the church at this point. Here we are concerned simply to note his form of approach. As before, he first sets out the principles involved (cf. 11.1–15), from which he attempts to prove his own point of view. It is noteworthy that Paul at first appeals to principles of action rather than to regulations. *Dei* does not appear, though both *opheilei* (indicating a moral obligation, vv. 7, 10) and *prepon estin* (a natural sense of fitness, v. 13) are used here. The same kind of principles are implicitly assumed in the short passage in 14.34ff. But in both cases, having outlined the principles and, therefore, at least by implication, having given expression to the ideals of Christian freedom, he ends the discussion with a very strong effort at compulsion: 'We recognize no other practice, nor do the churches of God' (11.16, cf. 14.36).[12] In Galatians, Paul had made the motivation for moral action the desire to please God; here, the ultimate moral sanction is the desire to please men.

ETHICAL BEHAVIOUR

In those places where Paul gives specific instructions on various aspects of conduct, we again find slight, though no less significant, differences here from his teaching in Galatians on the same, or similar, topics. In 1 Corinthians, we find the principle that Christians ought to limit their liberty in Christ depending on external circumstances, something that is altogether quite absent from Galatians. In that context, of course, Paul hardly expected the exercise of liberty to lead to quarrels and disturbances within the Christian fellowship (cf. 6.1ff.). At that stage in his ministry, Paul had assumed that if all Christians enjoyed the liberty to which Christ had called them, and renounced whatever allegiance they may have professed either to Judaism or to some other system, complete harmony would prevail in their fellowship. When at Antioch Cephas had broken off fellowship with Gentile Christians for the sake of the scruples of his Jewish brethren, Paul, far from condoning Cephas's attitude in thus limiting the exercise of his Christian liberty for the sake of weaker brethren, criticized him in no uncertain terms (Gal. 2.11ff.), something which runs quite contrary to Paul's instructions on the very same thing in 1 Corinthians 8.1–13, and his statement of his own procedure in 9.19–23. The reason for this change is, presumably, that the Corinthians had taken Paul's earlier teaching at its face value, and had applied the logic of Christian liberty to such an extent that an unrestrained liberty could not be tolerated; and so he set out to reformulate his own teaching, by redefining it in such a way as to preserve the original tenor of the theme, while yet emptying it of almost all positive practical content.[13] So we find in 1 Corinthians 6.12 that Paul both modifies and amplifies his Galatians teaching. He begins by quoting what are presumably his own words,

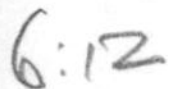

misapplied by the Corinthians: 'All things are lawful for me.' Though it may well be true to the apostle's mind to observe, as many commentators do, that 'all things' here includes only those things which were morally indifferent, we do well to remind ourselves that this is not the clear meaning of the phrase. Taken by itself, it could sanction any kind of behaviour, or misbehaviour. Though Paul had advised the Galatians not to use their Christian liberty as 'an opportunity for the flesh' (5.13), 'the flesh' had not been defined, and by claiming the inspiration of the Spirit, the libertine could justify any sort of immoral behaviour.[14] So Paul seeks to elaborate his teaching in such a way that the original declaration of Christian liberty is not lost, though the teaching is circumscribed with other moral rules so that, effectively, Paul is not now advocating the complete freedom that he had spoken of before. First, by way of modifying his original statements, he declares that 'not all things are helpful', i.e. certain types of action can cause grave concern to our fellow-believers, and can even be a hindrance to the gospel itself. Then, in an amplification of his previous teaching, Paul shows that by taking part in immoral activities (the point at issue here), the libertine is not in fact free, but has simply exchanged one kind of bondage for another: 'Christian liberty is not licence, for licence is not more but less than liberty' (Barrett, *1 Corinthians*, p. 146).

The same principles are outlined in respect of eating *eidōlothuta*, in chapter 8 where Paul declares that since the unrestrained exercise even of justifiable liberty can become a *skandalon* to the weaker brother, Christians ought to be prepared on occasion to sacrifice their own liberty in order to save the conscience of others. This was Paul's own practice in his ministry (9.19–23), and it should be the careful concern of Christians in everything: 'Give no offence to Jews or to Greeks or to the church of God. . . .' (10.32). The contrast with Paul's own attitude at an earlier stage in his ministry is obvious. Whoever they were, the non-eaters in Corinth had almost certainly been influenced by Jewish thought. They may even have been former Jews or proselytes. This means they were in *precisely* the same situation as Cephas at Antioch (Gal. 2.11ff.), though Paul's method of dealing with them was very different. In Galatians he strongly disapproved of such actions, probably because he wanted to discount the supposed value of keeping the Jewish Law in view of the heretics whom he was opposing. But here in 1 Corinthians he seems to go out of his way positively to encourage anything that leads to the following of rules and regulations, even if they have a Jewish tinge about them (cf. Longenecker, *Paul, Apostle of Liberty*, p. 239).

In summary, then, we may distinguish the teaching of 1 Corinthians from that of Galatians in three main areas:

1. In 1 Corinthians, the idea of tradition being handed down within the church, on the basis of which the truth of a given statement can be guaranteed, comes to the fore. This emphasis is so strong that one commentator can even speak of 'an unbroken chain of tradition' (Grosheide, *1 Corinthians*, p. 269), an expression that sounds strangely familiar from the later controversies of the catholic church Fathers with the second-century Gnostics. Coupled with this emphasis on tradition, we also find a consistent mention of practices and beliefs that are common to all the churches, as a sort of elementary ecclesiastical law.

2. Moral rules are brought in to explain and adapt the broad principles laid down in Galatians, though often these rules are of such a character as to constitute a substantial modification of the original principle of Christian freedom. Coupled with this we also find that the Old Testament is viewed in a more positive light than in Galatians, often (as in 1 Cor. 10.1ff.) with the intention of drawing moral guidance in contemporary situations.[15]

3. Specific behavioural patterns are laid down in respect of both social and ecclesiastical ethics:

On the social level, guidance is given on the problems faced by Christians in coming to terms with society as a whole, and also with one's fellow-Christians. The question of *eidōlothuta* was one that concerned not only Christian relationships but citizenship in general, and the problems faced by the Christian in coming to terms with a pagan society.

Instructions are given not only for the adjustment of Christian experience to the world but also in respect of the organization of the church. Though in the light of later developments few have been prepared to regard Paul's exposition of the *charismata* in 1 Corinthians 12 and the function of those who possessed these gifts within the congregation as a viable 'church order', we ought not to lose sight of the fact that this is precisely what Paul imagined it to be, at least within the context of a church like that at Corinth where these gifts were in evidence. In defining the operation of the *charismata*, Paul was able to combine his original teaching of complete liberty in Christ with a certain amount of organization, to the end that all things may be done decently and in order (14.40). He could do the same when he gave instructions for the conduct of church services (1 Cor. 14.26ff.). But he found himself in difficulties when he tried to do the same thing with his teaching on the equality of the sexes, and the outcome was that we now have two contradictory statements on the subject, one related to the essential elements of his teaching and the other directly conditioned by a more legalistic approach to the problems of the church at Corinth.

In these three points there are striking parallels with the reaction of the later catholic church against Gnosticism, and all three of them (with other elements) played an important part in combating the second-century heresy. Indeed, W. Bauer's comment on the content of 1 Clement could almost be applied directly to 1 Corinthians as opposed to Paul's earlier teaching in Galatians:

> In its positive exposition of the common faith of the church, markedly moralistic in approach, and based on the Old Testament and the Sayings of the Lord, *1 Clement* offers the best refutation of any gnostic-tainted Christianity. . . .[16]

The fact that such tendencies can be traced within Paul's teaching even at this early stage must have an important bearing on our understanding of the nature of Paul's opponents in Corinth. We ought, however, to recognize the limitations of this kind of evidence at the outset. For one thing, such tendencies as we have noted are not always very marked, and often there is but a slight change of emphasis from Paul's earlier teaching on Christian freedom. Some aspects of this change of emphasis could perhaps be explained in a different way. It could be argued, for instance, that since in 1 Corinthians 7—16 Paul appears to be replying to specific questions sent to him by the Corinthian church, he would in the very nature of the situation need to express himself in more direct fashion than he might otherwise have done. But this does not materially affect the argument here, for whether in reply to questions or as his own personal and independent observations, Paul appears to base his statements on a different moral premise from that employed in Galatians. Whether we put this down to experience in dealing with practical moral issues, or to a different moral outlook, the distinction is still there. If we had only Galatians we might suppose that Paul's answer to questions would be: 'Be conformed to Christ, and allow the Spirit to work out his own personality in your experience.' In 1 Corinthians, however, he tries to define in a quasi-legalistic fashion the ways in which the Spirit ought to do this, and therefore in effect he limits not only the exercise but also the substance of the liberty which he had earlier expounded in Galatians.

In addition, the tracing of tendencies of this sort is always, to a greater or lesser extent, a subjective business. Nevertheless, it seems to us that such changes of emphasis as we have drawn out here are real, and that it is no coincidence that the same changes, though in more drastic form and in conjunction with others, were made by the second-century church in combating Gnosticism. To what extent Paul used them to do the same thing must be confirmed by other, more objective, evidence about the Corinthian situation. This will be our concern in the next chapter, when we consider the historical problem of the Corinthian situation. First, however, we must turn our attention to 2 Corinthians to see if the same tendencies can be found there.

2 *Corinthians*

If we found significant differences between the ethical atmosphere of Galatians and that of 1 Corinthians, we find no less important distinctions between 1 Corinthians and 2 Corinthians, for in 2 Corinthians, at least in respect of the matters which we have considered above, we find ourselves back in something far more like the Galatians teaching, though not identical with it. By way of drawing attention to the variations here, we can best use the same divisions as we employed in our examination of 1 Corinthians, to facilitate direct comparison of the two epistles and their teaching.[17]

ETHICAL PRINCIPLES

In the course of his defence of his own apostolic authority in 2 Corinthians 3, Paul declares that ultimately he is dependent not on himself, nor on those who preceded him, but on God alone, and because of this he and his fellow-workers are 'qualified . . . to be ministers of a new covenant, not in a written code but in the Spirit; for the written code kills, but the Spirit gives life' (3.6). The whole of this statement at once brings us back into an ethical atmosphere very similar to that of Galatians. What Paul says about his apostolic authority is similar to what he says in Galatians 1, and the Holy Spirit is here said to be able to do the very thing which the Law, according to Galatians 3.21, was unable to do: the Law was incapable of giving life to sinful men.[18] Yet oddly enough, though the sentiment expressed here is wholly in line with Paul's statements in Galatians, there are no very clear parallels with the teaching of Galatians itself, while on the other hand there are many such parallels with Romans. A casual survey of the commentaries reveals that no commentator has found any material parallels with Galatians here, though references to Romans abound, and one scholar goes so far as to declare: 'This passage is almost a summary of the Ep. to the Romans.'[19] The new and distinctive element that appears in 2 Corinthians, in contrast to both Galatians and 1 Corinthians, is the emphasis on the ethical consequences of the 'new covenant', something which was mentioned for the first time briefly, and almost casually, in 1 Corinthians 11.25. This seems to suggest that Paul's thought had at this stage begun to move towards a conscious combination of the teaching of Galatians with that of 1 Corinthians. Both elements were necessary for a balanced view, which is indeed what we find in Romans, which is a kind of epitome of just these aspects of Paul's theology. Yet many things puzzle us in trying to assimilate Romans to Galatians. Whereas in Galatians Paul sees scarcely any value at all in the Old Testament Law, which did not even have God as its author (Gal. 3.19), in Romans, 'the law is holy and the commandment is holy and just and good' (7.12). Even more than this, Christians, albeit unconsciously, actually fulfil the requirements of the Law: 'God . . . sending his own Son . . . condemned sin in the flesh, in order that the just requirement of the law might be fulfilled in us, who walk not according to the flesh but according to the Spirit' (Rom. 8.3ff.). What Paul says in 2 Corinthians 3.6 is clearly the 'link passage' in the development of his thought between Galatians and 1 Corinthians, on the one hand, and Romans on the other. Though Paul is certainly contrasting two different kinds of moral authority in the use of the terms *gramma* and *pneuma*, the distinction is no longer that made in Galatians between a law-principle that cannot justify man before God (Gal. 3.11) and a principle of complete freedom releasing men from any 'yoke of slavery' (Gal. 5.1ff.); rather is it here 'the difference between the law as *externally* written at Sinai on tablets of stone and the *same* law as written *internally* in the heart of the Christian believer'.[20]

Again, further down in the same chapter, Paul brings up one of his catch-phrases from Galatians: 'Where the Spirit of the Lord is, there is freedom' (2 Cor. 3.17). Though admittedly the phrase itself does not occur in Galatians, it is the natural corollary to a statement like, 'if you are led by the Spirit you are not under the law' (Gal. 5.18). But, once more, there is a subtle change which can best be understood in the light of the emphases we noted in 1 Corinthians. A twin emphasis is made here. First of all, in view of the mention of 'the veil' in v. 16, and the 'unveiled face' of v. 18, there is perhaps here a reference to the freedom of access to God which Christians now have under the 'new covenant'. In addition, it is also a freedom to be conformed to Christ: 'Beholding the glory of the Lord, [we] are being changed into his likeness from one degree of glory to another' (v. 18). This again is very similar to the teaching of Romans 6.15—7.6, where Paul compares the position of Christians with release from slavery and marriage to a second husband (after the death of the first). In the one case, those who are 'set free from sin, *have become slaves of righteousness*' (6.18); in the other, Paul tells his readers: 'You have died to the law through the body of Christ, *so that you may belong to another*' (7.4). Though the basic sentiment of this verse is close to the tenor of Galatians, it has this qualification, that

> there is the substitution of new ties for old ones, not the abolition of all ties. Christian freedom is not licence; it is the free acceptance of the ties of affection instead of the enforced acceptance of bonds of fear (Plummer, *2 Corinthians*, p. 104).

Yet this addition is achieved without moving in the quasi-legalistic direction of 1 Corinthians. The comment of one scholar on a passage in 1 Corinthians, though hardly appropriate in that context, aptly describes Paul's ethical principles as brought out for us here in 2 Corinthians 2.6 and 2.17: 'In germ these two assertions contain a complete Christian ethic, which would be anti-libertine without being legalistic' (Héring, *1 Corinthians*, p. 46). The germ seems to have grown to full maturity in Romans.

ETHICAL MOTIVES

We find a similar distinction in the motivation for ethical behaviour given in 2 Corinthians, and the two important statements here are 5.14 and 8.8ff. Though in 5.14 Paul is again engaged in defending his own activities as an apostle, it is clear that what he says ought, in his view, to be true of the experience of every Christian. In v. 15, he applies it more or less directly to his readers. But the key phrase is in v. 14: 'The *love of Christ* controls us.'[21] No longer is the fear of criticism by other congregations, or even by some authoritative apostolic authority, the norm by which conduct is to be judged and regulated. Rather is Christian behaviour seen here as a natural response to the love which Christ has shown for the believer. Once again we are close to the kind of ethical statement made in Galatians. The reference to dying and rising with Christ at once recalls the similar reference in Galatians 2.20 ('It is no longer I who live, but Christ who lives in me') and 5.24

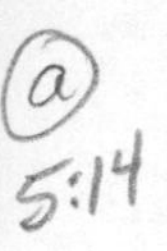

('Those who belong to Christ Jesus have crucified the flesh with its passions and desires'). There is, however, an important distinction, for whereas in Galatians the death and resurrection of Christ was applied to Christians in rather vague terms as meaning a denial of 'the flesh', here a more specific statement is made: the purpose of the Christian's association with Christ in this way is 'that those who live might live no longer for themselves' (v. 15), a theme which is elaborated in even more practical terms in Romans 6.1–14, especially vv. 12ff.

Another important statement on the Christian's ethical motivation is in 2 Corinthians 8.8ff., where Paul is urging the Corinthians to prepare their contribution to the collection which he is intending to take for the church at Jerusalem. In enjoining this duty upon them, Paul first mentions the faithfulness of the Macedonian churches in helping towards the relief of their poorer brethren in Jerusalem; but here the attitude of other churches is not the final moral sanction, nor does Paul apply it even as a subsidiary consideration. What Paul says about the Macedonian churches in 8.1ff. has all the marks of a genuine concern for the condition of those congregations. There is here a distinctly personal touch which is altogether lacking in Paul's statements about 'the churches of God' in 1 Corinthians, where that phrase is used almost as a stereotyped formula. Whereas Paul is here looking for what F. F. Bruce calls 'friendly emulation' (*1 and 2 Corinthians*, p. 222), in 1 Corinthians he was seeking an official conformity to a stated pattern. The real reason why the Corinthians ought to participate in this act of generosity is now said to be because Jesus Christ gave up everything for them in coming to earth at all (v. 9). We have already seen the importance attached by Paul to the incarnation as an ethical example to be followed by all Christians, and the occurrence of it here is the more striking in view of those places in 1 Corinthians where Paul urges the Corinthians to follow his own example, which is held up as an authentic reflection of Christ's own moral attributes. Nor does he even appeal, as he may well have done in such a context, to the generous actions of Jesus recorded in the gospel traditions. Rather does he go back to the very source of all ethical activity, found not in rules and regulations, nor even in authorized exemplars (and still less in the practice of other churches!), but in the person of Christ Himself.

ETHICAL BEHAVIOUR

In contrast with 1 Corinthians, this second epistle is almost completely lacking in direct moral instructions. Nowhere do we find directions for the conduct of Christian worship, or for one's relationship to society at large. Only two passages give us some kind of hint as to Paul's thought on practical problems, and neither of them is free from difficulties. 2 Corinthians 1.24 gives us a very general expression of Paul's feelings on how he ought to direct the Corinthians ('Not that we lord it over your faith . . .'), but this is hardly as specific as many of the statements of 1 Corinthians. In 6.14, one of the few direct instructions given in the epistle, we are faced with the problem of the unity of 2 Corinthians.[22] The statement in 1.24 was presumably brought out by the activities of the 'false apostles' who appeared in the church at Corinth, and who were acting in an arrogant fashion with the Corinthian Christians. On the contrary, Paul asserts, he was not the kind of apostle who would exercise compulsion on his converts. This was, of course, what he had said before in 1 Corinthians (7.35), though what followed there seems to have amounted to at least a strenuous effort at compulsion. In 2 Corinthians, however, Paul repudiates compulsion both in theory and in practice. In so far as 6.14 can be taken as a genuine part of this epistle, it continues the same pattern. The definite prohibition, 'Do not be mismated with unbelievers', is not followed up, as it might have been in 1 Corinthians, with a declaration that this is the practice of the rest of the churches, and so should be observed at Corinth also. Rather does Paul argue by a series of rhetorical questions and a quotation from Scripture that both common reason and the revealed will of God in the Old Testament support his own practice in the matter.

In summary, then, important distinctions must be drawn not only between Galatians and 1 Corinthians, but also between 1 Corinthians and 2 Corinthians. In terms of our overall interpretation of the situations presupposed by these three epistles, such an observation has significant implications. We have argued that the forms of expression used by Paul in Galatians were directly conditioned by the kind of opponents he was facing when he wrote that epistle. The fact that in 1 Corinthians he appears to have moved almost to the opposite extreme in the imposition of moral, social, and ecclesiastical law on his converts, can probably be taken to indicate that the opposition faced when Paul was writing 1 Corinthians was of an altogether different stamp. But 2 Corinthians is much more similar to Romans than it is to either Galatians or 1 Corinthians considered separately, though it can be seen as an important stage in the logical synthesis of the two strands of teaching represented in those two epistles. There is only negligible evidence to suggest that Paul was opposing any particular 'parties' when he wrote the Roman epistle (cf. Kümmel, *Introduction*, pp. 221ff.). But one cannot claim the same thing about the background of 2 Corinthians, since there are statements in the epistle itself which make it clear that Paul was actually opposing some specific individuals. Inasmuch as the variations in his moral and spiritual appeal to his readers provide a valid test of the character of the opposition, it would seem best to suppose that the opposition encountered in the writing of 2 Corinthians was of a different type again from that envisaged in 1 Corinthians. Since 2 Corinthians brings in various elements of the teaching of Galatians, albeit in a modified form, the presumption must be that the opposition in 2 Corinthians was more like that found in Galatia than that encountered in the context of 1 Corinthians. The question that must now arise is, Who were these different groups of opponents whom Paul was dealing with in the various churches? This brings us to the real heart of the matter, and presents one of the most important issues in Pauline theology. In view of its considerable importance, it must demand a full chapter to itself.

4

Who were Paul's Opponents—in Galatia and Corinth?

I

Galatia

The traditional answer to the question which we must now go on to consider has been to suppose that Paul's opponents in the Galatian churches were Judaizers, who had entered these churches more or less immediately after Paul's visit there, and by the promulgation of a Pharisaic type of Judaism-cum-Christianity had misled the believers into thinking that they needed to be circumcised and to keep the Law if they were to be fully qualified Christians at all. This was the general view of interpreters from the earliest times until the emergence of the Tübingen School under F. C. Baur, midway through the nineteenth century.[1] Even Baur's theory did not materially affect the prevailing ideas of the nature of the Galatian heretics, for he merely brought them into closer contact with Jerusalem, in order to draw out the implications of his own hypothesis of a radical break between Jewish and Gentile Christians in the first century. On the whole, this kind of view has been all but universally adopted, and is held by the majority of scholars at the present time. What Kirsopp Lake wrote sixty years ago can still be utilized as a fair comment on the situation:

> The nature of the controversy is clearly fixed by the whole trend of the Epistle. From beginning to end, it is engaged in controverting the proposition that Gentile Christians ought to be circumcised and observe the Jewish Law; it is also obvious

> that this proposition had been set up by Christian teachers who had come to Galatia after St. Paul had left his converts, and we can scarcely be wrong in identifying these teachers with those of the Jerusalem propaganda. . . . So much is plain . . .[2]

With this judgement, G. S. Duncan found himself in agreement: 'There is no need to doubt . . . that [the trouble] was caused by Jewish-Christian emissaries who came in from outside, probably from Jerusalem' (*Galatians*, p. xxxii). More recently, F. F. Bruce has expressed the same view, claiming that the traditional picture requires 'very little modification' ('Galatian Problems: 3. The "Other" Gospel', p. 257). At the same time, however, other views have been put forward, which merit serious consideration.[3] But first, we must look again at the evidence as we have understood it in Paul's actual words, and see where this may lead us. One of the most obvious flaws in the methodology of both sides of the debate has been the regrettable tendency to formulate theories first, and then to fit the evidence of the epistle into them. Thus, for instance, Ropes elaborates his own theory first and then proceeds to make a brief exposition of the epistle on the basis of the theory. But since the epistle is our only evidence for the Galatian heresy, any valid impressions of its character must in the nature of the case be based on an exegetical understanding of the epistle itself. Crownfield is even bolder than Ropes. After outlining his theory, he comments: 'The final test of any such hypothesis would be the construction of a detailed commentary in which each word and phrase is seen to find an explanation in terms of the general position' ('Singular Problem of the Dual Galatians', p. 496). This is an uncritical approach. The test of any hypothesis should be whether it is a natural and necessary outcome of the evidence, as that can be objectively determined. To construct the theory and then read the evidence on the basis of it can lead to any result we wish to reach, since we have put the evidence in before pulling it out.

From our own exegetical approach to the epistle, five main points may be drawn out here, which we can take as a foundation for understanding the nature of Paul's opponents. Detailed exegetical arguments for all these points have been put forward in chapter 2.

1. Paul had no fundamental disagreement with the Jerusalem apostles. His message was precisely the same as their message: a

fact which is emphasized by the charge he was answering in 1.10—2.21, i.e. the suggestion that he had received 'his' gospel as a merely academic tradition from Jerusalem, and so at secondhand. Paul never tried to deny that 'his' gospel was identical with that of the other apostles, but rather emphasized that, though the outward form of his message was inherited from others, the inner ethical and spiritual reality of it belonged to his own experience. The whole of 1.10—2.21 shows that Paul was not basically opposed to the mission of the Jerusalem church; and, since this is also made clear in Acts, we may assume it to be a true picture (cf. Gal. 2.7ff., and Acts *passim*). The incident with Peter at Antioch does not cast doubt upon this assertion, but rather confirms it, for in 2.13 Paul uses of Peter the verb *sunupokrinomai* (a *hapax legomenon* here in the New Testament) which clearly implies that such behaviour was not typical of Peter, who was in fact being false to his own principles. The mention in 2.12 of 'men from James' does not necessarily mean that James had sent messengers for the purpose of prohibiting table fellowship between Jews and Gentiles.[4] On every account of the chronology of Galatians, the incident mentioned in Galatians 2.11ff. took place before the Apostolic Council of Acts 15, and such an occurrence would simply give vivid illustration of one of the reasons for that Council being convened at all.

2. If we are right in concluding that the tension between tradition and revelation that comes out in Galatians 1.12 and 1 Corinthians 15.3 is not an outright contradiction, we must still give some account of why Paul emphasized the revelatory aspect of his message in Galatians, and the traditional links of it in 1 Corinthians. The most obvious explanation for this is that he was facing different kinds of opponents. We know that, whatever we may ultimately call them, Paul's Corinthian opponents were more 'Gnostic' than those in Galatia, and were laying considerable stress on existential spiritual experiences.[5] Against that, Paul emphasized the continuity of the traditions which he handed on. It is therefore reasonable to assume that in Galatia the opposite force was at work, and this was why Paul emphasized the revelatory nature of his message in that context.[6]

3. Unless we are to suppose that, at some stage in his ministry,

Paul had made a complete volte-face with regard to the Law, we must conclude that his extreme devaluation of it in Galatians (especially in 3.19) *must* have been conditioned by factors in the situation with which he was dealing. Though Schmithals (*Paul and the Gnostics*, pp. 41ff.) argues that the section 3.1—5.12 is a compilation of odds and ends culled from Paul's debates with Jews about the Law, this cannot be sustained, for it is clearly the central part of the whole epistle (cf. Wilson, 'Gnostics—in Galatia?', p. 365). We would be unrealistic to imagine that we can isolate the teaching of Galatians from the rest of Paul's epistles, unless we are to suppose that the apostle was exceedingly inconsistent. What, then, are we to make of such statements as the following, when viewed against the background of Galatians: 'So the law is holy, and the commandment is holy and just and good' (Rom. 7.12); or, 'The law is spiritual' (Rom. 7.14); or again, 'I delight in the law of God' (Rom. 7.22)? The simplest answer is that, in Galatians, the situation was such that it was necessary for Paul to make this complete devaluation of the Law's character, and the obvious conclusion to draw from this is that the Galatian heretics must have been insisting on the observance of the Jewish Law.

4. One of the most striking features of the epistle is the section 5.13—6.10, which is remarkable for its general ethical teaching as opposed to the detailed instruction which Paul often gives elsewhere. Both the grammatical form of the introductory section here, and its position in the epistle, together with its vague content, suggest that Paul was merely anticipating possible objections to his attitude towards the Jewish Law. In our view, there is no reason to suppose that Paul is here replying to any specific allegations at all, whether from Jews or Gentiles. As a former Pharisee he would be fully aware of the moral consequences that would normally follow when the Torah was discounted, and he therefore pointed out that this was not what would happen when those concerned had the Spirit of Christ within them. This, of course, is in sharp contrast to the position of Ropes, who declares:

> It sounds like a straightforward warning against lax tendencies, addressed to persons who really needed it; it does not sound like an exhibition, for the purpose of argument, of the way in

which Paul would be capable of treating the matter if he were actually writing to readers who did need the warning (*Singular Problem*, p. 23).

Such a suggestion has nothing to commend it, except the subjective judgement of those who make it. In 1 Corinthians Paul was facing opponents who were quite definitely embarking on a course of antinomian libertinism, and they might well have welcomed such a diluted, imprecise attack as he makes in this section of Galatians. As is obvious throughout 1 Corinthians, however, this was quite different from the way Paul would argue in the heat of a battle with libertines. We can hardly conceive that the Paul of 1 Corinthians could have been faced in Galatia with opponents of the same stripe, only to issue this vague kind of denunciation of what they represented.[7] O'Neill's judgement is certainly the right one here, though he draws unjustified conclusions from it: 'Here there are in fact no particular opponents in mind at all. . . . This section is directed to all Christians, to meet the common human temptations' (*Recovery of Paul's Letter to the Galatians*, p. 67).

5. Several elements have been brought to light in our exegesis of the main body of the epistle which combine to suggest that there was a considerable confusion in the Galatian churches:

(*a*) The fact that the false teachers held out some hope of Christians (Jews and Gentiles) becoming 'sons of Abraham' by being circumcised and following the Law, shows the confused nature of at least part of their teaching: no real Jew would ever have taught that Gentiles could become 'sons of Abraham', while no Gentile would want to be such, or see any advantage in it.[8]

(*b*) We have noted that certain parts of Paul's argument are somewhat peculiar, inasmuch as he proves the same things elsewhere in a more logical and more forceful fashion. Especially is this true of 4.21—5.1, which we therefore assumed to have some connection with the false teaching.[9]

(*c*) The confusion of the situation is brought out further in the way that Paul tells his readers to keep the Law if they are also circumcised (5.3), though according to 4.21 this is exactly what they want to do. Our solution to this discrepancy was to suggest that there were two groups, the educated members of the churches who had worked out the whole matter theologically, and the others, who were willing to do anything to escape persecution (cf. 6.12). In any event, for Paul it was impossible to believe that any man could fulfil the Law in a meaningful sense, and even Jews were recognized by him to be sinners like everyone else (cf. Rom. 3.23).

(*d*) The problematic verse, 5.11, suggests that Paul's opponents were at one stage actually claiming his own authority in support of their position on circumcision. This would doubtless be an inconsistent thing for them to do, but it need not lead to the conclusion that Ropes draws, i.e. that it was a group of radical antinomians who were making this charge. The same can be said of the argument that Paul's opponents could not appeal to Jerusalem for some superior authority to Paul, if Paul was in fact in agreement with the Jerusalem apostles. This would mean that the opponents were opposing the very ones whose support they claimed! (Ropes, *Singular Problem*, pp. 19ff.). But this discrepancy, and that which Ropes finds in 5.11, is more apparent than real, and fails to take adequate account of the facts. Ropes writes as if Jerusalem was just round the corner from Galatia, whereas in fact it was at some considerable distance, a distance at which false teachers could claim almost anything without anyone being able either to confirm or deny their claims. The same explanation applies to their apparent appeal to Paul himself in 5.11. Paul was far enough away not to pose any threat to such appeals, while his new converts were insufficiently acquainted with the niceties of his thought to be able to contradict the false teachers in this. Far from being 'extraordinary', as Ropes claims (p. 20), such a situation is perfectly understandable when people are wanting to establish a doctrine for which otherwise there would be singularly little support.

In summary, our own exegesis of the epistle seems to suggest a situation somewhat as follows. Quite soon after Paul's departure, there had come into the Galatian churches a group of false teachers. They came on no authority but their own, though they did, in at least one instance (5.11), claim support from some alleged teaching of Paul himself, which he had not included in the message he preached in Galatia. Perhaps they also appealed to the Jerusalem leaders for some sort of authority, suggesting that in any case Paul was inferior to them, and all that he knew he had learned by rote at Jerusalem. Because of this, they argued, Paul was not aware of the full implications of the gospel, which required the observance of the Jewish Law and circumcision. This was the only ground on which Christians could be incorporated into the true People of God, designated under the all-embracing term 'the sons of Abraham'. This message was favourably received by some of the better educated Christians in the Galatian congregations who, as an added bonus, soon discovered that circumcision could also release them from persecution (6.12), presumably at the hands of local Jews, not from the false teachers. When this became known, many of the less perceptive church members also showed an interest, not so much in the theoretical teaching as in the practical escape from persecution which it could secure. At this point, just as many were contemplating circumcision, Paul heard of the situation and wrote his epistle.

This general impression of the situation in the Galatian churches clearly fits into the traditional assumption that Judaizers of some kind were at work, though the evidence is insufficient for us to try to specify the precise relationship of such Judaizers to the Jerusalem church and its leaders. We cannot, however, leave the subject here, without dealing first with the alternative theories that have been put forward. These can be divided into three main groups. There is that represented particularly by Ropes, and including Lütgert and Crownfield. Then there is the position of Schmithals, which itself owes much to the work of Lütgert and Ropes. Finally, there is the old position recently revived by O'Neill, who argues that Galatians as we now have it is not the original work of Paul.

We shall deal first with the views of Lütgert, Ropes and Crownfield. Since Ropes takes over almost all of Lütgert's theory, and in turn expands and develops it further himself, and since Crownfield merely amends Ropes's theory, we shall confine ourselves largely to a consideration of Ropes's work. In his relatively short monograph, Ropes sees three basic difficulties in the Judaizing theory:

1. In 3.6ff., Paul goes to some pains to emphasize that Christianity has a positive relation to the Hebrew traditions of the Old Testament, and even to the Law itself; and so,

> If we are to suppose that Paul is here guided purely by the purpose of his controversy against judaizing tendencies, it must

> be admitted that at this juncture he makes a concession, the concession, namely, that sonship to Abraham is needed in order to obtain a right to the promises of God (*Singular Problem*, p. 7).

According to Ropes, what then follows in 3.13–29 'seems to constitute at least a qualified admission, and a dangerous one, of some degree of plausibility in the contentions of those who seek to pervert the Galatians' (p. 8). Two comments may be made on this:

(*a*) Ropes correctly sees that, though the references to Abraham in 3.6ff. are brought in as a reply to Paul's opponents, nevertheless they reveal an essential part of his own theological convictions. But this hardly complicates the situation for the interpreter, and certainly it need not involve Paul in any approval of the false teachers and their message. The most that it can suggest is that the character of Christian believers as a part of the 'true Israel' had been a significant element in Paul's original preaching,[10] and that it had subsequently been perverted by Judaizers.[11] Accordingly, Paul seeks not to abandon it but to expound it correctly. We have a close parallel to this procedure in the case of circumcision, a rite which Paul flatly rejects here in its literal sense, but which he can still take up and adapt as a 'circumcision of the heart'.[12]

(*b*) Ropes's second assertion, that 3.13–29 now takes the form of a concession to a Judaizing opposition, is a completely subjective judgement. It is quite impossible to regard what Paul says here about the Law and its significance as any kind of concession to Jews. The text itself suggests quite the opposite, and one can hardly imagine that any adherent of the Jewish Law and circumcision would have been greatly comforted by what Paul says here.

2. The point out of which Ropes attempts to make most capital is the question of the alleged appeal of Paul's opponents to the Jerusalem authorities. He argues that

> the judaizers are represented as trying to undermine Paul's work by declaring that he had accepted authority and received influence from the very group with which they themselves had substantial sympathy. Dependence on such authorities, it would seem, ought rather to have been a merit in their eyes than a source of discredit (*Singular Problem*, p. 21).

This claim does have more substance than most of the rest of Ropes's arguments, but on closer examination of it the most we can reasonably say is that it is 'not proven'. Three points must be made:

(*a*) There is in fact no unequivocal evidence to prove that the Judaizers did appeal to the Jerusalem leaders over and above Paul. We have noted above that it is perhaps a reasonable conjecture to suppose that this had happened, but it must always remain no more than just a conjecture.

(*b*) Our understanding of the epistle has shown that Paul's opponents did not argue that he had some kind of derived authority from the Jerusalem apostles, but that he had no real authority at all because he had simply taken over the externals of the Jerusalem gospel without any spiritual comprehension of its message. This is quite different from the suggestion that Paul was in some fundamental way dependent on Jerusalem. In addition, the supposed monolithic structure of the Jerusalem 'authority' is a figment of the scholarly imagination, since Paul himself makes it clear that the so-called 'pillars' themselves were but human, and even Peter was capable of yielding to pressure from the other side on one occasion (2.11ff.).

(*c*) This observation leads us on to our third point, for it is clear that in a sense both Paul and a Judaizing opposition could have appealed to the Jerusalem leadership. Paul could claim that the Jerusalem apostles were against circumcision being imposed on Gentile converts, and that they had recognized his own ministry on that basis. Judaizers could claim that the actions of Peter at Antioch at least proved there was some kind of difference between circumcised Jewish Christians and uncircumcised Gentile believers. Moreover, we have seen reason to think that the Galatian heretics would be willing to grasp at any straw that could be used to support their position, with no scruples as to the honesty of such tactics, in which case Ropes's argument must fall to the ground.

3. The other main criticisms which Ropes makes of the Judaizing theory can conveniently be grouped together, since we have already dealt with them at some length, and we include them here only for the sake of completeness. These comprise the charge against Paul which lies behind 5.11, which, according to Ropes, is 'a most extraordinary charge for judaizers to bring . . .' (*Singular Problem*,

p. 21), and the question of the ethical exhortations of 5.13—6.10. We have already seen that Ropes's explanation of these two points is by no means the only one, nor is it the most likely.

In addition to the facts to which we have already drawn attention, four major criticisms of Ropes's theory may also be made on more general grounds. The combination of these, together with the points already made, forms a decisive case for the rejection of the theory.

(*a*) The most fundamental criticism has already been mentioned, namely that Ropes follows an uncritical procedure in approaching the subject. He adopts the quite arbitrary method of producing the theory first, and then attempting to make the exegesis of the epistle fit into the theory.

(*b*) The epistle itself gives no indication at all of the addressees being divided into two groups. We have ourselves suggested that evidence is available for the sub-division of the one basic group into what may be called, for want of better terms, the 'intellectuals' and the 'pragmatists'. But both these 'groups' were orientated in the same Judaizing direction. This is very different from the assumption made by Ropes that Paul switches from addressing Judaizers and then turns to antinomian radicals, with not the slightest hint that he is constantly changing his tack to accommodate such varied sources of opposition. Especially is this the case in 5.11 where, according to Ropes, Paul is addressing not 'Judaizers', but 'radicals', though there is no suggestion in the text that would make one think this verse should be isolated from its context, which is allegedly dealing with the Judaizing section of the opposition!

(*c*) Ropes bases his work on one major presupposition that simply cannot be upheld. He was writing at a time shortly after the discovery that some kind of radical 'Gnostic' antinomianism may have formed a part of Paul's opposition in Corinth, and he seems to have been unduly influenced by this. It is no coincidence that eleven years before the publication of his monograph on Galatians, which forms the basis of Ropes's work, W. Lütgert had been the first to suggest that the key to the Corinthian situation lay in the assumption that Gnostics were at work there.[13] Ropes too easily assumed that this was the key to the understanding of the Galatian situation as well: 'The same general tendency would naturally present itself elsewhere' (*Singular Problem*, p. 10). The research of the ensuing forty years has shown that what for Ropes and his contemporaries was thought to be the solution to the problem is itself the most problematical element in the entire investigation of the background of Paul's epistles.

(*d*) There are certain psychological improbabilities in Ropes's suggestion that Gentile 'radicals' who themselves were in some sense the spiritual offspring of Paul were opposing him here. Whatever date we give to Galatians, 1.6 makes it clear that the difficulties in the Galatian congregations arose very soon after Paul's departure, and presumably therefore, very soon after the conversion of those people whom Ropes would like to see as 'radical' opponents of the apostle. According to Ropes, these opponents 'were led to take a position of direct, and indeed bitter, hostility to him and to his leadership of gentile Christianity' (*Singular Problem*, p. 26). Presumably he would say the same thing of the Judaizing opponents, for he claims that they also were local Gentile Christians, who in this case had succumbed to the overtures of the Jews from the local synagogue. But it is unlikely that people of such limited Christian experience would in so short a time have gone to such extremes as Paul himself ascribes to the leaders of the opposition.[14] At the same time, it is more than likely that, in the face of some sort of false teaching coming into the church from outside, such young and inexperienced believers would be turned into a state of confusion such as we have described above.

Before leaving this particular theory, we ought briefly to turn our attention to Crownfield's adaptation of it. He saw the importance of the fact that the epistle itself gives no evidence that two groups of people were being attacked, and so he concluded that only one group was involved, who misrepresented Paul's teaching in two quite different ways. According to Crownfield, Paul's opponents were basically syncretists, practising Jewish rites, including circumcision, though with a view to gaining some kind of illuminatory experience after the fashion of the pagan Mystery-cults. This reconstruction, while avoiding one of the criticisms made of Ropes's theory, still does not escape the others, and it must accordingly be rejected, and for the same reasons. Following Ropes, Crownfield sets out his theory first, and then manipulates the evidence to fit the theory. He draws parallels from the

Colossian heresy, in which he finds a combination of Jewish rites and moral laxity, a procedure which is no more justifiable than is Ropes's effort to read the Corinthian situation into the Galatian churches. Finally, he is forced to the unlikely conclusion that for this kind of perversion to have taken place so soon in the Galatian churches, Paul himself must have been some sort of Jewish Mystery adherent before his conversion![15]

Walter Schmithals has attempted to evade all these difficulties by supposing that the opponents faced by Paul in the Galatian churches were actually Jewish-Christian Gnostics. This removes the Judaizing element as a real force in the situation, while still leaving Schmithals in a position to give some sort of explanation for the presence of Jewish-based ideas in the heresy. This theory has a distinct advantage over that of Ropes, both in its content and in the way Schmithals works it out. If it could be accepted, it would certainly provide a more or less coherent picture of the situation in Galatia, and it would also eliminate many of the difficulties otherwise encountered in trying to relate what Paul found in the Galatian congregations with, say, the situation in Corinth. In contrast to Ropes, Schmithals has at least made a serious effort to lay an exegetical foundation for the theory though, as we have already seen, the presuppositions of his exegesis are far from acceptable in many instances. He begins by pointing out several discrepancies in the traditional Judaizing theory, mostly the same problems to which Ropes had already drawn attention. The familiar problem of how Judaizers could accuse Paul of being dependent on the Jerusalem apostles is raised. Schmithals also suggests that, since they were evidently opposed to the Gentile mission of Paul and his companions, Judaizers would never have actually promoted it by travelling from Jerusalem to far-flung regions in order to correct what they saw as aberrations among Gentile Christians (*Paul and the Gnostics*, p. 15). Here Schmithals seems to be using a very narrow definition of 'Judaizers'. So far as we can see, they need not necessarily have resisted the idea of a Gentile mission *per se*, but only on the basis on which Paul was conducting it. One gets the distinct impression that they would have been perfectly happy to have conducted such a mission themselves, calling Gentiles first to become Jews and then to join themselves to the Christian church within Judaism.[16]

Schmithals realizes, however, that such apparent difficulties in the Judaizing theory, even if they can be shown to be of substance, are no substitute for the detailed working out of the possibilities presented by the text itself, and he seeks to find a fresh understanding of the situation partly by direct exegesis of the epistle, and partly by a sometimes indiscriminate use of parallels and analogies drawn from Gnostic sources. Four main points emerge, at which Schmithals claims to have found definite signs of Gnostic influence, and we shall briefly enumerate each of these in turn.

1. Paul's statement on his apostleship in 1.12 is said to be a Gnostic argument. We have already dealt with this assertion at some length, so it need not detain us unduly here. Schmithals, of course, is arguing on the assumption that a fully developed Gnosticism preceded the emergence of the Apostolic Church, and so while Paul's opponents may have been Jewish-Christian Gnostics, even the 'orthodoxy' which the apostle claimed for himself was hardly orthodox in the later sense of the term, but was simply a different form of Gnosis. Schmithals does not explain why one Gnostic (Paul) should have tried to correct other Gnostics, but presumably he is meaning to indicate that by describing his apostolic calling in 'Gnostic' terms, Paul was directing some sort of *ad hominem* argument to those with whom on certain things he would share the same outlook.

2. The second point here has also been dealt with above at some length. This is the interpretation of 5.3 which, according to Schmithals, proves that before Paul's intervention, the Jewish-Christian Gnostics of Galatia had never thought of keeping the Law in addition to being circumcised. This would suggest that his opponents were not Judaizers, and since circumcision could in certain instances be used by Gnostics to refer to symbolic release from the flesh, this must have been its background here. We have seen, however, that not only is the evidence adduced by Schmithals inconclusive in itself, but its late date rules out its potential value for deciding the matter.

3. The observance of *hēmerai*, *mēnes*, *kairoi*, and *eniautoi* (4.10) cannot, according to Schmithals, be traced to Pharisaic practices, but to Gnostic rites which also enjoyed popularity among the Essenes (*Paul and the Gnostics*, pp. 43ff.). This verse is a kind of

exclamatory summary of what Paul meant in the preceding verses when he referred to the Galatians' continued desire to be the slaves of *ta stoicheia tou kosmou*. We noted in dealing with that phrase that Paul was probably gathering up everything, of whatever origin, that could possibly separate his converts from the use of the freedom in Christ to which they were called. Schoeps has suggested that in speaking of the enslavement of humanity under the rule of the *stoicheia* Paul was unconsciously using Gnostic terminology, and there is no reason why this may not have been the case (*Paul*, p. 21). But he can still remain convinced that there is a distinctively Jewish background to the terminology of 4.10, and he suggests that the *hēmerai*, *mēnes*, *kairoi*, and *eniautoi* which the Galatians were keeping were, respectively, sabbaths, calendar months, Jewish festivals of various kinds, and jubilee years.[17] In the light of the rest of our exegesis of Galatians, it seems more reasonable to accept this interpretation than that put forward by Schmithals, though, of course, even Jewish calendrical calculations were invariably based on the kinds of astronomical data that would naturally form useful source-material for any would-be Gnostic.

4. The fourth main point made by Schmithals is the contention that libertinism, as envisaged in 5.13ff., was a Gnostic characteristic. We have already argued that it is unnecessary to postulate any specific situation as the background of this section of the epistle, and that Paul was doing no more than giving a reasoned defence of his doctrine of freedom at the practical level. In any case, it is quite absurd to claim, as Schmithals seems to do, that Gnostics were the only libertines. Even they did not have a monopoly on immorality.

We need go no further, since it is clear that the theory put forward by Schmithals cannot be sustained without recourse to the unfounded assumption that Gnosticism existed in its developed form prior to the emergence of the apostolic community. The conclusion reached by F. F. Bruce in a recent study seems to be the only one possible: 'Gnosticism has really to be read into the teaching of these people as reflected in Paul's attack on them before it can be read out of it' ('Galatian Problems: 3. The "Other" Gospel', p. 260).

In his book, *The Recovery of Paul's Letter to the Galatians*, J. C. O'Neill has tried to avoid all the difficulties of other theories by suggesting that the present text of Galatians is an expanded version of what Paul originally wrote. He recognizes the peculiarities to which we have drawn attention in our own exegesis, and which have formed the basis of much of Ropes's argument. The letter that Paul originally wrote must, according to O'Neill, have been an entirely logical and consistent composition. By contrast, the Galatians we know is 'full of obscurities, contradictions, improbable remarks, and *non sequiturs*' (p. 8). What happened was that Paul's original letter was subjected to reinterpretation at various stages of its history, and marginal glosses and sermonic explanations have now been merged with the original text.

In the hands of O'Neill, this hypothesis about the origin of Galatians becomes the key to unlock all its mysteries. He can dispose of every exegetical problem at a stroke, simply by suggesting that the text is not original to Paul. By excising 3.19, 4.1–3, 8–10, 12, 24b–27, and 5.13—6.10, the evidence for the theories of Ropes and Schmithals is skilfully removed. The question of inconsistencies and peculiarities in Paul's argument, and the problem of who his opponents were is no longer of any consequence, for the difficulties can now be seen to be the work of some late interpolators.

If it could be accepted, such a theory would have obvious attractions. The following points, however, appear to speak decisively against any such hypothesis:

1. The dissecting of any biblical text in this way can be justified only on the ground of expediency, and not of principle. To cut out those passages which present exegetical difficulties to the interpreter is a valid method only when there is some kind of textual support for such an excision. Here in Galatians, there is strikingly little MS. evidence for the kind of interpolation that O'Neill proposes. It is odd, to say the least, that not one ancient MS. has, on this theory, preserved anything like the original text of this epistle.

2. By accepting this theory, it becomes hard to account for the acceptance of Galatians into the canon of the New Testament. What O'Neill suggests is not that one specific group rewrote

Galatians for their own purposes, but rather that the epistle has been subjected to alteration and interpolation from many different sources. On the one hand, he argues that 3.19 was a gloss inserted by some Gnostic group to support their view that the Law of the Old Testament had been given by angels and not by God (p. 52); while on the other hand, 4.1–3, 8–10 is the product of an early Christian writer who was opposing a Jewish-Christian Gnosticism similar to that practised by the Elchasaites (p. 58). 5.13—6.10 emanates from a similar context, and is of a piece with the moralistic teaching of the Didache or the Epistle of Barnabas. By allowing that the original Galatians has been altered by such diverse groups of people, O'Neill makes it impossible to posit any realistic *Sitz im Leben* either for the production of the present text of the letter, or for its acceptance by the catholic church of the second century as a valid part of Scripture. If this letter was ever re-edited in an anti-Gnostic context in the second century, it is hard to believe that the editor(s) would have made such a bad job of it. Far from enabling us to see Galatians as a more coherent letter, on this theory it becomes little more than an implausible collection of theological titbits drawn from incredibly diverse sources.

3. This view does not do justice to the fact that Paul was a real man, dealing with a real-life situation in which the issues were highly complicated. We have already drawn attention to the fact that the confusion that is to be found in Galatians was nothing more than a reflection of the confusion in the Galatian churches, and that this is a perfectly understandable situation in the historical context. To suppose that Paul was writing the letter in some haste and wrote things that, on further reflection, he may have wanted to express differently, requires less imagination than to envisage a man writing a completely logical, consistent theological treatise which was at the same time so inexplicit that later generations could add to it at will without anyone ever guessing what they were up to. Since the former view has the support of all the major New Testament MSS., it appears to be a far more likely explanation of the problems than is O'Neill's drastic rewriting of the Galatian epistle. O'Neill defines the whole problem too sharply by suggesting that the options lie between 'supposing that Paul was confused and contradictory and supposing that his text has been commented upon and enlarged' (p. 86). This is not the real

choice we have to make. The real issue is whether Paul was a real man reacting to a specific set of historical circumstances, or whether he was a twentieth-century academic writing books about theology. On this account of the situation, we can have no hesitation in choosing the first alternative.

Our conclusion, therefore, is that, in broad terms, the Judaizing hypothesis which has been held by interpreters from the earliest times is still more likely to be the correct one. We have found it necessary to adjust it in places, but unless some kind of fresh and indisputable evidence is forthcoming, it must remain the only plausible explanation of the circumstances in which Paul wrote the epistle to the Galatians.

II

Corinth

In view of our earlier remarks about the distinctive nature of the teaching of the two Corinthian epistles over against Galatians, the conclusion just reached about Paul's opponents in Galatia is obviously going to be of crucial significance in the understanding of the Corinthian situation. Before going on to draw conclusions about Paul's opponents in Corinth, however, we should first take account of some of the conclusions reached by other scholars, working on a different basis from that adopted here.

At the beginning of the era of scientific biblical criticism, F. C. Baur attempted to fit the Corinthian epistles into his theory that Paul was everywhere faced with Judaizing opposition. So he viewed these epistles, along with the other genuine Pauline letters, as 'earnest and trenchant polemics against an anti-Pauline Judaising Christianity' (*Paul*, I, p. 292). Though Baur's work has in many ways exercised a deep influence on the course of later scholarship, in this instance his ideas were relatively short-lived, for the work of W. Lütgert, published in 1908, introduced an altogether different element into the interpretation of the Corinthian situation, and one that was rapidly espoused by many scholars, so that it came to be the 'critical orthodoxy' at least of German scholarship from the time when it was first promulgated.[18] Lütgert argued that both the practical and doctrinal difficulties of the Corinthian church could best be explained by the assumption that they had been subjected to some sort of Gnostic influence, which was especially to be associated with the 'Christ party' (1 Cor. 1.12), and which operated by introducing a subtle distortion of Paul's own message.[19] At the time, this thesis was taken up and modified by A. Schlatter,[20] and Reitzenstein also made use of it.[21] Bultmann was quick to adopt this interpretation of the Corinthian epistles, and claimed to have found the Gnostic redeemer myth lurking behind 1 Corinthians 2.8.[22] Others have tackled the problem in a more or less piecemeal fashion, and, *inter alios*, Schniewind, Haenchen, Dinkler and von Soden have made significant contributions.[23] In his study *Weisheit und Torheit*, U. Wilckens examined the Christology of the Corinthian heretics as it is reflected in 1 Corinthians 1–2, and concluded that it grew out of Jewish Sophia speculation. It was the pre-existent Sophia that spoke through Jesus, and which was recognized only by such people as the Gnostics in Corinth. Other elements said to point to the presence of some sort of Gnostic thought in Corinth are the Pauline use of *psychikos* and *pneumatikos* (1 Cor. 2.14ff.; 15.21, 44–9), and the reference to the 'deep things of God' (1 Cor. 2.10); while the view taken by the Corinthians of morality and the sacraments, not to mention the question of resurrection dealt with in 1 Corinthians 15, all point unmistakably to the presence of Gnostic influence.

The most thoroughgoing and systematic interpretation of the Corinthian situation along these lines has been that of W. Schmithals, in his book *Gnosticism in Corinth*, originally published in German in 1956. According to Schmithals, 1 Corinthians and 2 Corinthians were actually compounded out of a series of six separate letters written by Paul in the course of his dealings with the Corinthian church in the middle of the first century, though they were not collected together until about A.D. 96, when they were edited for use in the anti-Gnostic struggle.[24] Despite the diversity of the literature, however, there was but one set of opponents, who are especially prominent in 2 Corinthians 10–13, and whom Schmithals characterizes as Jewish-Christian Gnostics, with a totally Gnostic outlook on the gospel (op. cit., pp. 113–16). The main practical demonstrations of their theological beliefs were to be found in their pride in *gnōsis* (cf. 1 Cor. 8.1ff.), which in turn was manifested in libertine behaviour in both social and individual morality. They demonstrated their spirituality by speaking in tongues (1 Cor. 14),[25] and in their ecstasies resorted to their native Aramaic to curse the human Jesus, because they honoured only the heavenly aeon, Christ (1 Cor. 12.3).[26] The use which Paul made of the distinction of *psychikos* and *pneumatikos* in 1 Corinthians 2.14ff., 15.44ff., shows that his opponents must have been Gnostics, while even Paul himself must have had some Gnostic tendencies, for he never explicitly attacked their radical cosmic dualism.[27] The account in 1 Corinthians 10.16ff. describes not a Christian communion, but a Jewish Gnostic rite in which the broken bread represents the scattered pneumatics, and even 10.16b–17 does not make the rite a Christian one, since 'Jesus' is not mentioned, and the use of 'Christ' could possibly indicate the Jewish Messiah, divorced from any belief in Jesus.[28]

It is unnecessary for us to enter into any detailed discussion of these assertions made by Schmithals. For one thing, our purpose here is simply to indicate the trends of scholarly opinion on the subjects we have dealt with, and to show where our own evidence would best fit in. But in any case, most of what Schmithals says has been well described as 'a curiosity of exegesis'.[29] The same objections which we noted to Schmithals's interpretation of Galatians can also apply here, and they are of such a fundamental character as to require the discounting of much of what he says. Here again, we find the unfounded assumption that there was a system of pre-Christian Gnosticism as fully developed as the systems known to us from the second century. Moreover, not only does Schmithals assume that the evidence of the second-century systems can simply be applied *en bloc* to the situation at Corinth, but he also assumes, without any warrant in the evidence, that Paul was facing the same sort of opponents in every area of his ministry, and so if Jewish-Christian Gnostics were to be found in Galatia, Thessalonica, Ephesus and Philippi, they are automatically the cause of the trouble in Corinth also.

Not all scholars, however, have taken this line of approach to the Corinthian situation, and of those who have not, the most important is undoubtedly J. C. Hurd, who has argued in his book *The Origin of I Corinthians* that the complete explanation for the difficulties encountered by Paul is to be found in his own teaching and behaviour. Hurd traces four stages in the dealings of Paul with the Corinthian church:

1. His first preaching there, and the founding of the church. The Corinthians stuck rigidly to his initial teaching, and it may even have been the source of such contentious ideas as the denial of the resurrection of the dead (*The Origin of I Corinthians*, pp. 285ff.).

2. The 'previous letter' (1 Cor. 5.9ff.) to the Corinthians, part of which is preserved, according to Hurd, in 2 Corinthians 6.14—7.1, was quite different from stage 1, and was a legalistic effort to get the Corinthians to adopt a practice in line with the provisions of the Apostolic Decree.

3. Oral and written information in reply to this was brought to Paul by Stephanas, Fortunatus, Achaicus and Chloe's people, which tended to move in the opposite direction, towards an extreme expression of Christian freedom.

4. 1 Corinthians was written as Paul's response to the situation, expressing a viewpoint halfway between the two extremes of freedom and caution: 'Paul warned the Corinthians of the various dangers involved in the conduct they advocated, but in the end he allowed them to continue very much as they were' (*The Origin of 1 Corinthians*, p. 273).

On this reconstruction of the evidence, Gnostic influence must be ruled out as a possible element in the situation, which can be interpreted purely in terms of Paul's own inconsistencies over the Apostolic Decree.[30] Several points suggest, however, that this cannot be a complete explanation of the situation:

1. It is difficult to see how everything in the Corinthian situation could have been derived from the original Pauline teaching there which, after all, is known only from Hurd's hypothetical reconstruction of it. It is far more reasonable to suppose that some external influences were at work here, which found a foothold through the Apostolic Decree and Paul's teaching in the epistle to the Galatians (which would presumably have approximated to Paul's original teaching in Corinth).

2. If the Apostolic Decree played such a direct part in the Corinthian situation as Hurd suggests, it is next to impossible to explain why Paul did not simply refer to it in 1 Corinthians 6.12ff. and 7. If he had already delivered it to Corinth in person, this would surely have been the natural thing to do.[31]

3. Professor Barrett has pointed out that this reconstruction allows a very short time for the development of Paul's thought in the way suggested.[32] To his observation we may perhaps add that if, with Hurd, we assume that Galatians came immediately after 1 Corinthians, we are left with a picture of Paul as a man with few moral scruples, willing to change not only his approach, but his basic principles at a moment's notice.[33] If we are to see the pattern of thesis plus antithesis resulting in synthesis in Paul's theology, it is preferable on theological grounds to see Galatians as the thesis, 1 Corinthians as the antithesis, with the synthesis coming in 2 Corinthians and Romans.

Despite our reservations about the Gnostic background proposed for 1 and 2 Corinthians by Schmithals and others, this line of approach still seems to offer the most fruitful understanding of the Corinthian situation, at least as it is depicted in 1 Corinthians. Though the historical facts speak against the identification of the Corinthian heresy with any form of Gnostic theory known to us, or even with an amalgam formed out of theories that are known to us (such as the 'system of pre-Christian Christ Gnosticism' formulated by Schmithals, *Gnosticism in Corinth*, pp. 36–86), at least five pieces of evidence seem to point very strongly to the presence of some kind of Gnosticizing tendency in the background of 1 Corinthians. The first two considerations here are of a circumstantial nature, and the other three are more or less direct, but the combination of both types of evidence forms a very strong case for the existence of some kind of 'Gnostic' belief in the Corinthian church. The evidence is as follows:

1. Our own analysis of the theology of Paul's writings has shown that there is a considerable difference of emphasis in his teaching in 1 Corinthians on the questions of tradition, the Old Testament, and the exercise of Christian morality, when this is compared with his teaching on the same subjects in Galatians. Such varying expressions of theological principles must have been directly conditioned by the forms of opposition which Paul encountered in the communities which he was addressing. In Galatians, there is conclusive evidence that he was opposing the introduction of Judaizing teaching into the Galatian churches. This teaching had been brought in by people from outside, and was concerned mainly with the validity of his own authority as an apostle, the question of kinship to Abraham, with its related problems of the Old Testament Law and circumcision, and the question of Christian social morality. In opposing such teaching, Paul stated firmly that he had been directly appointed by Christ Himself to his apostolic office, and that not only were Christians the 'sons of Abraham' by virtue only of their faith, but that their relationship to Christ would automatically and inevitably produce within their experience the kind of morality that was fitting for a Christian. All external rules and regulations were, therefore, irrelevant. Moreover, much of the Old Testament was of little direct value to the Christian, and even the supposedly divine origin of the Law was by no means certain. In contrast to this, in 1 Corinthians Paul emphasized that he stood within the traditions of the church, he used the Old Testament

as both practical example and theological source book, and he introduced forms of ethical teaching that laid emphasis on the very things that in Galatians he had so much deprecated. These observations suggest not only that some of Paul's opponents in Corinth were libertines (a fact we can learn directly from 1 Corinthians anyway), but also, because of their close resemblance to the ways in which the catholic church of the second century opposed the Gnostic menace, there is a prima facie case for supposing that 'Gnostic' ideas were also the target of Paul's attack in 1 Corinthians. The fact that there was also an element of asceticism in Corinth is likewise possibly to be linked to Gnosticizing tendencies. Christian freedom could be expressed in either extremity, and both could be deduced from Paul's teaching in Galatians 3.28. The fact that in 1 Corinthians Paul finds himself more in line with the ascetic viewpoint only serves to emphasize the precarious nature of his own position, attempting to defend the truth of his teaching, but denying the logical outcome of much of it.[34]

2. At the time of the troubles in Corinth, the Christian churches had very little literature of any kind to guide them in matters of either belief or practice. The Old Testament (LXX), while known to the Gentile churches, can hardly have exercised much influence if Paul's advice in Galatians was heeded, and in any case it could be made to speak directly to the Gentile Christians only by a tortuous process of exegesis that, though familiar to the Jewish rabbi, would hardly have meant much to the average Gentile convert. The real sources of information about the Christian faith, in addition to oral teaching, would therefore be Paul's epistle to the Galatians and the gospel traditions of the source known as Q, which many think were reduced to writing by this time. It will be shown in our next chapter that Paul's epistle to the Galatians, when taken in isolation from his other epistles, could form a very strong basis for 'Gnostic' ideas. If, therefore, we find Gnosticizing tendencies in Corinth, it is legitimate to describe at least some elements as 'Paul's gospel overdone'.[35] J. M. Robinson has convincingly argued that the same outcome could result from the understanding of Jesus' ministry and teachings that is presented in the gospel source Q, which by its very nature would have done much to encourage the Gnostic outlook. It is, among other things, the only

gospel source which gives to Jesus the name *sophia* (Luke 11.49; Matt. 11.19=Luke 7.35) and, while the implication of that in its original context may well have been far removed from any Gnostic ideas of Sophia, it is nevertheless easy to see how this kind of thing could have encouraged the development of dormant Gnostic seeds.[36] If we add to this the introduction of the Apostolic Decree, with its implicit recognition of higher and lower grades of Christians, it is easy to see that, given but slight encouragement, the Gnostic seeds which were at the time floating around the religious atmosphere of the Roman empire could find here a very congenial plot in which to germinate.

3. At least a section of the Corinthian church was indulging in sexual excesses and the indiscriminate eating of *eidōlothuta*, claiming that since by *gnōsis* they were pneumatics, anything was permissible to them (cf. 1 Cor. 8.1ff.; 10.23ff.; 6.12ff.). These traits are also enumerated in Revelation 2.14, 20, where many scholars see a reflection of some form of Gnostic teaching. Behaviour of this kind was characteristic of the later Basilideans (Irenaeus, *Adv. Haer.* I.24.5) and, according to Justin, *Dial.* 35.1–6, of Gnostics in general. The concepts of *sophia* and *gnōsis* were also prominent in Corinth, and though the latter was probably a mere catchword connected more with the question of eating *eidōlothuta*,[37] the former seems to have had a certain speculative content in relation to the divisions of 1 Corinthians 1–3. Though it is probably going too far to agree with Wilckens that 1 Corinthians 1.17 envisages a Gnostic pneuma-Christology, Paul does recognize the existence of a kind of *sophia* which, since it refuses to be ruled by Christ crucified, 'arises within this *aiōn* or . . . within the *kosmos*. Like other Gnostic systems it is a way of escape from this world to the upper world of divine existence, based upon the authority of the *archontes*.'[38] But for him, the true meaning of *sophia* is to be found only in Christ (1.24, 30), the central character in the divine plan of salvation (cf. Barrett, *1 Corinthians*, pp. 67ff.). Other elements of Gnostic terminology are also encountered in 1 Corinthians, and their presence suggests that Paul was opposing people who used them in a more Gnostic fashion than he himself could do.[39]

All these linguistic parallels, of course, can prove nothing of themselves, though taken together with the other evidence adduced here they can be of secondary value. It is notoriously difficult to base anything on a mere comparison of terminology. This was what led to the absurd results of the earlier work of the *Religionsgeschichtliche Schule*, and in order to appreciate fully the exact significance of such terms here we would need to make a careful comparison of Paul's language with that of later Gnosticism. This would involve not merely the observation of the occurrence of linguistic terminology, but also an analysis of the significance attached to it in every possible context.[40] Only on the basis of such an examination will we finally reach anything like a definitive answer to the linguistic problem of Gnostic elements in the New Testament. Meanwhile, however, the two other points which remain to be considered here provide evidence that these terminological nuances were connected at Corinth with two important doctrinal deviations, and this gives us more confidence in supposing that they were, therefore, somehow a part of the Gnosticizing thought of a section of the Corinthian church.

4. One of the clearest indications of the existence of a group of people in Corinth who considered themselves to have been released from the ties of normal morality because of their character as *pneumatikoi* is found in the excesses associated with the celebration of the sacraments in Corinth. The problems connected with the Eucharist, for example, can best be explained if it is assumed that the Corinthians looked upon this as a magical performance, which gave them release from the flesh and endued them with *pneuma* so that they no longer needed to be concerned with the norms of personal and social morality.[41] It is striking that at one of the points where Paul brought in the Old Testament to prove a point in his argument in 1 Corinthians, he did so with precisely this implication in mind. In chapter 10, he implied that both immorality (v. 8) and the social problems involved in the eating of *eidōlothuta* (vv. 23ff.) had arisen out of 'a mistaken idea that baptism and the Eucharist are automatic prophylactics against sin and ensuing judgment' (F. F. Bruce, *1 and 2 Corinthians*, p. 90; cf. E. Käsemann, *ENTT*, pp. 108–35). In doing so, Paul once again took up a theme familiar from Galatians, and basing his argument on the assumption that Christians are now the true 'sons of Abraham' and, therefore, the 'true Israel', he took the experience of Israel in the wilderness as an analogy of Christian experience.[42]

Israel herself had adopted this very attitude, for she had relied on the fact that 'all ate the same supernatural food and all drank the same supernatural drink' (v. 3) as a guarantee that she was immune from God's judgement on sin. History had proved her wrong, just as it would prove the Corinthians wrong if they persisted in their 'Gnostic' idea that their reception of the Spirit and their Christian freedom had released them from the bonds of normal morality. True Christian obedience should find its source and fulfilment in Christ Himself, who can be known only through the experience of faith, and not through the legalistic framework even of a sacramental system or a false claim to spiritual liberty:

> The Christian is saved through the connection with God's historical act of salvation in the cross and resurrection of Christ, . . . not by the possession of supernatural powers, but by the acceptance in faith of that divine act and by proving its truth in his life (Dibelius/Kümmel, *Paul*, pp. 136ff.).

5. Alongside a false view of the sacraments as possessing a kind of magic spirituality for the present, there was also at Corinth a conviction that there would be no future resurrection of the dead (1 Cor. 15.12ff.). It is unnecessary for us to consider this passage exegetically, as much of it is of only secondary relevance to our subject (cf. Schmithals, *The Office of Apostle*, pp. 73–9). Three points, however, emerge here as fundamental in regard to the Corinthians' beliefs on the subject:

(*a*) The Corinthians believed in the resurrection of Jesus. To be sure, Schmithals has contended that the Corinthian 'Gnostics' doubted even this, since according to him no Gnostic could ever have accepted the resurrection of a man (*Gnosticism in Corinth*, pp. 155–9). For them, the ascended Christ was all that mattered. Two points must be set against this, however: (*i*) Paul emphatically states at the outset of his argument that what he is about to say is not something new, but what he had told the Corinthians before (cf. the occurrence of *euēngelisamēn* twice in vv. 1ff., and the *kērussomen* of v. 11), and included in this statement was the odd fact that Christ 'was buried' (v. 4). Doubtless this was simply a part of the original tradition as Paul had received it, but its inclusion would surely deal a death-blow to any Gnostic idea that Paul had in fact been referring not to resurrection but to the ascension of Christ.[43] (*ii*) The tone of vv. 17–19 clearly implies that the

Corinthians whom Paul was addressing had a hope of some kind of future life after death, and the question, therefore, was whether or not this would be attained by resurrection. According to the predominant Gnostic view, at death the *pneuma*-self simply departed from the body, to be absorbed into its original Source, or into the Godhead (cf. Irenaeus, *Adv. Haer.* I.24.1, on Saturninus), while the body returned to its elements in the ground (cf. Irenaeus, *Adv. Haer.* I.24.5, on Basilides). This is a viable content for the view that Paul was opposing here.[44]

(*b*) Paul's opponents in Corinth also evidently did not accept that there was any reason for the resurrection of Christians.[45] This much is perfectly clear, for it is stated in unequivocal terms: 'How can some of you say that there is no resurrection of the dead?' (v. 12). Paul then goes on to take the resurrection of Christ as the basis of his argument that Christians also must have some kind of future resurrection experience.

(*c*) The Corinthians seem to have adopted what Käsemann has called a 'sacramental realism' (*NTQ*, p. 126), by which 'as participants in the cross of Christ, the baptized are at the same time participants in his Resurrection and Enthronement, liberated from the old aeon of death and the powers, and translated into the new aeon of the Kingdom of Christ' (ibid., p. 125). This was perhaps connected with the doctrines of people like Hymenaeus and Philetus, who at a later date also declared that the resurrection was already past (2 Tim. 2.18). This view has been advocated by many scholars, and rejected by many.[46] But there is much to be said in its favour: (*i*) It is an understandable development of, and deviation from, Paul's teaching in Galatians, especially in 2.19ff. Though Paul makes it clear in 1 Corinthians 15 that in his view there was to be a certain tension between the present 'resurrection' of Christians and their future expectations, he had not done so in Galatians. Since so much of what he taught there was open to abuse by those of 'Gnostic' bent, there is no reason to suppose that this had not been the case in this connection also. In Romans 6.4, on the other hand, Paul makes it clear that the 'resurrection' of which he speaks is exclusively concerned just with the moral aspect of the present, physical life: the Christian is raised 'to walk in newness of life'. (*ii*) 1 Corinthians 4.8 shows that this kind of 'Gnostic' eschatology was already present in Corinth. (*iii*) Denial of the resurrection of the dead was a common Gnostic trait, and the view of Simon Magus, expressed in the Clementine *Homilies* 2.22, is typical of perhaps the majority of Gnostics: 'He does not believe the dead will be raised.' Cf. also Polycarp, *Phil.* 7.1; Justin, *Dial.* 80.4. (*iv*) We do have evidence of the acceptance of some such doctrine in Corinth at a slightly later date (cf. *1 Clem.* 23–6). If W. Bauer's theory can be maintained, that the Gnostics in the church at that time had a direct lineal descent from the 'strong' referred to in Paul's correspondence, the value of this evidence is enhanced.[47] Though its worth is doubtful, the apocryphal correspondence between Paul and the Corinthians in the *Acts of Paul* also shows the apostle fighting two Gnostic teachers in Corinth, a prominent part of whose doctrine was the denial of the resurrection of the dead (cf. *NTA* II, pp. 341ff.).

It therefore seems most likely that there was a 'Gnostic' element in the Corinthian church, which maintained that by virtue of the pneumatic character of its members it was released from the normal rules of society and ethics, and that this was coupled with a quasi-magical view of the sacraments and a realized eschatology whereby the possessor of *gnōsis* was considered to have been raised already and to be living an enlightened, 'spiritual' existence in this present world. The suggestion made by some (including R. McL. Wilson, *Gnosis and the New Testament*, p. 53), that what Paul was opposing here was the old Greek philosophical view that there could be no such thing as physical resurrection, is untenable. The Corinthians *did* accept the resurrection of Jesus, and in any case there is no evidence for the influence of Greek thought of this kind on the Corinthians. It is more likely that the sort of popular ideas present in Gnostic thought would have been widely known in a congregation such as that at Corinth seems to have been (cf. 1 Cor. 1.26: 'Not many of you were wise according to worldly standards . . .').

So far we have confined our attention to 1 Corinthians. When we come to 2 Corinthians we find a slightly different situation. Though Schmithals argues that the opponents of Paul in 2 Corinthians (especially 10–13) were Gnostics (*Gnosticism in Corinth*, pp. 113–16), others have tried to distinguish the two sets of opponents. D. Georgi is representative of several scholars in seeing Paul's opponents in 2 Corinthians as Hellenistic Jewish-Christian missionaries.[48] As we have indicated above, our own observations on the variations of Pauline teaching between 1

Corinthians and 2 Corinthians also seem to point in this general direction. In support of this view, three main points deserve our attention here:

1. In addition to the theological distinctions to which we have already drawn attention, other pieces of evidence in 2 Corinthians itself also support this interpretation:

(*a*) In 2 Corinthians 11.5 (12.11), the opponents are called 'superlative apostles' (*huperlian apostoloi*), a term which is, according to C. K. Barrett ('Christianity at Corinth', p. 294), 'precisely parallel to that of *hoi dokountes* (Gal. 2.6)'; and there is no doubt that in the Galatians context Paul was speaking of the Jerusalem apostles. It is therefore reasonable to suppose that these are the people in mind here.

(*b*) 2 Corinthians 11.22 'undoubtedly proves that at least some of Paul's opponents were Jews' (Lake, *Earlier Epistles*, p. 220). Moreover, the language used suggests that they were probably Jews of at least a Palestinian background, if not a direct Palestinian origin (cf. F. F. Bruce, *1 and 2 Corinthians*, pp. 296ff.).

(*c*) According to 2 Corinthians 11.4, these people were preaching 'another Jesus' and 'a different gospel', terms reminiscent of Galatians 1.6ff., and terms which are used by Paul only to refer to Jews.

2. Arguments that have been brought against the suggestion that there was a Jewish element involved in the opposition faced in 2 Corinthians have been unconvincing:

(*a*) Lütgert (*Freiheitspredigt und Schwarmgeister in Korinth*) argued that since there is here no mention of circumcision, these people cannot have been Judaizers. The point is well taken, though the absence of a reference to circumcision does not prevent them from having been Jews. Not all Jews (let alone Jewish Christians) held circumcision in high regard and, as Barrett has pointed out ('Christianity at Corinth', pp. 296ff.), Cephas himself had sought to impose a Judaistic way of life, without circumcision, on the Gentile Christians of Antioch (Gal. 2.14). Not only is there evidence that this kind of watered-down Judaizing demand could be made, but we also have clear evidence of such a demand being made by someone with a close connection with the church in Corinth.[49]

(*b*) Paul's opponents seem to have argued that he did not have the same visions and revelations as they did (2 Cor. 12.1–10), nor did he work miracles such as were appropriate to the office he claimed (12.11ff.). It is often supposed that such claims are 'Gnostic' (cf. Schmithals, *Gnosticism in Corinth*, pp. 187–92), but this is not necessarily the case, for even the Jewish rabbis could lay claim to this kind of activity.[50]

(*c*) Though Bultmann[51] has argued that Paul's opponents here had some kind of mythological Gnosis which the apostle simply took for granted, the fact still remains that there is no explicit mention of the kind of question that played such an important role in 1 Corinthians. Nor is it even implied. Rather is the question now directed solely to Paul's authority as an apostle, something which we know to have been a deep concern of certain Jewish Christians (cf. Gal. 1–2).[52]

3. Finally, it should be added that, in the light of our own suggestions about the situation, the assumption that some kind of Jewish-Christian (though not Judaizing) influence was involved here, seems to be the more likely. Whatever may have been the exact course of events in Paul's dealings with the Corinthian church between the writing of 1 Corinthians and 2 Corinthians, it is clear that 2 Corinthians was written in a time of severe crisis for the church (cf. Lake, *Earlier Epistles*, pp. 120ff.). This is shown not only by the character of the epistle,[53] but also in the way Timothy and Titus, and even Paul himself, were engaged in visiting the congregation. The deep concern which Paul seems to have had at the time when he himself probably made a flying visit to the church at Corinth, is much easier to understand on the assumption that a group of Jewish Christians had come in than it would be on the assumption that there had merely been an extension of the problems dealt with in 1 Corinthians. Probably a group of Jewish Christians with a personal animosity towards Paul (the 'false apostles' of 11.13ff.),[54] seeing the apparent inconsistency of Paul's approach to the varying situations in Galatia and in Corinth, had come in with the accusation that he was such an inconsistent man that his complete spiritual bankruptcy was now demonstrated for all to see. The very charge that Paul had directed against his opponents in Galatia (cf. Gal. 3.3) could now be directed against Paul himself (2 Cor. 10.2), for he was simply seeking to gain whatever advantage he could in every situation.[55] It was against such an idea that Paul penned 2 Corinthians, the character of

which was determined by the situation. Paul was now aware of the subtlety of his opponents on both sides of the theological fence, and so, while attacking this new Jewish opposition, he still had to guard against possible Gnosticizing misrepresentation of his teaching,[56] a balance which he achieved with considerable success, and which was to lay the foundation for his *magnum opus* in the Roman epistle.

5

Theological Diversity in the Pauline Correspondence

It has already been suggested above that at least some elements in the heresy opposed in 1 Corinthians could be attributed to a misunderstanding or a deliberate misuse of Paul's own teaching in Galatians, and that when in 2 Corinthians he came to oppose something more like the Jewish opposition he had met in Galatia, he was making a conscious effort to avoid being branded by one side or the other as either a Gnosticizer or a Judaizer. This process in his thought reached its fulfilment in Romans, an epistle in which Paul was consciously trying to produce a 'neutral' theology, taking account of the valid claims of both sides while avoiding the pitfalls that he had encountered in writing both Galatians and 1 Corinthians. In considering the implications of this hypothesis, we must now inquire into four main questions:

1. Could Paul's teaching in Galatians have been claimed as 'Gnosticizing', or even explicitly 'Gnostic' in any sense?

2. Is there any historical evidence known to us which would indicate that Paul's teaching in Galatians could have been taken this way in his own lifetime?

3. Is there a valid method for detecting such change in the historical situation behind the theological arguments of Paul's epistles?

4. What was the outcome of this for Paul's own theological position?

We shall consider each of these questions in turn.

I

How Gnostic is Galatians?

We have already seen that the apostles, especially the Twelve but also Paul, were held in high esteem in perhaps the majority of the Gnostic theories. For the Gnostics, the apostles and other leaders of the early church held supreme authority not because of their established position in the ecclesiastical theory of the catholic church, but because they themselves were held to have been Gnostics *par excellence*, often superhuman figures, and always with the divine spark enlightened by *gnōsis* as their distinguishing mark (cf. *Exc. Theod.* 3.2). It is not surprising, therefore, to find that Paul and his teachings feature quite prominently in much of our literature. Valentinus claimed a close connection with Paul through one Theodas,[1] and the Valentinians, believing that Paul used the basic ideas of their system, treated his epistles with great respect.[2] Though a recent author has shown that they misunderstood Paul's teaching, and interpreted it in the light of the Valentinian system,[3] the very fact that they were able to do so suggests that there must have been within the Pauline corpus the seeds of the kind of doctrine which they were seeking to propound. Marcion's teaching is, of course, the *locus classicus* for the use (or misuse) of the Pauline epistles, and the fact that he placed Galatians at the head of his collection of these epistles can surely be no accident, for it was in this epistle that he probably found most to support his own ideas.[4]

The *actual* use of the New Testament by these later figures is not our concern here, and the definition of such use is a highly complex matter.[5] But the fact that both the Church Fathers and the Gnostics, and others who stood midway between the two, could find some justification for their position in the Pauline epistles does show that the possibility of such misunderstanding was built into Paul's thought right from the start. Those who have investigated the matter most fully have all reached similar conclusions:

> Gnostic exegesis is largely *eisēgēsis* . . . The number and variety of their Biblical quotations is superficially impressive, but it is rather a matter of embellishing Gnostic material with scriptural

references than of constructing systems out of genuinely Biblical materials.[6]

When we turn to the text of the epistle to the Galatians, it becomes clear that at almost every point in Paul's statements there is the possibility of a genuine misunderstanding on the basis of 'Gnostic' thought. In many crucial connections Paul expresses himself either in a vague way, or in a very extreme fashion, both of which leave him open to misinterpretation. By taking his words at face value, it is easy to see how Gnostic ideas could have claimed apostolic foundation in Pauline teaching. Doresse's comment goes to the heart of the matter when he says of the Gnostics:

> Their interpretation, far from being the product of wild imagination, as at first sight one might suppose, must have been the result of exegesis, *literal* to the point of falsification, applied to the smallest details and biased by cabbalistic speculations (*Secret Books*, p. 108).

Little wonder then that Schoeps could describe Paul's thought as 'the theology of multiplied misunderstanding' (*Paul*, p. 262).

Each of the three main areas of Pauline teaching in Galatians was immediately susceptible to this kind of interpretation. In the defence of his authority as a properly accredited apostle (1.10–2.21), Paul laid an extraordinary emphasis on the revelational character of his mission: he was the one who had a direct encounter with the risen Christ, and who on that account was sent into the world to proclaim the gospel with authority. Though we have rejected Schmithals's claim that this was a reflection of Gnostic thought by Paul, it is clear that his teaching in Galatians 1.12, especially when taken in isolation from the rest of his epistles, could form the basis of a Gnostic idea of the apostle and his functions. Schmithals has shown quite convincingly in his study, *The Office of Apostle* (pp. 122–92), that one of the signs of a Gnostic messenger was his prophetic character, and it was essentially this kind of claim that Paul was making for himself in Galatians 1–2. Like Paul, the Gnostic messenger brought a special revelation, proclaiming the secrets of an alien world and its God to a lost humanity, embodied in a series of unique truths made known to the elect. This, in the broadest sense, is what Paul was saying in

Galatians 1.11–12. We must not, of course, lose sight of the differences, to which we have drawn attention in a previous chapter. Nor must we overemphasize the prophetic character in Gnostic speculation, for certain elements fundamental to Paul and to the New Testament writers in general were absent or insignificant for the Gnostic:

> The eschatological, the ethical, and the communal aspect of the prophetic address have become completely neglected for the sake of the first and last, the proclamation of gnosis. . . . Because of the inherent dualism, the kerygma of this alien world can never reach prophetic concreteness (Laeuchli, *Language of Faith*, p. 28).

Paul's teaching on the Old Testament was, if anything, even more susceptible to a Gnostic interpretation, and indeed, taken in isolation from his other epistles, Paul's statements on the Law in Galatians can with a great deal of justification be called blatantly Gnostic. There were in the second century two main lines of development from Paul's teaching on the Old Testament. On the one hand, there was a development of the kind of thought found in the Pastoral Epistles of the New Testament, so that Paul could be depicted especially as a teacher of 'the Law of Christ'. This approach was taken over by Ignatius of Antioch, 1 Clement, Hermas, and the 'orthodox' church in general. Such a development, however, was not based on Galatians, but on Galatians interpreted in the light of Romans and 1 Corinthians. On the other hand, in the *Epistle of Barnabas*, something like Paul's teaching in Galatians 3.19, that the Law was given by angels, seems to have been taken as a basis for the total devaluation of the Law and the covenant in their original setting. According to this author, the Jewish view of the Old Testament rested on a fundamental misunderstanding, and in fact the Law and circumcision had never been intended literally, but were to be given a 'spiritual', and Christian, interpretation. Though the *Epistle of Barnabas* postulated no direct antithesis between the Old and New Testaments, such a view of the Old Testament led on naturally to Marcion, and thence to the various radical Gnostic groups such as the Carpocratians, the Cainites, and the Ophites.

The devaluation of the Old Testament, and, therefore, the rejection of law in any sense for the Christian community, was an inevitable outcome of Paul's teaching. For one thing, Paul seems to have made but little use of the Old Testament in his missionary activity, laying most of the emphasis on the pre-existent Lord Who came from above, died on the cross, rose from the dead and ascended back to heaven. This was a perfectly understandable thing for him to do, of course, for the whole ethos of his mission was determined primarily by his conversion experience, in which he had met this risen Christ whom he now proclaimed (cf. Bauer, *Orthodoxy and Heresy*, pp. 238ff.). But this, coupled with his extreme statements in Galatians 3, especially v. 19, would naturally mean that his converts were particularly susceptible to a slide in the Gnostic direction, even at the earliest stage of his ministry. The natural and logically necessary outcome of Paul's statement that the Law of the Old Testament was 'ordained by angels through an intermediary' (Gal. 3.19), whatever may have been its original justification in the face of legalistic Judaizers, was the belief that the Law was the product not of the supreme God, but of some evil angelic Demiurge. Though Duncan (*Galatians*, p. 115) is right to observe that 'Paul does not assert that the angels in question were demons or spirits of evil', it was but a short step from Paul's statements to the assumption that the Law was the work of some evil angelic Demiurge. Schlier (*Galaterbrief*, p. 158) and Bultmann (*Theology* I, p. 268) both contend that Paul was actually taking up some kind of gnostic myth regarding the Law's origin, though there is in fact no definite evidence that the angels who gave the Law according to Galatians 3.19 were ever identified with an evil Demiurge before the second century (Wilson, *Gnosis and the New Testament*, p. 61).

It is hardly surprising that Marcion treasured Paul's writings, and especially Galatians, when his Gnostic theories were presented for him in such a palatable fashion. Though he went further than Paul by tracing the antithesis of Law and gospel back to two different gods, and to that extent perverted the Pauline gospel, one's judgement on him (and others like him) must be tempered with considerable sympathy in view of the exceedingly loose forms of expression employed by the apostle. In addition, in 4.21—5.1 Paul used a form of Old Testament interpretation which was to become the standard way for Gnostics to deal with the Old Testament, and so here again, whatever may have been Paul's original intention in emphasizing this 'allegory', his use of it could easily have added grist to the mill of any who were inclined to move in a Gnostic direction. The same methods were, of course, employed also by the 'orthodox' Christians. Indeed, this was one of the main causes of contention:

> It is not surprising that Gnostic exegesis provoked the early Fathers to exasperation, for the Gnostics were using the Church's books and employing the self-same methods of interpretation, but producing very different results (Wilson, *Gnosis and the New Testament*, p. 77).

The only difference was that the orthodox insisted that the apostolic tradition was public and, therefore, a more or less objective standard was available, whereas the Gnostics' insistence that secret revelations had been divulged to selected individuals left the door open for them to introduce their own systems and theories.

We have barely scratched the surface in pointing to elements of Pauline teaching in Galatians which could easily be taken to provide justification for a move in a Gnostic direction. Many other, slighter examples have been pointed out by Schmithals in his study. Though he regards these as the *basis* of Paul's thought, most of the parallels which he adduces are in fact better understood as the *outcome* of Pauline teaching in certain Gnostic contexts.[7] It seems likely, therefore, that Paul's teaching in Galatians could be construed almost as an open invitation for Gnosticizing influences to enter the first-century church, especially in the matters of the nature of spiritual authority, and the position and values of the Old Testament and its Law, and, therefore, the place of law as such in the Christian life.

II

Were Paul's Opponents Gnostics?

It is one thing to show that Paul's teaching here was open to Gnosticizing tendencies, but quite another actually to prove that it was in fact subjected to such misunderstanding at an early stage. Indeed, in the nature of the case, it is all but impossible to prove that this happened, though there is a certain amount of evidence which makes it easy to believe that this could have been the outcome. Here, we shall first consider what we know of the history of the early church, to see if there are any incidents known to us which might have provided the foothold that Gnostic ideas would have needed for Paul's Galatian teaching to be taken up in a Gnostic sense; then we shall go on to mention some other elements in Paul's teaching to see if there is any internal evidence that this was actually the case.

In the search for some other, external evidence which may shed light on the meaning of Galatians and its historical situation, we are inevitably forced to consider the question of the relationship of this epistle to the Acts of the Apostles, and particularly the question of Paul's various visits to Jerusalem, outlined in Galatians 1–2, and the possibility (or impossibility) of fitting his account into the Acts narrative. Particularly is our attention directed here to the so-called Apostolic Council reported in Acts 15, which was directly concerned, if the account in Acts can be believed, with the very same questions of the Law and the Old Testament which we have seen to be in Galatians a possible starting-point for Gnosticizing ideas in the early church. Not only is this passage notable for the many difficulties which it raises, but also for the fact that, if it contains reliable traditions, it depicts Paul adopting an attitude towards the imposition of the law-principle on Christians which at best is inconsistent with his teaching in Galatians, and at worst could be taken as evidence of an outright contradiction.[8] While in Galatians Paul argues against the application of any kind of law-principle to the Christian, who must on the contrary find the source of his morality in Christ Himself, in Acts 15 we find the same Paul implicitly accepting the application of the law-principle to Christian experience, and openly advocating the imposition of certain legal requirements on Gentile Christians.

B. W. Bacon was certainly right in describing this complex of events as 'the crux of apostolic history'.[9] If our observations are correct, it is of even more crucial significance than has generally been supposed for, quite apart from the light which it sheds on Paul's personality and on the intentions of the author of Acts, it can also be seen to contain within itself part of the answer to the problem of how and why Gnosticizing tendencies first entered the Christian church. Since our main interest lies more in drawing out the implications of this complex of events in the light of our own study, we merely refer here to the not inconsiderable body of literature on the subject of the exact correlation between Galatians and Acts, summaries of which are available in concise form in Kümmel, *Introduction*, pp. 195ff. In our view, the most plausible explanation of the situation so far put forward is that proposed by W. M. Ramsay, who equated Galatians 2.1–10 with Acts 11.27–30; and on the basis of our own approach, from a very different direction, we shall shortly see reason to accept this view essentially as Ramsay propounded it, and suppose not only that Galatians was the first of Paul's epistles, but that it was written immediately before the Apostolic Council described in Acts 15.[10]

On reading the account as it now stands in Acts 15, the clear impression that one gains from the first three verses is of a large-scale controversy in the Gentile churches between Paul and Barnabas in concert with the Gentile Christians, on the one side, and 'some men [who] came down from Judea' (v. 1), on the other, and that the specific point at issue was the question of circumcision. We cannot tell from the bare statement of v. 1 whether the demand for circumcision was coupled with a demand also for the Gentiles to observe the whole of the Jewish Law, though the sequel may well suggest as much.[11] The outcome of this disagreement is, however, clear: Paul and Barnabas were sent along with certain others to make representations at Jerusalem to 'the apostles and the elders' (v. 2), a group of men who throughout the entire narrative are the ones who make the decisions, and who carefully and consistently are distinguished from Paul and Barnabas and their companions (cf. vv. 4, 6, 22, 23). Following the report given by Paul and Barnabas to the church as a whole (v. 4), the 'apostles and elders' then convened a private meeting to discuss the problems. The outcome of this meeting was that after Peter had declared in favour of the Gentiles and against the

Pharisees on the basis of his experience with the Gentile mission, especially with Cornelius, Paul and Barnabas gave their evidence (not as members of the Council, but simply as witnesses, vv. 12ff.). Their general position was supported by James, who quoted Scripture to support the case.[12] But he then went on to suggest a compromise solution, that the Gentiles should 'abstain from the pollutions of idols and from unchastity and from what is strangled, and from blood' (v. 20)—all prescriptions of the Levitical Law.[13]

The sequel now follows that 'the apostles and elders, with the whole church' (v. 22)—still distinguished from Paul and Barnabas, who do not seem to have figured in this part of the proceedings—chose men to take the message to Antioch in the company of Paul and Barnabas. The fact that no mention is made of Paul and Barnabas agreeing with the verdict *may* suggest that Judas and Silas were entrusted with the job of conveying the message either because Paul and Barnabas would not do it, or because they could not be trusted to convey the entire message; though it seems more likely that these others were sent in accordance with the Mosaic legal requirements for the establishing of evidence which had, after all, been commended by Jesus himself (Matt. 18.16). The final outcome was that after the Decree was read in Antioch, the church there 'rejoiced at the exhortation' (v. 31). Not that the Gentiles accepted the Decree with unreserved acclamation. Yet even this concession was more than they had hoped for, and that in itself would be no small cause for rejoicing. Nor was this sense of relief restricted to the church, for Paul on his next missionary expedition took upon himself the task of delivering the decision of the Council to some of the churches he was visiting (16.4).

The problem, however, is not solved quite so easily, for in the only context in his own writings where Paul deals with the issues raised by the Apostolic Decree, he does not mention the Decree itself, nor does he allude to it or hand on the views of the Jewish-Christian church (Rom. 14.1ff.; 1 Cor. 8.1ff.). In these contexts he prefers rather to argue from first principles, on the basis of which he appears to reach rather different conclusions from those which, according to Acts 15, he evidently accepted at the time of the Jerusalem Council, conclusions which also seem to be in opposition to his insistence in Galatians on the freedom of the Christian believer. At the same time, running parallel with Paul's change of emphasis (if not actually a change of mind), there is a certain amount of evidence for a hardening of Jewish-Christian practice in insisting on the observance of the rules of the Apostolic Decree, and often even upon the observance of more of the Old Testament Law.[14] Two possible explanations suggest themselves here. We could take the line proposed by several scholars, and argue that Acts 16.4–5 is a Lucan interpolation for the purpose of giving universal application to a Decree originally intended for just a few specific churches.[15] But Acts 16.4ff. scarcely suggests that Paul committed this message to *all* the churches he visited and established. Indeed, there is no further mention of Paul doing so even in the rest of the book of Acts. A more plausible explanation, which also has the advantage of requiring no conjectural emendations to the text either of Acts or of the epistles, is to suppose that between Paul's acceptance of the Apostolic Decree and the time of his letters to the Roman and Corinthian churches, an emergent historical situation forced him to change his approach to the matter. This new situation was brought about by the intrusion of 'Gnostic' ideas into the Gentile churches. Such ideas may have gained a foothold in the Gentile churches as a reaction against the terms of the Apostolic Decree and also against Paul's evident acceptance of them, claiming in its favour the argument of Paul in his epistle to the Galatians, which had been written just before the Jerusalem Council. This development led to two different ways of dealing with the situation. For Paul it meant a clearer expression of his own approach to Christian liberty, emphasizing that the would-be Gnostics had misinterpreted his intention. For the Jewish Christians, on the other hand, this new situation led to a strengthening of the position of the more extreme Judaizers, which in practice led to an even greater insistence on the indissoluble (almost sacrosanct) nature of the terms of the Apostolic Decree.

It was Sir William Ramsay who pointed out long ago that the effective outcome of the Apostolic Decree was to create two grades of Christians: a lower class of weaker believers, who could not observe the whole of the Law but only the obligatory parts of it, and a higher class who were spiritual enough to obey the whole Law. Thus Ramsay concluded:

> It was almost inevitable that a Decree, which lays down no clear and formal principles of freedom, should in practice be taken as

making a distinction between strong and weak, between more and less advanced Christians; and it is certain that it was soon taken in that sense.[16]

It is equally certain that, once such a Jewish spiritual élite had been established in the church, the most natural reaction for the Gentile believers would be to try to produce a similar élite on their side of the ecclesiastical fence. It was just such an opportunity as this that Gnosis had been waiting for, and it can therefore tentatively be suggested that it may have been at this point that Gnosticizing thought first began to penetrate Gentile Christianity, as a counteraction against Jewish legalism. Far from effectively dealing with the prevalent heresy of the day, Paul's letter to the Galatians served only to heighten the tension between Jews and Gentiles, and provided the would-be Gnostics with a theological foundation on which to base their spurious arguments, which were to emerge for the first time as a viable 'Gnostic' movement within the church at Corinth.

Before going any further in the development of this hypothesis, we must pause to answer two possible objections that may be raised:

1. Perhaps the most obvious difficulty is the fact that scholars are by no means agreed on the authenticity of the account in Acts 15 of the so-called Jerusalem Council and of its sequel in the Apostolic Decree.[17] Many commentators look upon this as a part of Luke's hortatory purpose to show that the apostolic age was one of complete harmony in matters of doctrine and practice and that Paul, far from being the 'lone wolf' whom he can be made to seem from his epistles, was actually under the firm jurisdiction of the foundation apostles at Jerusalem. It is instructive, however, to note the view of C. H. Talbert in this connection.[18] Though he undoubtedly regards this section of Acts as being 'unhistorical' in its stated context, he does see a close connection between it and what he takes to be Luke's anti-Gnostic intention in writing. He rightly points out that, even if the incident actually happened as stated, Luke devotes an inordinate amount of space to this circumcision issue, an issue which can hardly have had much relevance when Luke wrote (whether we date this in the sixties or later in the first century). Talbert (who dates Acts *c.* A.D. 75–100), noting that the heresies reflected in both Colossians (cf. 2.11–14)

and the Pastorals (cf. Titus 1.10) are concerned with circumcision, concludes that Luke elaborated this theme in such detail because:

> There was a Gnostic group in the Aegean basin near the time of Luke-Acts that practiced the rite of circumcision. It is not at all unlikely therefore that the Lucan emphasis upon the apostolic rejection of circumcision as a necessity for Christians should be seen as another attempt by Luke to form a defense against Gnosticism (op. cit., p. 95).

What Talbert says here may contain an element of truth. Taken in conjunction with our own observations it at least suggests that the historical difficulties over the Apostolic Decree need not be so great as may at first be supposed. Moreover, the evidence of Paul's correspondence points clearly to the origin of Gnosticizing movements within the church in the very period of which we are speaking. The evidence of the Church Fathers, such as it is, also points in the same general direction. Simon the Samaritan (cf. Acts 8) is supposed to have been the first Gnostic (Irenaeus, *Adv. Haer*. I.23), while the heretics of Revelation 2 were allegedly connected with the later Nicolaitans (cf. Irenaeus, *Adv. Haer*. I.26.3, III.11.1; Eusebius, *H.E.* III.29). Though the historical reliability of these traditions is in doubt, their very existence shows that it was thought that Gnosticizing ideas penetrated the Christian church at a fairly early stage in its history. R. McL. Wilson (*Gnosis and the New Testament*, pp. 54ff.) is expressing a fairly common consensus of opinion (at least among English-speaking scholars) when he traces in the Pauline corpus a kind of progression of Gnostic influence from just the slightest appearance of Gnosis in Galatians, through Corinthians with more of a Gnostic element present, to Colossians/Ephesians and the Pastorals, where Gnostic thought is said to be fairly clearly in view. The deduction from this is that Gnosis must first have impinged on Christian belief at about the time of the writing of Galatians, which in turn suggests that if the Apostolic Council never took place, we may find it necessary to invent something very much like it to put in its place as an adequate explanation for the rise of 'Gnostic' ideas in the Gentile churches at just this period.

2. This leads on to a consideration of the second difficulty that may arise in the application of the hypothesis set forth here.

Talbert, in the context already mentioned, goes on to say: 'Though heresy did not exist in the apostolic age, yet there was a tendency, the demand for circumcision, which later came to be a part of Gnosticism, which did exist. This tendency was opposed by all the apostles' (p. 95). This points up what is a crucial issue, and one that must be faced if we are not to be accused of begging the question, or even of arguing in a circle. If Gnosis really did enter Christian thought as part of a Gentile reaction against a Jewish legalism which in its extreme forms demanded, among other things, circumcision, how is it that circumcision was plainly an obligatory rite (or, if not quite obligatory, at least a desirable 'optional extra' for the superspiritual) in the Gnostic heresies represented by Colossians/Ephesians and the Pastorals, as also in many of the classical Gnostic heresies of the second century? Not only did circumcision come to play a large part, but also the eating of *eidōlothuta* on which many Gnostics took a line which actually agreed with the terms of the Apostolic Decree, over against such as the Nicolaitans of Revelations 2 who took a different view.[19]

The solution to this problem is to be found in the history of Jewish Christianity and its relation to the Gentile churches. In a sense, Jewish Christianity was embodied in the person of James, the brother of our Lord, and though after his death Symeon, another relative of Jesus, was appointed in his place, the martyrdom of James effectively sounded the death-knell of a Jewish Christianity of the type which he had represented, and from this point onwards, such Jewish Christians as did survive were to be found mostly in various local and sectarian movements.[20] It is perhaps not without significance that it was just about this time, when Jewish Christianity was losing its influence on the church world-wide, that we have our first evidence of circumcision and food laws coming into Gnosis. It may be that by this time the controversy which initially sparked off the Gnosticizing reaction had been forgotten in the Gentile churches. In addition, the Jewish Christians had so little influence by now anyway, that those Gnostics who were seeking new ways in which to subdue the material flesh could find an acceptable supply of ideas in the old Jewish-Christian approach based on the Old Testament (which by this time was probably also becoming a regular source book for Gnostic mythology, particularly in regard to the Creation narratives of Genesis).[21] R. M. Grant, though he approaches the subject of early Christian Gnosis from a very different angle, and reaches conclusions which we would by no means endorse *in toto*, has argued that the period from *c.* A.D. 62 to 70 was crucial for the development of Christian Gnosis, with the failure of Jewish eschatological hopes and a subsequent influx of Jewish ideas into the mainstream of Gnostic thought.[22] Though we would disagree with him by placing the initial Christian-Gnostic involvement at least a generation earlier, the evidence does seem to point in the same general direction as that adduced by Grant, i.e. that there was in the sixties of the first century an influx of Jewish ideas into Christian Gnosis, which may have played a constructive role in the development of classical Gnosticism out of the initial stirrings encountered in the Pauline churches.[23]

This leads us on to a brief statement of some of the advantages which our hypothesis appears to have over other theories that have been propounded. Unless a new interpretation has the capacity of answering questions which already existing approaches are incapable of meeting satisfactorily, there is little point in adopting it, save for the sake of mere novelty. Our own reconstruction of the historical process has at least three important points in its favour:

1. The problem of Jewish elements in the context of early Christian Gnosis is one of the most difficult to resolve, and is the Achilles' heel of all theories except those which actually see a Jewish origin for Gnosticism. The reconstruction set forth here does full justice to both Jewish and Hellenistic elements in Gnosis, without expressly limiting the function of either in the rise of Christian forms of the heresy.

2. The great prominence given in the New Testament to the business of purchasing and eating *eidōlothuta* has often caused some difficulty, for in the context of a Gentile city like Corinth much, perhaps most, of the meat sold in the markets would have only a slight connection, if any at all, with idols, so far as we are able to tell. C. K. Barrett observes that, in normal life, the question 'would never have arisen in a Gentile church like that of Corinth if Jewish Christians . . . had not raised it' ('Things Sacrificed to Idols', p. 146). This being the case, it is difficult to see why so much contention should have been caused over an issue which

would but rarely present itself even to Gentile Christians. But if we assume that it was just at this point that Gnostic ideas had been called in by the Gentile believers to reassert their spirituality over against the élitist attitude of their Jewish counterparts, we can see why the Jews remained so stubborn and dogmatic on their part, and why the Gentiles were equally firm on theirs: to the former it was a question of orthodoxy to abstain from *eidōlothuta*, while to the latter it was an integral part of their doctrine of spiritual freedom and liberty in Christ that was at stake.

3. When, towards the end of the first century and on into the second, the catholic church organized itself in the fight against its Gnostic opponents, it is remarkable that it did so by the revival of the old Jewish-Christian form of church government, in preference to the charismatic order advocated and practised by Paul.[24] It is remarkable, firstly, because the catholic church was largely the heir not to Jewish Christianity, but to the very Gentile Christianity which had so prized the Pauline charismatic order; and, second, because by the time of the emergence of the catholic church at the end of the first century, Jewish Christianity had ceased to be much of a vital force, and had been more or less ineffective outside its own circles for some considerable time before that. It is not enough, therefore, to say that the catholic church was merely being reactionary in establishing the monarchical episcopate on the basis of the Jewish presbyterianism of an earlier period. There must have been a more fundamental reason than that. This we may suppose to have been a desire to go back to the beginning of the church's history and attempt to make a fresh start altogether. They knew of the influx of Gnostic teaching as a result of the legalistic decision of the Jerusalem Council, and aimed at getting back to something like that situation, in the hope that they could make wiser decisions than their predecessors had done. But this attempt was also a failure, as the catholic theologians became caught up with their own brand of legalism and the Church Fathers attempted to rewrite Christian history from the tendentious standpoint of their own *status quo*.

The evidence which we have examined here therefore suggests that the historical pattern of events lying behind the major Pauline epistles was as follows:

(*a*) Paul's mission to the churches of south Galatia, in his first missionary tour (Acts 13.1—14.23).

(*b*) The influx of Judaizers into the Galatian churches, and Paul's immediate response to their teaching in the epistle to the Galatians, emphasizing the bankruptcy of both the Old Testament itself and the law-principle which it represented, over against the complete spiritual freedom of the believer in Christ.

(*c*) The Council at Jerusalem (Acts 15.1–29) in the course of which Paul, for whatever reason, accepted the imposition of a certain limited legal requirement on Gentile Christians.

(*d*) A Gnosticizing movement arose among Gentile Christians, stimulated by two factors: the establishment of a kind of Jewish-Christian élite who could keep the whole Law, over against Gentiles who could keep only the basic Noachic commandments; also the growing conviction that in agreeing to this arrangement, Paul had himself been unfaithful to his own beliefs as outlined in Galatians, which could now form a textbook capable of being interpreted in the light of extreme ideas brought in from the Gentile environment of the Roman empire.

(*e*) Paul's efforts in the Corinthian correspondence, first to repress such views by an enforced legalism (1 Cor.), and then to give a more balanced view of the matter in the face of new Jewish opposition (2 Cor.).

(*f*) Paul's epistle to the Romans came slightly later. Writing to Christians he had not met, he attempted to give a completely balanced exposition of his theological position, which would be susceptible of misunderstanding by neither Judaizers nor Gnosticizers.

III

Can we Reconstruct History out of Theology?

Such evidence as we have just outlined here is more circumstantial than direct, though when it is taken in conjunction with the internal evidence of the theological variations of the major Pauline epistles, it can be seen to fit into the overall picture of Paul's ministry which we have gained from the evidence of his own writings. Before we go on to show how the circumstances of Paul's ministry have affected the expression of his own theological convictions, however, one further question remains outstanding. So far, we have taken it for granted that the variations to which we have drawn attention can be interpreted as valid pointers to the character of Paul's opponents in Galatia and Corinth, and that if Paul adopted one method in dealing with the Judaizers in Galatia, when he adopted a different method in 1 Corinthians he must have been facing opponents who stood at the opposite extreme of the theological stage, and whom we have characterized as 'Gnostics'. Are the criteria that have been employed here valid for this purpose?

The most notable difficulty encountered by any reconstruction of the circumstances dealt with in the Pauline letters is the fact that in every case we have only one side of the argument now available to us, and that is the side which eventually came out on top. It is a simple matter to see that Paul's authority in the Corinthian church was being questioned by people with different ideas, but when we come to ask who they may have been and what their ideas were, we are faced with a mass of speculative theories. The truth is that we will probably never be able to produce anything like a definitive account of Paul's relations with most of the churches addressed in his letters, for the simple reason that we know virtually nothing of his opponents other than what we can deduce from his replies to their arguments. It is just this fact that makes nonsense of the approach of people like Schmithals or Marxsen (cf. his *Introduction to the New Testament*, Eng. trans., Oxford, 1968), who assume that Paul actually misunderstood the nature of the opponents with whom he was dealing. Perhaps he did not always appreciate the full consequences of the teaching of his opponents, or indeed of his replies to such teaching; but if he had no idea of the essential ingredients of the teaching he was opposing, we are deceiving ourselves if we imagine that there is even a remote possibility that we can recover the details of their belief at this late stage.

Happily, on the matter of Paul's disputes with Judaizing Christians there is now a fairly wide area of general agreement for, after all, we are not left entirely at the mercy of our own subjective judgements in uncovering the historical situation. We also have a certain, if limited, number of more or less factual statements made in Paul's correspondence and, for what it is worth, we have the account in Acts. On Christian Gnosis, however, we have no such help in the New Testament, and the word 'Gnostic' and its derivatives are hardly ever used, even in the latest New Testament documents. The nearest the New Testament comes to an explicit technical mention of the term must be 1 Timothy 6.20, which speaks of 'what is falsely called *gnōsis*'. Yet the study of the New Testament from many different directions has shown that an incipient Gnosis must have existed at this period, otherwise it is difficult to understand the widespread emergence of Gnostic groups at the end of the first century, groups with such strong foundations that they could withstand the whole weight of the catholic church for several decades.

Since the only *direct* evidence that we have for the Church-versus-Gnosis controversy comes from the second century, we must inevitably take this as our starting-point. The catholic church of the second and following centuries had its genesis largely in the Gnostic controversies, and since its own defence mechanism against Gnostic belief fell into a very regular and predictable pattern, it has been assumed that by tracing this pattern back into the first century, there can be distinguished two main groupings within the New Testament canon: the 'apostolic' writings, produced at an early stage in Christian history, when the existence of Gnostic ideas was simply taken for granted, and the so-called 'early catholic' writings, which are said to represent the stage later in the first century when Gnostic beliefs became a real threat to the whole church. These two stages are usually clearly differentiated, and many would claim that the 'apostolic' stage is the only truly Christian one, while the supposed 'early catholic' writings represent a retrograde step in the development of the faith. This belief is based on the common idea that there was some sort of

Gnostic *system* ante-dating the rise of Christianity. The first, 'apostolic' period of the New Testament thus represents a time when already existent Gnostic ideas were assimilated and adapted by the early church, while the later, 'early catholic' period was a time when the church hardened its attitude and began to oppose any form of Gnostic theology. One of the most vigorous contemporary advocates of this view of early Christian history in relation to Gnosis and the Church is Ernst Käsemann, whose views have been popularized in English with the translation of some of his papers in two volumes of essays.[25] According to Käsemann, several features of ecclesiastical life and organization which later came to be characteristic of the catholic church can be traced in the New Testament. These are so different from the earlier, 'apostolic' New Testament writings that he can speak 'not merely of significant tensions, but not infrequently of irreconcilable theological contradictions' within the New Testament canon itself (*ENTT*, p. 100). The main features of this 'catholic' intrusion into the New Testament can be grouped together under four headings, though there are very many other minor features which also are often claimed to be 'early catholic'.[26] Here we confine our attention to the three main types of thought which are said to be catholic intrusions. Though we have dealt with two of these at greater length elsewhere, it will nevertheless be worth while in this present context to repeat and reinforce our earlier conclusions.[27]

1. Perhaps the most important change perceived between the 'apostolic' and 'early catholic' New Testament writings is in the eschatological position: futuristic in the apostolic age, realized in the early catholic era. Arguing from this premise, Käsemann declares:

> I can acknowledge as earliest Christianity only that which still has its focus in an eschatology determined by the original imminent expectation in its changing forms. When this focus shifts, a new phase is to be established.[28]

Thus, while the Paul of the epistles is 'a possessed man . . . pursuing a feverish dream' (*NTQ*, p. 241), that the focus has shifted and that a 'new phase' has been established is 'undoubtedly the case with Luke and the Pastorals'.[29] But if we compare the Pauline view with that of the Pastorals we will find that, though there is undoubtedly more realized eschatology in the Pastorals than there is in many of the Paulines, nevertheless there are clear traces of the same eschatological *tension*. In the genuine Paulines we find that though the apostle had a future hope of direct divine intervention, yet the presence of the Holy Spirit in the believer was in some way the agent by which the *eschaton* could be inaugurated in Christians here and now.[30] We find precisely this kind of tension in 2 Timothy 4.1, where there is a future expectation of 'God and of Christ Jesus who is to judge the living and the dead . . . by his appearing and his kingdom', and where also we learn that God has 'saved us and called us with a holy calling, not in virtue of our works but in virtue of his own purpose and the grace which he gave us in Christ Jesus ages ago, and now has manifested through the appearing of our Saviour, Jesus Christ' (2 Tim. 1.9–10). On the basis of this, Christians are to 'guard the truth which has been entrusted to you by the Holy Spirit who dwells within us' (2 Tim. 1.14). The main question to be asked is not which part of the eschatological spectrum is in the sharpest focus, but whether in fact the whole spectrum is held in perspective. However the main focus may have shifted in the course of the first century, the spectrum was undoubtedly always there, along with its attendant tensions, and this is the important thing.

2. Another alleged distinguishing mark of 'early catholicism' is its insistence on organizational church order, with its legitimate succession and duly ordained ministry as opposed to the earlier charismatic order (typical of the truly apostolic age). Käsemann claims that in the later writings of the New Testament there is no emphasis on the gift of the Holy Spirit to all Christians, but rather on the Spirit given to those who have been properly ordained by the laying on of hands. Thus,

> An office which stands over against the rest of the community is now the real bearer of the Spirit; and the primitive Christian view, that every Christian receives the Spirit in his baptism recedes into the background and, indeed, for all practical purposes disappears (*ENTT*, p. 87).

This stands in sharp contrast to the Pauline situation with no official ministry, in which even the great apostle himself was simply 'one charismatic among many' (*ENTT*, p. 81). It also stands in sharp contrast to another statement made by Käsemann himself in the same volume of essays:

> . . . the hypothesis that there was ever a Christianity without cultus or official ministry is not only incapable of proof but contradicts directly the role of apostolate and prophecy on the one side and of the sacraments on the other, as far back as we are able to see (*ENTT*, pp. 140ff.).

Käsemann himself would probably not see a contradiction here, for he seems to make a distinction between the type of 'official' ministry that existed in the 'apostolic' period and the later kind of 'official' ministry which was a mark of 'early catholicism'. But he can hardly have it both ways. If in fact an 'official' ministry existed at an early date, we must seek to define the relationship between it and the later developments, rather than simply dismissing the latter out of hand.

3. Following on from this assertion is another, which need not engage our attention unduly here, i.e. that great emphasis came to be laid on the tradition of the church being properly handed down. This could take several forms, of which we mention four:

(*a*) The primitive Christian kerygma, with its dynamic understanding of the role of faith in the Christian life, was replaced by a strict code of faith expressed more and more in static terms ('*the* faith'). But we do have evidence from an undoubtedly 'apostolic' context that Christian belief could be spoken of in the same manner, even if not in the same language (Rom. 6.17, cf. Phil. 1.27; Col. 2.7; Eph. 4.5). It is widely recognized that Paul himself cited current statements of doctrine in his letters,[31] and so again, while there may be more emphasis on this kind of thing in the so-called 'early catholic' writings, it is not sufficient to justify the making of a sharp distinction between them and the rest of the New Testament.

(*b*) In order to oppose more effectively the growing Gnostic menace, 'early catholic' writers would often cast simple statements about the situation of their own day into the form of prophetic speech (as, for instance, in 2 Pet. 2.1ff., 'False teachers also arose among the people, just as there will be false teachers among you . . .'). The reasoning behind this subterfuge was, according to Käsemann, twofold: (*a*) in order to 'characterize the existing state of affairs as not accidental but, seen within the framework of salvation history, as necessary'; (*b*) 'in order to contrast it with that which obtained in the apostolic age' (*ENTT*, pp. 169ff.). Here again, this contention doubtless has its element of truth, for such 'prophetic insights' were certainly more popular in the later New Testament writings than in the earlier. But it is going too far to claim that it is therefore a *distinctive mark* of 'early catholicism'. If doctrinal differences did exist in the apostolic age, whether connected with Gnosis or with anything else, there would be no difficulty in believing that someone as intelligent as Paul appears to have been could have made 'prophecies' of this kind. There is no adequate evidence for taking this to be a clear sign of the presence of 'early catholicism' over against 'apostolic' Christianity.

(*c*) This third aspect of the development of catholic tradition is really the basis of the one just mentioned, i.e. that the belief soon developed that heresy of any kind was unknown in the apostolic age, and the emergence of such was a sign of inevitable decay. But the earliest possible instance of anything like this belief is in *1 Clement* 44.1–3, a passage which probably reflects a much earlier New Testament passage with no connection at all with 'early catholicism'.[32]

(*d*) There also grew up an emphasis on the finality of the church's own tradition. What was believed and accepted by the early apostles had been handed down 'once and for all' by these apostles, who were now caricatured as the only true repository of the genuine and authentic Christian tradition. This is but a refinement of 3 (*a*) above, and the comments made there are sufficient to put this argument also in its proper perspective.

It is apparent, therefore, that the whole issue of so-called 'early catholic' writings in the New Testament has been grossly overrated, and that it can be resolved more in terms of tension than of contradiction. These writings are undoubtedly different in emphasis from the earliest New Testament literature, but not so very different as to be hounded out of the canon, as Käsemann would like them to be.[33] Nevertheless, though we cannot go anything like as far as Käsemann does in the development of these distinctions, the plain fact is that it is only by an application of some such test as this to the New Testament that we can hope to make any kind of progress in seeking to discern the spread of various theological influences in the early church. However precarious such a course may be, it is a risk that must be taken if we are to reach any conclusions at all. To take the risk in the same way as Käsemann has done would presumably lead to the same conclusions, and our approach is to be distinguished from his in so far as we have attempted, however inadequately, to base our historical judgements on an exegetical approach to the literature. To some extent, Käsemann approaches the New Testament with the theory already firmly established, on the basis of which the documents can be forced into the mould of either 'apostolic' or 'early catholic' contexts. Such an approach must inevitably lead to a subjective criticism, and this kind of broad generalization can never be an adequate substitute for detailed exegesis.

Between the epistle to the Galatians, with its emphasis on the complete freedom of the Christian believer from any kind of law-principle, and the epistles to the Corinthian church, Paul has made a significant shift in the direction of what, for want of a better term, we can only describe as 'early catholicism'. So we find emphasis in 1 Corinthians on the handing-on of traditions in the church context (15.3ff.), specific instructions on how to behave in given legal and moral situations (6–8), and elementary forms of what can only be called 'ecclesiastical law' (e.g. in 1 Cor. 11–14), all of which are not only absent from Paul's Galatian teaching, but which would have been a logical impossibility at that stage in Paul's ministry. It is these developments, and their sequel in Paul's Roman epistle, to which we must finally direct our attention.

IV

How did Paul's Theology Develop?

To give a complete exposition of Romans to show how it fits into Paul's theology in the Galatian and Corinthian correspondence is beyond the scope of this study. Here I have been trying to set the stage for a thoroughgoing examination of Pauline theology, and a comprehensive exegesis of the Roman epistle must form the subject of a future volume. Nevertheless, it is possible here to indicate the general trends of Paul's thought. Attention has already been drawn to several passages of Romans where Paul's teaching in that context can be seen as a combination of teaching given earlier in Galatians, 1 Corinthians and 2 Corinthians. I have already suggested the following possible combinations:[34]

Gal. 2.19ff./5.24 + 1 Cor.	= Rom. 6.12ff. (cf. 2 Cor. 5.14)
Gal. 3.19, etc. + 1 Cor.	= Rom. 7.12 (cf. 2 Cor. 3.6)
Gal. 3.21 + 1 Cor. 11.25	= Rom. 7.5–12, 8.3ff. (cf. 2 Cor. 3.6)
Gal. 5.14 + 1 Cor. 7.14	= Rom. 13.9ff.
Gal. 5.18 + 1 Cor.	= Rom. 6.15—7.6 (cf. 2 Cor. 3.17ff.)

But the evidence is by no means restricted to just a few comparatively isolated texts, for the whole tenor of Paul's theology in Romans can be seen to depend on a combination of his earlier teaching in very diverse contexts.

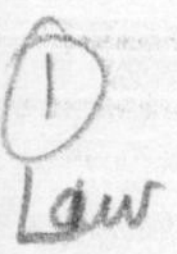

Especially is this the case with Paul's teaching on the Law of the Old Testament in Romans. Here we find a restatement and an elaboration of the quite diverse viewpoints of Galatians and 1 Corinthians respectively, with the difference that the two are now allowed to coexist as a natural tension in Paul's thought. Many statements in Romans could just as easily have appeared in the Galatian epistle without appearing to be alien to that context. Paul still insists that legalism is not the way to find favour with God: 'No human being will be justified in his sight by works of the law' (3.20). Even those who are Christians need pay no special attention to the teaching of the Old Testament, for they are 'not under law but under grace' (6.14b), 'discharged from the law, dead to that which held us captive, so that we serve not under the old written code but in the new life of the Spirit' (7.6). Not that the Law did not have its value, for its introduction had shown sin to be what it really was, violation of God's holy will (5.13ff.), a theme familiar from Galatians also (cf. 3.19a). But when we reach Romans 10.4, and read that 'Christ is the *telos* of the law', it becomes evident that Paul was here going beyond his Galatians teaching, and may well have been moving in the opposite direction altogether. What is meant by describing Christ as the Law's *telos*? Opinion is generally divided on this, some claiming that *telos* here means 'goal', in which case the Law would not be abolished at all by Christ's coming,[35] though others take it to mean 'end', which would certainly fit in with Paul's statements in Galatians and elsewhere in Romans. But in view of some of the other things Paul says here about the Law it is possible, even likely, that he was deliberately using the ambiguity of the word to cover up a subtle change in the direction of his thought on the matter. Every new beginning is in some sense an end, as something disappears and something is preserved. Paul seems to be implying that, though the function of the Law has been radically altered by the coming of Christ, it has not been altogether abolished. How else can we account for the fact that the Law, so much despised in the Galatian epistle, can now be described as 'God's law' (8.7, cf. 7.22), and as such its character is spiritual (7.14), holy, just, and good (7.12)? In 3.21 Paul regards this divine Law as having a part in the production of the salvation that has come in Christ, for though 'the righteousness of God has been manifested apart from law', in fact 'the law and prophets bear witness to . . . the righteousness of God through faith in Jesus Christ for all who believe'. Paul is here holding together the teaching of Galatians, that Christ had abolished the Law once and for all, and his teaching in 1 Corinthians that the principle of law as such was necessary for the Christian, so that while he may not be 'under the law', he was 'under law to Christ' (1 Cor. 9.21).[36]

This has important consequences for the Pauline ethic as it appears in Romans. When an imaginary opponent demands, 'Do we then overthrow the law by this faith?', Paul can retort: 'By no means! On the contrary, we uphold the law' (3.31). The very reason why Christ came was 'that the just requirement of the law might be fulfilled in us, who walk not according to the flesh but according to the Spirit' (8.4).

In the ethical teaching of Romans, we find a slight though important shift of emphasis from the position held in Galatians.

In Galatians, the primary aim of the Christian was said to be Christ-likeness, expressed most clearly in Paul's own claim that 'it is no longer I who live, but Christ who lives in me; and the life I now live in the flesh I live by faith in the son of God, who loved me and gave himself for me' (Gal. 2.20). In 1 Corinthians, on the other hand, one of the most important aims of the Christian was to be like his fellow-Christians, something that was achieved by observing the rules and regulations laid down by the apostle for 'all the churches'—a principle which we have seen to be closely allied to the very legalism that Paul opposed so bitterly in Galatians. In Galatians, the primary motive for Christian morality was gratitude for the love of God in Christ. In 1 Corinthians, the keeping of recognized rules was a major concern. Now in Romans, the two are combined to produce something which owes much to each of these earlier positions, but which has a distinctive character all its own.

In 12.1 Paul lays down the foundation of Christian ethics, which is found only in a complete surrender of self-will to the direction of the Holy Spirit. Just as in Galatians Christian morality found its source and basis in a new and different approach to life, 'life in the spirit' as opposed to 'life in the flesh' (Gal. 5.13–24), so here also the Christian's life is to be 'transformed by the renewal of your mind' so that he operates on a completely different level of existence from the non-Christian. But whereas in Galatians such statements had not led to the promulgation of any real ethical code, in the rest of his ethical teaching here Paul goes on to describe in some detail the ways in which the Christian ought to behave, for 'love is the fulfilling of the law' (13.10). The distinction must not be overemphasized, of course, and it is by no means to be drawn in monochrome tones, though it is clear that in principle Paul's Galatians teaching is distinct from anything found in other parts of his correspondence.

As he expounds the principle of love fulfilling the Law, Paul enunciates an ethical system which is not free from moral rules and directives, but which manages to combine these with the freedom of the Christian to act in accordance with the directives of the Holy Spirit in his own life. This synthesis is achieved by once more drawing attention to Christ Himself, this time laying emphasis on His own moral teachings. At many points in Romans 12—14 Paul's teaching is virtually identical with that of our Lord:

(*a*) The principle of returning good for evil (Rom. 12.14, 17=Matt. 5.39, 44).

(*b*) The payment of taxes (Rom. 13.7=Mark 12.17).

(*c*) Love of one's neighbour as the fulfilling of the Law (Rom. 13.9=Mark 12.29ff.; cf. also Gal. 5.24).

(*d*) Censorious judging of others (Rom. 14.4, 10, 17=Matt. 7.1).

(*e*) Clean and unclean foods (Rom. 14.14=Mark 7.15).

The fact that Paul makes so much use of the teaching of Jesus as recorded in the gospel traditions[37] must also be important for the question of Paul's authority as an apostle. Here he appeals neither to his own subjective experience, for that could have been susceptible to Gnosticizing interpretations, nor to his relationship with the Jerusalem apostles, which could have led to some sort of Judaizing view. Instead he emphasizes his own direct contact with the Jesus of history, who was also the Jesus of the church's experience, and whose words can be taken as a foundation for the Christian ethic.

No doubt much more could be said in the effort to explain Romans as a synthesis of the thesis and antithesis of Galatians and 1 Corinthians respectively. But the facts to which attention has been drawn are sufficient to indicate that in some of his most important teaching in Romans, Paul was heavily dependent on his previous experiences in other churches.

Finally, we must answer the question posed in our title: Was Paul a libertine or a legalist? What has been said already in this study will provide the answer. He was at heart neither. He was simply 'a man in Christ' (2 Cor. 12.2), whose main aim in life was to serve the One who had so radically affected his life on the Damascus road. From that day on, Paul was convinced that the end-product of Christian faith was the production of a life that was Christlike. In his encounter with the Galatian Judaizers, as with the Gnosticizers of Corinth, that was his main ambition. They were all 'my little children, with whom I am . . . in travail until Christ be formed in you' (Gal. 4.19). In his enthusiasm for his vocation Paul made many blunders, as we would expect from even the best of men. He wrote many things that could be construed as either antinomian or legalistic, things which, on later reflection, he may have expressed quite differently, or not have expressed at all. But through all his problems, he had the same goal before him to the end of his life, 'that I may gain Christ, and be found in him, not having a righteousness of my own, based on law, but that which is through faith in Christ, the righteousness of God . . .' (Phil. 3.9). If the gaining of divine righteousness meant that he needed to be at times either a libertine to win back the Judaizers, or a legalist to restore would-be Gnostics, that was a risk he was prepared to take: 'I do it all for the sake of the gospel, that I may share in its blessings' (1 Cor. 9.23).

APPENDIX A

The Argument of Galatians

1.1–9 INTRODUCTION

(*a*) Usual salutation (vv. 1–5)

(*b*) Paul expresses his surprise at the Galatians' acceptance of 'another gospel' (vv. 6–9)

1.10—2.21 THE FIRST FALSE DOCTRINE

Paul deals with the attack on his authority as a properly accredited apostle.

3.1–5 A PERSONAL APPEAL

Paul appeals to the Galatians' own experience to tell them that they received the Holy Spirit because of their faith in Jesus, and not because of their obedience to the Torah.

3.6—4.7 THE SECOND FALSE DOCTRINE

Paul tackles the suggestion that, since the promise of the messianic kingdom was given to Abraham and his descendants, those wishing to be in that kingdom must become members of his family by circumcision and continued obedience to the Torah. He answers this by appeal to three arguments from Scripture:

(*a*) *3.6–14* The blessings promised to Abraham belong to 'men of faith' (v. 9), because Abraham had faith. At the same time, 'all who rely on works of the law are under a curse' (v. 10).

(*b*) *3.15–24* Since the Torah came long after Abraham's time, it cannot possibly affect a direct promise made to him by God. The 'inheritance' cannot be by both Law and promise (v. 18). But nevertheless, the Law does have a function: (*i*) to reveal sin as a transgression against God (v.19, cf. Rom. 4.15; 5.13); (*ii*) to be man's custodian 'until Christ came, that we might be justified by faith' (v. 24), i.e. by trying to gain salvation by their own efforts at keeping the Law, men realized that it was an impossible task, and so the way was prepared for God's act of grace in Jesus Christ.

(*c*) *3.25—4.7* Since the Law was only effective 'till the offspring should come to whom the promise had been made' (v. 19), and since 'the offspring' had come in Jesus Christ, the era of the Law was now finished, and to those who had faith in Him, Christ would impart freedom from the Law. Whereas before they had been slaves to the *stoicheia tou kosmou*, they were now sons and heirs of the promise made to Abraham.

4.8–20 ANOTHER APPEAL

A further personal appeal by Paul to the Galatians, urging them not to go back to the legalism from which they have been freed.

4.21—6.10 THE THIRD FALSE DOCTRINE

Paul now deals with the argument that Christians ought to keep the Torah and to be circumcised. He deals with this as follows:

(*a*) *The Question of the Law* (*4.21—5.1*) Another appeal to the Abraham saga, this time using the story of the free woman Sarah driving out the slave woman Hagar, as an allegory of the superior position of the good news in Christ over against the legalism of the Jewish Torah.

(*b*) *The Question of Circumcision* (*5.2–12*) Paul declares that circumcision is of no value either way to the Christian (v. 6), and in some cases could even lead to a negation of the work of Christ (v. 2). In any case it involved an observance of the complete Torah (v. 3), the very thing that Paul has just rejected. The freedom which Christ imparts is clearly incompatible with the 'yoke of slavery' (v. 1) brought by circumcision and the Torah.

(*c*) *The Question of Christian Social Ethics* (*5.13—6.10*) Paul again deals with this in various ways:

(i) *5.13–15* Freedom in Christ does not mean an antinomian freedom, but the opportunity to serve one another in love.

(ii) *5.16–26* Though the Christian gospel lays down no specific imperatives, 'those who belong to Christ Jesus have crucified the flesh with its passions and desires' (v. 24), and so their moral imperatives are formulated by the fruit of the Spirit, which manifests itself in their lives.

(iii) *6.1–6* Christians should beware of judging others, because of their own recognized weakness. The Christian's part is to 'fulfil the law of Christ' in everything (v. 2).

(iv) *6.7–10* In order to reap the harvest of eternal life, one must sow not to the flesh but to the Spirit.

6.11–18 A LAST TRIUMPHANT APPEAL

Paul clinches the argument in his own writing. First he scores two points against his opponents:

(*a*) *Verse 12* The *spiritual bankruptcy* of those who were corrupting the Galatians: they 'want to make a good showing in the flesh', the very thing that Paul has denounced in the previous section (cf. 'He who sows to his own flesh will from the flesh reap corruption', v. 8).

(*b*) *Verse 13* The *inconsistency* of his opponents: though they emphasize the outward fleshly sign, they are not willing to accept even such spiritual discipline as would be involved in keeping the Torah.

Then, as a foil to these, Paul makes two positive statements of his own belief and practice:

(*a*) *Vv. 14–16* The only legitimate cause of glorying before God is that the Christian has been crucified to the world, through the cross of Christ. This kind of 'new creation' is the only thing of any value in the sight of God, and the sole qualifying mark of 'the Israel of God'.

(*b*) *V. 17* Paul himself may be criticized because he is a renegade Jew, but he has the mark of true spirituality before God: 'I bear on my body the marks of Jesus.'

APPENDIX B

The Date of Galatians

Our intention in this brief consideration of the date of the epistle to the Galatians is not primarily to argue from first principles in establishing the evidence. That has already been done so well by such a large number of scholars of all shades of opinion that to repeat the basic facts of the problem would serve no useful purpose here.[1] But at an early stage in the course of this investigation into the theology of the four major Pauline epistles, it soon became evident that our analytical approach to this subject would inevitably have certain consequences for the relative dating of the epistles. It therefore seems appropriate to include this excursus to indicate the direction in which our conclusions point in respect of the Galatian epistle. Two alternative dates are generally assigned to this epistle. On the one hand some, following W. M. Ramsay, date it as early as *c.* A.D. 49, addressed to the South Galatian congregations founded by Paul on his first missionary journey. Others, however, disputing the possibility that these people could be called 'Galatians' in a very meaningful way, date the epistle later, during the third missionary journey, and so within the same period as the Corinthian and Roman epistles. In so far as our conclusions on the theological structure of those epistles has any direct bearing on the matter, it clearly supports the early date for Galatians.

It was J. B. Lightfoot who first introduced the possibility of ascertaining the relative dates of these epistles by considerations of style and doctrinal content and whenever these criteria have been employed since his time, Lightfoot's conclusions have more or less been taken for granted. He argued that the letters to Corinth and Rome were written in the following order: 1 Corinthians in the spring of A.D. 57 from Ephesus; 2 Corinthians in autumn A.D. 57 from Macedonia; Romans early in A.D. 58 from Corinth, with Galatians fitting in after 2 Corinthians and before Romans, written from Macedonia or Achaia in the winter or spring of A.D. 57/58.[2] Several parallels were drawn out by Lightfoot between Galatians and 2 Corinthians. Most of them were simply questions of expression,[3] which could hardly prove that the two epistles were necessarily written at the same time. The most they could show was that the same man was responsible for both. But in any case, once the integrity of 2 Corinthians was challenged, Lightfoot's observations tended to be forgotten. C. H. Buck attempted to revive them some twenty years ago by pointing out that, even on the basis of only 2 Corinthians 1–9, Lightfoot's argument would still stand.[4] Buck argued that there was 'ample evidence' to show that Galatians was both prior to Romans and subsequent to 2 Corinthians 1–9. This evidence consisted mainly of the Pauline antithesis of spirit/flesh and faith/works, as used in 1 Corinthians, 2 Corinthians 1–9, Galatians and Romans.[5] The frequency of the terms shows that faith/works occurs in its classical Pauline form only in Galatians and Romans, and not in 1 Corinthians and 2 Corinthians. According to Buck, this means that unless Galatians was written after 2 Corinthians 1–9, we should have to imagine that Paul first formulated the antithesis in Galatians, then changed his mind and rejected it in writing 1 Corinthians and 2 Corinthians, and then changed his mind again in writing Romans. Such an argument, however, carries little weight, and is simply groundless supposition. If our analysis of the historical situation is correct, the reason Paul does not use it in 1 Corinthians and 2 Corinthians is because in 1 Corinthians he was attempting to introduce some form of elementary moral code of 'works' in the face of a Gnosticizing interpretation of Galatians, while in 2 Corinthians he was still aware of the need to express himself cautiously in order to avoid misrepresentation. In Romans, on the other hand, he was making a studied statement of his basic Christian beliefs, and so he had to try to combine both elements, which he did with a large measure of success.[6]

We are still left, however, with the question of the resemblances of Galatians and Romans, which according to Lightfoot are 'much more striking and definite': 'Almost every thought and argument in the Epistle to the Galatians may be matched from the other Epistle.'[7] But the kind of parallels cited by Lightfoot hardly prove the point. The mention of Abraham's place as the progenitor of those who have faith in God (Gal. 3, Rom. 4) proves nothing more than that this was a part of Paul's basic beliefs. Moreover, the parallels which Lightfoot emphasizes in connection with the place of the Law are significantly different, for though the same thought may well be present, in each case the Romans statement is a diluted version of Galatians, and more favourably disposed to the Law.[8] In some ways Lightfoot realized this, for he conceded that 'the Epistle to the Galatians stands in relation to the Roman letter, as the rough model to the finished statue . . .'[9] But the two or three months which Lightfoot's dating would leave for Paul's shift of emphasis is hardly adequate for this kind of change to have taken place. To allow sufficient time for Paul's thought to undergo such a change of emphasis would need a much longer period, which is what our study has shown.[10]

In brief, then, four reasons may be given for supposing that our consideration of the theological distinctions in the major Pauline letters points to an early rather than a late date for Galatians:

1. Though it is possible to understand the different emphases on the role of revelation and tradition as a total and consistent part of Pauline theology,[11] there are nevertheless distinct differences between the teaching of Galatians 1.11ff. and 1 Corinthians 15.1ff. on this subject. It is inconceivable that Paul moved from an emphasis on the tradition of the church duly handed on in 1 Corinthians to the opposite emphasis on an individualistic revelatory experience in Galatians. Nor, after his experience with the Gnosticizing tendencies met in Corinth, is it likely that Paul would subsequently have made such an unguarded statement as that in Galatians 1.11ff. But it is easy to think that the Galatians statement was earlier than the Corinthians passage, written at a time when Paul was unaware of the possibly Gnostic understanding of his words, and that in the meantime such an understanding had come into the Corinthian church, to which his statements in 1 Corinthians 15 were in part the reply.

2. Paul's teaching on the Law in Galatians is very negative by comparison with his teaching on the same subject in Romans, even in the places where he seems to be saying the same things. If we compare, for instance, Romans 5.20ff. with Galatians 3.19a, the positive function of the Law as seen in the Romans passage is absent from Galatians.[12] Now it is easy to understand how Paul could have had a very pessimistic view of the Law at a relatively

early stage in his ministry, before he had experienced some of the immorality into which 'free' Christians could fall. But it is almost impossible to think either that he initially held a positive attitude to it, which later changed, or that (as would be required if Galatians is dated close to 1 and 2 Corinthians and Romans) he could have held the two together at one and the same time.

3. The Christian moral code as outlined in Galatians 5.13—6.10 is broad in scope, and is expressed in terms of principles rather than rules, a contrast with 1 Corinthians and Romans. In Galatians there is an emphasis on more or less complete freedom within the moral limitations set by the indwelling person of Christ Himself. Quotations from Jesus' teaching, which in both 1 Corinthians and Romans are used in the form of moral rules to draw out the implications of the basic principles of Christian morality, are absent from Galatians.[13] Nor does Galatians have any mention of the principle of limiting one's liberty in order to avoid offence to fellow-Christians.[14] In Galatians Paul adopts the idealistic view that, if all believers are under the control of the Holy Spirit, they will naturally do what is right both individually and socially. In 1 Corinthians and Romans, and to a lesser extent 2 Corinthians, he adopts a more realistic position, and introduces elementary moral rules to form guidelines for behaviour in specific situations, a process which again is more easily explicable in terms of an early date for Galatians than the other way round.

4. If we accept Lightfoot's (and Buck's) view that Galatians was written after 1 Corinthians and 2 Corinthians, certain elements of the Galatian epistle would be hard to understand, particularly Paul's stated surprise at the unexpected way in which the Galatians had deserted his message (Galatians 1.6).

We must therefore conclude that such evidence as our investigation provides would tend to support an early date for Galatians, over against the late date which places it in close proximity to 1 and 2 Corinthians and Romans.

APPENDIX C

The Apostles

In the course of the exegesis of Galatians, it was found necessary to refer from time to time to the concept of 'apostleship' and, though it is beyond the scope of this study to examine the complex problems that surround the concept in the early church, we append here a few notes on the trends of recent debate.

W. Schmithals has himself produced a history of the apostolate which is both masterly in expression and comprehensive in scope, in which he presents a vast amount of evidence from many sources (*The Office of Apostle in the Early Church* (London, 1971), Eng. trans. and revised edition of *Das kirchliche Apostelamt* (Göttingen, 1961), FRLANT NF 61). A useful summary treatment is provided by W. Schneemelcher in *NTA* II, pp. 25–31, in which Schmithals's work is rejected as too extreme ('fantastic hypotheses', p. 25), though Schneemelcher has no new positive approach to suggest. He contends that 'the institution and conception of the apostles do not have their roots in the *historia Jesu*' (p. 28), and so Paul must have been the one who really gave the office its theological importance. A recent example of a more positive approach to the problem is R. Schnackenburg's 'Apostles Before and During Paul's Time', in *Apostolic History and the Gospel* (F. F. Bruce *Festschrift*), eds. W. W. Gasque and R. P. Martin (Exeter, 1970), pp. 287–303. K. H. Rengstorf's article on *apostolos* in *TDNT* I, pp. 407–47, is still of value, though now dated. Cf. also A. Ehrhardt, *The Apostolic Succession* (London, 1953), pp. 11–34. The problem of the relationship between 'the apostles' and 'the Twelve' is ably dealt with by P. Vielhauer, 'Gottesreich und Menschensohn in der Verkündigung Jesu', in *Festschrift für Günther Dehn*, ed. W. Schneemelcher (Bonn, 1957), pp. 51–79, with the result that Vielhauer separates the Twelve from the apostles, and can trace neither group back to the ministry of Jesus Himself.

C. K. Barrett, *The Signs of an Apostle* (London, 1970), has a useful summary of most of the different viewpoints, combined with a fresh assessment of the matter. For a more recent survey of the continuing debate, cf. A. Lemaire, 'The Ministries in the New Testament', in *Biblical Theology Bulletin* III (1973), pp. 140–43.

APPENDIX D

The 'Parties' in Corinth

We have deliberately avoided the temptation to link up the various groups of heretics in the Corinthian church with the 'parties' of 1 Corinthians 1.12, since their character and composition are matters of some doubt. It seems likely that there was some kind of Jewish 'party' represented by the name of Cephas, in which case Paul will have been fighting a battle on two fronts. But the evidence drawn out in our own study suggests quite plainly that the Jewish problem was not at this stage the most important. T. W. Manson made a complete analysis of the Corinthian situation along these lines, though it is doubtful whether we can go along with him in seeing at the time of 1 Corinthians a 'concerted move to instil Palestinian piety and Palestinian orthodoxy into the Corinthian Church' (*Studies in the Gospels and Epistles* (Manchester, 1962), pp. 190–224; quotation from p. 205). Lake, some fifty years earlier, had asserted that 'there is no trace in these Epistles that the party of Cephas (or any other party) was Judaistic, or represented the principles of the stiff Jerusalem Church' (*Earlier Epistles*, p. 116). According to N. A. Dahl, the only real 'parties' were a pro-Pauline group, with its slogan, 'I belong to Paul', and the rest of the party slogans were more in the form of declarations of independence of Paul than statements of confidence in the people named. Thus, 'I belong to Christ' should also be taken not to signify a special 'Christ party', but simply hostility to Paul's authority (N. A. Dahl, 'Paul and the Church at Corinth in 1 Cor. 1:10–4:21', in *Christian History and Interpretation: Studies Presented to John Knox*, eds. W. R. Farmer, etc. (Cambridge, 1967), pp. 322ff.).

Presumably not all would be hostile to Paul on the same grounds, though our concern has been only with those who seem to have had Gnosticizing inclinations. See C. K. Barrett's article, 'Cephas and Corinth', in *Abraham unser Vater*, p. 9, where it is pointed out that there must have been a Jewish party of some kind connected with Cephas, though Barrett is himself more prepared to see a diversity of opposition behind 1 Corinthians than some others have been. For a more radical view, cf. Schmithals, *Gnosticism in Corinth*, pp. 36–80, 193ff., and *The Office of Apostle*, pp. 173ff. According to his view, the statement, 'I am of Christ', is a Gnostic formula whereby the speaker expressed his own identity with the Primal Man, of whom a prominent description was the use of the term 'Christ' or 'Messiah', originally used altogether independently of the Christian application of it to Jesus. W. Bauer took a different view again, and in addition to the four usual 'parties' traced a group called 'the strong', who were dominated by Gnostic ideas. At first they were kept in check by the combined efforts of Pauline and Jewish Christians, but by the end of the first century, *1 Clement* reflects a situation in which 'the strong' had taken over the Corinthian church, and their Gnostic Christianity had become the Corinthian 'orthodoxy' (*Orthodoxy and Heresy*, pp. 99ff.).

Notes

CHAPTER 1

1 In Eng. trans., Baur's book *Paul the Apostle of Jesus Christ* (London/Edinburgh, 1875, vol. II and 1876, vol. I, 2nd edn) may be consulted. For a valuable assessment of his work, cf. S. Neill, *The Interpretation of the New Testament* (Oxford, 1964), pp. 19–28.

2 W. D. Davies, *Paul and Rabbinic Judaism* (London, 1948), *Christian Origins and Judaism* (London, 1962). R. N. Longenecker, *Paul, Apostle of Liberty* (New York, 1964). Cf. also, *inter alia*, D. Daube, *The New Testament and Rabbinic Judaism* (London, 1956).

3 *Paul*, Eng. trans. (London, 1961).

4 J. C. O'Neill, *The Recovery of Paul's Letter to the Galatians* (London, 1972), p. 9.

5 For a different view of Paul's debt to the Hellenistic world, cf. W. L. Knox, *St. Paul and the Church of Jerusalem* (Cambridge, 1925), pp. 136–49, *St. Paul and the Church of the Gentiles* (Cambridge, 1939), and *Some Hellenistic Elements in Primitive Christianity* (London, 1944).

6 So C. H. Dodd, 'The Mind of Paul: I and II', in *New Testament Studies* (Manchester, 1953).

7 So E. Käsemann, *Essays on New Testament Themes* (London, 1963: *Studies in Biblical Theology*, 41), *New Testament Questions of Today* (London, 1969).

CHAPTER 2

1 A. E. Harvey, 'The Opposition to Paul', in *Studia Evangelica IV*, ed. F. L. Cross (Berlin, 1968) (= *TU* 102), pp. 319–32.

2 Especially Josephus, *BJ* II.454. Bauer, in loc., gives a more extended list of other occurrences.

3 R. M. Hawkins, 'The Galatian Gospel', in *JBL* 59 (1940), p. 143.

4 G. Friedrich, *TDNT* II, p. 733.

5 J. B. Lightfoot, *St. Paul's Epistle to the Galatians* (London, 1865), p. 77.

6 Cf. J. Jeremias, *anthrōpos*, in *TDNT* I, p. 364. E. D. Burton, *A Critical and Exegetical Commentary on the Epistle to the Galatians*

(Edinburgh, 1921) (ICC), pp. 37ff., favours the implication of 'the general idea "human" without more exact discrimination'. But in view of what follows here, it seems likely that Paul also has in mind the argument that his gospel had developed as a human elaboration of the Jewish religion, and the denial of this is therefore included in the assertion that his gospel was not *kata anthrōpon*.

7 Both *tēs akrobustias* and *tēs peritomēs* in v. 7 are 'genitives of connection', being the equivalent of *tois en akrobustia* and *tois peritetmēmenois* respectively (cf. Burton, *Galatians*, pp. 92ff.).

8 See Appendix C for a brief survey of the contemporary debate about the concept of apostleship.

9 For what follows, cf. A. Ehrhardt, *The Apostolic Succession*; H. von Campenhausen, *Ecclesiastical Authority and Spiritual Power in the Church of the First Three Centuries*, Eng. trans. (London, 1969).

10 *Ptolemy to Flora*, in Epiphanius, *Pan.* xxxiii. A convenient Eng. trans. is in R. M. Grant, *Gnosticism: an Anthology* (London, 1961), pp. 184–90.

11 Cf. W. Bauer, 'The Picture of the Apostle in Early Christian Tradition', in *NTA* II, pp. 40ff.

12 Cf. *Gospel of Thomas* 114, where he appears as a Gnostic misogynist.

13 *Strom.* VII.106.4. According to VII.108.1, another source was Matthias, who, according to Hippolytus, *Ref.* VII.20 also gave secret teaching which he received in a special instruction from Jesus.

14 Clement of Alexandria (*Strom.* VII.106.4) says that the Valentinians claimed a close affinity with Paul through one Theodas, who was supposed to have been the apostle's disciple.

15 This seems to be a more plausible definition of the Gnostic concept of apostleship than that put forward by Schmithals in his *Office of Apostle*, where he argues (pp. 114–89) that the apostolate was based on the Gnostic redeemer concept, within which he distinguishes a heavenly and an earthly apostle concept. Though he provides much documentation for each, Schmithals's argument fails to convince because he gives no real grounds for supposing that such redeemer figures were actually called 'apostles'. Indeed, he admits himself that this title is not very common (pp. 191ff.) in the literature he has cited, and that in Gnostic literature generally the term is reserved exclusively for the Twelve of the New Testament traditions. This, coupled with the complete absence of any Gnostic evidence from the New Testament period, makes it difficult to believe that the church's apostolate was based on some pre-existent Gnostic concept.

16 *The Office of Apostle*, p. 255: '. . . there is no reason for placing Luke earlier than about 120–130. In no case may one move it up into the first century . . .' (!)

17 Cf. his 'Basic Shifts in German Theology', in *Interpretation* 16 (1962), pp. 76–97. On Schmithals: 'He presupposes in an uncritical way the Bultmannian solution of the gnostic problem centered in the pre-Christian origin of the Gnostic redeemer myth. But the time is past even in Germany when this can be presupposed without further ado simply by allusion to Reitzenstein' (p. 80).
On the whole question of pre-Christian Gnosticism, cf. E. M. Yamauchi, *Pre-Christian Gnosticism* (London, 1973).

18 M. Dibelius (and W. G. Kümmel), *Paul*, Eng. trans. (London, 1953), p. 60.

19 R. N. Longenecker, *Paul, Apostle of Liberty*, p. 39.

20 Paul quotes Jeremiah 1.5 in v. 15 here. Cf. also 1 Corinthians 9.16 and Jeremiah 20.9.

21 Cf. A. K. Helmbold, *The Nag Hammadi Gnostic Texts and the Bible* (Grand Rapids, 1967: *Baker Studies in Biblical Archaeology*, no. 5), pp. 80ff.

22 Cf. especially J. Jeremias, *The Eucharistic Words of Jesus*, Eng. trans. (Oxford, 1955), pp. 128ff.

23 *The Apostolic Preaching* (London, 1936), 1st edn, pp. 19ff.

24 Cf. R. Bultmann, *Theology of the New Testament*, Eng. trans. (London, 1952), vol. I, § 33, 'Christ's Death and Resurrection as Salvation-occurrence'; and in H. W. Bartsch (ed.), *Kerygma and Myth*, Eng. trans. (New York, 1955), pp. 112ff.

25 In *JBL* 76 (1957), pp. 181–91.

26 'Revelation and Tradition in Paul', in *Apostolic History and the Gospel*, p. 224.

27 D. Guthrie, *Galatians* (London, 1969) (*NCB*), p. 66.

28 H. N. Ridderbos, *The Epistle of Paul to the Churches of Galatia* (Grand Rapids, 1953) (*NIC*), has rightly seen the importance of this: 'The *nor was I taught it* is a specific reference to academic instruction. In this connection, the immediately preceding *received* is presumably to be taken as referring to the general, as distinguished from the school, tradition' (p. 58, n. 3). Cf. also Burton, *Galatians*, p. 40.

29 Cf. G. E. Ladd's comment on the nature of the Christian tradition: 'The Christian tradition is not mere instruction passed on like Jewish oral tradition from one teacher to another . . . [but it] has a two-fold character: it is *both* historical tradition and kerygmatic-pneumatic tradition at one and the same time. It is historical because it is tied to events in history and the tradition preserves the report of these events. It is kerygmatic because it can be perpetuated only as *kerygma* and received as a confession of faith. It is pneumatic because it can be received and preserved only by the enabling of the Spirit' (art. cit., above).

30 E.g. the Syrophoenician woman, Matthew 15.21–8 (cf. Mk. 7.24–30). Though there are many problems connected with the setting of the various synoptic utterances on this subject, which we can hardly begin to consider here, the fact that alongside this saying referred to above, Jesus is recorded in Matthew as having commended the woman for her faith, at least shows that this kind of tension did exist within the same corpus of traditions. Indeed, it is striking that here Matthew has a more explicit commendation of the woman (*megalē sou hē pistis*, v. 28) than does Mark.

31 Cf. also J. Munck, 'Israel and the Gentiles in the New Testament', in *JTS* ns. 2 (1951), pp. 3–16.

32 But there is no trace in Paul of that particularism which characterized the post-apostolic age, and which insisted that, while all men were given equal opportunity, the Gentiles were now to be more equal than the Jews, whose day was finished. He was not suggesting that the days of Israel were finished, but that all men, whether Jews or Gentiles, could become a part of the true 'Israel' of God, by incorporation through Christ into the family of those who were obedient to God.

33 On the significance of the phrase *kai elogisthē autō eis dikaiosunē* in the second half of v. 6, we can make only brief comment here. It is clear that the background of Paul's thought is the Old Testament picture of God as a judge requiring obedience, and on this basis issuing rewards or punishments; cf. L. Morris, *The Apostolic Preaching of the Cross* (London, 1965), 3rd edn, pp. 253ff. The use of the verb *logizomai* for a commercial transaction (the LXX equivalent of Hebrew *ḥashabh*) led the rabbis to interpret Genesis 15.6 as the basis for a doctrine of merits, whereby Abraham gained divine favour. But Paul sees the *dikaiosunē* which Abraham gained not so much as a righteousness of character: rather was his faith *dikaiosunē* in the sense that it gave him a ground of acceptance whereby he could stand before God. Cf. Burton, *Galatians*, pp.154, 469ff. This is far removed from any doctrine of merits, and perhaps explains Paul's more radical rejection of the possibility of keeping the Law than was found in Judaism. Though he did preserve what he took to be the basis of Old Testament faith, Paul contended that with Christ there had been a dramatic change of emphasis: 'He still maintains that only the righteous can enjoy true fellowship with God. But the Gospel now adds that it is not man's own work which establishes this fellowship with God. It is God's own sovereign and gracious and decisive intervention for man in Christ' (G. Schrenk, *dikaiosunē*, in *TDNT* II, p. 203).

34 On this understanding of Paul's argument, and for what follows, see H. J. Schoeps, *Paul*, Eng. trans. (London, 1961), pp. 177ff. Though Schoeps is arguing as a Jew, and reaches conclusions which would never have been acceptable to Paul (perhaps because of

this?), his approach to Paul's argument in Galatians is in general most illuminating.

35 This is the clear implication of *hosoi gar ex ergōn nomou eisin hupo kataran eisin* and the following quotation (with a few insignificant variations) from Deuteronomy 27.26 LXX. According to the premise on which those who keep the Law must argue, they stand condemned by the very Law in which they profess to find their salvation. In contrast with this, God's own attitude is quite different (vv. 11ff.). Though man (whether Jew or Gentile) likes to rely on Law, since it ministers to his pride, God's way is altogether different. In its original setting, of course, Deuteronomy 27.26 was more of an incentive to observance of the Law than an invective against those who were unable to keep it all. But Paul is right in drawing out the implication he does here: 'The very thing that had been for Israel, so long as it lived out of grace, an impetus to living a life of grateful obedience to God, meant for those who looked to human merit for the fulfilment of expectation, the end of all hope – this according to the absolute norm, by which God judges' (Ridderbos, *Galatians*, p. 124).

36 In more optimistic moments even as a Christian, Paul could say as much: cf. Philippians 3.4ff.

37 Op. cit., p. 40. Longenecker goes on to argue that 'we need not insist that this understanding was entirely different from that of Pharisaism' (pp. 41ff.). But in all these discussions we need to remember that there are no accounts of Pharisaic belief and practice at this period independent of the New Testament itself.

38 In introducing the principle of Leviticus 18.5, Paul can hardly be taken to be contradicting what he has said with regard to the possibility of keeping the Law in vv. 10–11. The point is that he is quoting the kind of basis on which the legalist would have to operate, with the object of making a *reductio ad absurdum* of the entire legalistic structure. Longenecker's distinction between this kind of legalism and what he has called 'nomism' is helpful here though, as Paul goes on, it becomes clear that even 'nomism' (i.e. the pious and faithful honouring of the Law in the true covenant setting) must be at an end with the coming of Christ.

39 The mention in v. 14 of *hē epangelia tou pneumatos* as corresponding to *hē eulogia tou Abraam*, shows that all the time Paul is using the Old Testament passages retrospectively, with most of his attention focused on their fulfilment in Christ. Cf. H. Schlier, *Der Brief an die Galater* (Göttingen, 1965), *KEK*, 13. Aufl., pp. 140ff. Since the Spirit was the earnest of the blessing which is given to those who are acceptable to God (2 Cor. 1.22, 5.5, etc.) it also becomes the basic gift of the new life in Christ (v. 2) and therefore the fulfilment of the promise (v. 14).

40 *Contra* Schoeps, op. cit., who follows G. Klein, *Studien über Paulus* (Stockholm, 1918), pp. 62–7.

41 *Contra* Ridderbos, *Galatians*, p. 127, who argues: 'That Christ . . . became a curse Paul infers from the Scripture of Deut. 21:23'.

42 *St. Paul and the Church of the Gentiles* (Cambridge, 1939), p. 108, referring to Philo, *De post. Cain* 8 and 17. Knox goes on to suggest that Jesus, 'being a denizen of the spiritual world, had accepted of His own free will the curse of a material nature, and so liberated from that curse, and the consequent subjection to the Torah, those who had been plunged into matter by the sin of their first parent.'

43 *TDNT* I, p. 450. He continues, 'Obviously, then, Paul is stating a view of substitution.' To consider this passage in the context of Paul's soteriology would take us too far from our main objective here, and we can only refer to the commentaries for full treatment of the question. Cf. especially Burton, *Galatians*, pp. 136ff. and Schlier, *Galaterbrief*, pp. 168ff. Also L. Morris, *Apostolic Preaching*, *passim* but especially pp. 62ff.

44 There are difficulties as to precisely how Paul arrived at this figure of 430 years between the promise and the Law. Cf. Schlier, *Galaterbrief*, pp. 147ff.

45 Lightfoot, *Galatians*, on 3.15. Followed by Burton, *Galatians*, pp. 179, 496ff. But there is a legal background in much that Paul is saying here, e.g. justification (v. 11), adoption (v. 13), etc. The phrase *kata anthrōpon legō* (v. 15) suggests the same thing (cf. Rom. 3.5). Though Guthrie (*Galatians*, p. 105) protests that the meaning 'will' here is 'too restricted because no mention is made of the death of the testator', it fits better with what Paul says in v. 17, where the emphasis (as in a human will) is on the one-sided nature of the divine covenant (*diathēkēn prokekurōmenēn hupo tou theou*).

46 D. E. H. Whiteley, *The Theology of St. Paul* (Oxford, 1964), pp. 85ff.

47 Paul's approach to the relationship of promise to Law was, of course, not the only one. But even here we can see how the traditional Jewish beliefs have been remodelled in the light of God's action in Christ. Cf. G. S. Duncan, *The Epistle of Paul to the Galatians* (London, 1934) (*MC*), p. 110: 'In whatever way . . . the Law might be related to the Promise, it was God's gracious Promise which provided the unalterable basis of the covenant-relationship between Him and His people; the inheritance thus offered to Abraham and his offspring would come as the result of God's free gift; . . . The inheritance ceases to be a free gift from God when men think that their obedience gives them a claim on it.'

48 Loc. cit. But cf. B. Reicke, 'The Law and This World According to Paul', in *JBL* 70 (1951), p. 260: 'One certainly ought not to go so far as not to believe that Paul means what he says, nor should one, under any condition, utilize reference to the particular circumstances of the letter as a means of evading the question whether the ideas referred to may have their objective basis in Paul's general theological

outlook' (an article originally in *Svensk Exegetisk Årsbok* 8 (1943), pp. 43–70).

49 Hebrews 2.2 has the same intention as Paul, of showing the secondary character of the Law.

50 A. T. Hanson, *Jesus Christ in the Old Testament* (London, 1965), pp. 96ff.

51 Though he unjustly regards this verse as a later gloss, J. C. O'Neill's judgement on its meaning is a sound one: 'The purpose . . . was to show that the Law had been given by angels and not by God' (*Recovery of Paul's Letter to the Galatians*, p. 52).

52 Guthrie, *Galatians*, p. 111. The reason that the Law could not give life was simply that it had no power to give a man the moral ability to do what it demanded (Rom. 8.3ff.). Later in the epistle, Paul goes on to show that it is only through the fulfilment of the promise in the person of Jesus Christ that men can be given the moral power to do what is right in God's sight (Gal. 5.13—6.10).

53 Duncan goes so far as to see every part of this verse, including the Law's function as a revealer of sin, as a part of Paul's depreciatory purpose here (*Galatians*, pp. 111ff.). But this is probably too extreme.

54 Burton, *Galatians*, p. 200. According to A. Oepke, *Der Brief des Paulus an die Galater* (Berlin, 1964), 2. Aufl., *THNT* 9, pp. 86ff., the very term *paidagōgos* itself may have carried some pejorative implication, since the *paidagōgos* in Greek life was often a slave who was no good for anything other than disciplining small children. Though Paul is here giving the Law some definite positive function, it is still the case that at least a part of his intention is 'to bring clearly to the fore the inferior function of the Law as compared with Christ. Law was essentially a disciplinarian' (Guthrie, *Galatians*, p. 114).

55 *Kyrios Christos* (Göttingen, 1967), 6. Aufl., FRLANT NF 4, pp. 148ff.

56 The matter is not quite as simple as this, for in neither Hebrew nor Greek did the plural or singular of such a term change its essential meaning (cf. Burton, *Galatians*, pp. 505–10). That Paul was not unaware of this factor is shown by the present verse. In a very real sense, Christ could be the singular fulfilment of the promise of descendants to Abraham, while yet preserving the corporate overtones of the promise, for Christ was a representative personality incorporating with His own person all those who believed in Him.

57 Lightfoot, *Galatians*, 6th edn (1880), p. 163.

58 The precise legal analogy which Paul is here intending to draw is uncertain. For useful surveys of the evidence, cf. Burton, *Galatians* pp. 211ff., and S. Belkin, 'The Problem of Paul's Background', in *JBL* 54 (1935), pp. 52ff. The best explanation may well be to assume that Paul is not thinking here of any specific legal code, but just of

a general custom. Whether the exact background here may ever be established, we cannot tell, but there is no doubt of the spiritual lesson that Paul wishes to draw from it.

59 This does not necessarily lead to the conclusion that the 'elements' here are the same as the angels who gave the Law in 3.19 (as Reicke and Schlier). But Reicke is correct in seeing that in this context (and in what follows, vv. 8–10), 'We . . . must accept the analogy between the Law and the "elements" of the universe and between Judaism and heathendom as a fact' ('The Law and This World', p. 260). Paul certainly recognizes a close affinity between the angels and the elements. He would probably have said that the angels of 3.19 were a *part* of *ta stoicheia tou kosmou,* but not that the *stoicheia* had given the Law. Cf. Duncan, *Galatians*, pp. 134ff. Paul's statements certainly left the door wide open for this kind of implication to be introduced, but it is doubtful whether Paul was here intending to make the association himself.

60 A. J. Bandstra makes the interesting suggestion that by the *stoicheia* Paul meant to indicate the Law and the flesh, both of them forces inherent in the world and operating among men before and apart from Christ, and each dependent on the other for its full operation: Law operates in the context of flesh, on the one hand to declare God's will, and on the other to stimulate latent sin into external activity (*The Law and the Elements of the World*, Kampen, 1964).

61 Cf. R. McL. Wilson, *The Gnostic Problem* (London, 1958), pp. 72ff.

62 For this and what follows here, see E. E. Ellis, *Paul's Use of the Old Testament* (London/Edinburgh, 1957), pp. 51ff., 130.

63 It is at just this point that Philo can be most closely compared with the later Gnostics, for both of them were embarrassed by the biblical emphasis on *Heilsgeschichte*. Neither of them could understand how God, Who is, in absolute existence, could even participate in the 'becomingness' of ordinary history. While Philo sought to remove the idea of God entering history by an allegorization of the redemptive events of the Old Testament so that they became illustrations of timeless eternal truths, the Gnostics did the same thing by declaring that the centre of divine revelation was to be found not in certain historical events, but rather in an immediate and personal *gnōsis* of God, which was to be gained through mystical and ritual procedures. Paul's approach was very different from both of these.

64 Duncan, *Galatians*, p. 144. The contrast in vv. 25ff. between *hē nun Ierousalēm* and *hē anō Ierousalēm* is a case in point. Though the idea of a new Jerusalem in contrast to the present one was found in pre-Christian Judaism, and indeed could be found in the Old Testament itself, one verse of which (Isa. 54.1 LXX: there may have been an original, though vague, allusion here to Sarah and Hagar, cf. 51.2) Paul quotes to support his case, Paul speaks not of a Jerusalem coming in the future, but of an already existing reality over

against the Jerusalem which he associates with Sinai, Hagar, and legalism. But this is not to be taken in any Platonic sense, as if *hē anō Ierousalēm* was the heavenly reality behind *hē nun Ierousalēm*. Rather is Paul meaning to draw a contrast between two realities which actually existed in tangible form, and the fact that he opposes them as representatives of two entirely different ideas of religion speaks against the supposition that he was thinking in terms of any Doctrine of Ideas here. In the light of what we said above (pp. 25ff.), Paul's use of Isaiah 54.1 here is instructive. It has parallels in Justin, *Apol.* I.53 and Cyprian, *Test.* I.20, both of which are similar, though different from Galatians. According to them, the verse shows that Gentile Christians would be 'more numerous and more true' (Justin) than Jewish or Samaritan Christians, whereas for Paul the contrast is seen between the true Israel, both Jews and Gentiles, and the unbelieving nation of Jews.

65 Guthrie, *Galatians*, pp. 130ff., makes two suggestions which deserve attention: (a) Paul's extreme representation of the Hagar/Sinai relationship in vv. 24–5 can perhaps be accounted for on the assumption that Jews would *never* have identified the Law of Sinai with Hagar's descendants (not even in the light of Paul's statements in the preceding verses here), and so Paul is forced to stress the identification to its ultimate logical limit, which is possibly more than he wanted to do. Thus the question could be resolved by explaining the difficult phrases as exaggerated language designed to meet the special situation in Galatia.

(b) Since Sinai is a wilderness, not only would it be a fitting picture for spiritual dearth, but it may also have reminded Paul of the desert to which Hagar fled from Sarah.

Though such considerations may not provide a conclusive answer to the problem, they at least suggest that the linguistic approach commonly adopted by commentators is perhaps not the most fruitful way of trying to understand Paul here.

66 'A Problem of Interpretation', in *Studiorum Novi Testamenti Societas Bulletin II* (1951), p. 11. Burton, *Galatians*, pp. 261ff. makes a similar point, though is less convinced that it is an acceptable solution to the difficulty. Cf. also Duncan, *Galatians*, pp. 145ff. On the suggestion that there is also a Gematria here (i.e. a numerical valuation of the letters) between *nun Ierousalēm* and *Agar Sina*, cf. Oepke, *Galaterbrief*, p. 113.

67 Yet another element is introduced in v. 29, with the statement *ho kata sarka gennētheis ediōken ton kata pneuma*. If this is to be interpreted on the basis of a Jewish Haggadah of Genesis 21.9 (cf. Strack-Billerbeck III, pp. 575ff.), we must conclude that the Galatian heretics were actually persecuting in a physical way the more 'orthodox' members of the congregations. But this seems to be against 6.12, where the 'heretics' themselves are under threat of persecution from a third party. Perhaps we should follow Ridderbos and take *diōkō* in a

mitigated sense, as 'not so much a threat to life as one to freedom and security. It was so that Ishmael had persecuted Isaac. He did not leave Isaac in peace, grudged him his priorities, his privileges' (*Galatians*, p. 181).

68 1 Corinthians 10.1ff. is the only possible parallel, but this seems to have been an early Christian commonplace, and not peculiar to Paul. Cf. Hebrews 2–4 and Jude 5 for similar applications of Israel's wilderness wanderings to the Christian experience.

69 *Paul, Apostle of Liberty*, p. 158: 'Whatever Christian convictions went into the foundation and structure of his thought, and whatever Greek terms and ideas embellish his theology, the Jewish conviction that freedom must be theocentric if it is to be freedom at all undergirds the whole.'

70 The addition of *palin* in the second half of 5.1 shows that Paul was thinking of a bondage that had been common to both Jews and Gentiles, which naturally directs our attention to this context.

71 H. Schlier puts it succinctly: 'Man attains to self-control by letting himself be controlled' (*TDNT* II, p. 496).

72 For the Jewish background to all this, see above, pp. 28ff. Not all Jews, of course, made such an unbending demand for circumcision. The more liberal ones could on occasion forgo it. Philo, *De Migr. Abr.* I.450 refers to a class of Jews who attached only symbolic significance to the Law and circumcision, though he himself urged both a literal observance of it and a symbolic interpretation (cf. a Christian comment on this in *Ep. Barnabas* 9.4). The *Or. Sib.* 4.24–33, 162–70 (probably late first century A.D.) lists conditions on which Gentiles can enter the blessings of the messianic kingdom, but with no mention at all of circumcision or the Torah. Cf. also Josephus *Ants.* 20.2.4. For a discussion of some of the points raised, cf. also F. F. Bruce, 'Galatian Problems: 3. The "Other" Gospel', in *BJRL* 53 (1971), p. 265.

73 J. H. Ropes, *The Singular Problem of the Epistle to the Galatians* (Cambridge, Mass., 1929).

74 The problem of Jewish elements in Gnosticism is a vast and difficult one. But if we think of Gnosticism as involving some kind of radical dualism, we can hardly find it here. Though Daniélou (*Theology of Jewish Christianity*, Eng. trans. London, 1964) speaks of a pre-Christian Jewish Gnosticism, on the premise just stated the features to which he draws attention would not be Gnostic, but simply the ideas of an unorthodox Judaism which later came to be incorporated into Gnostic systems.

75 H. J. Schoeps, *Theologie und Geschichte des Judenchristentums* (Tübingen, 1949).

76 This is a fact which many of the Bultmannian scholars have failed to notice. In the overwhelming majority of cases, it is not the ideas which the Gnostic propounded that were 'Gnostic' *per se*, but the

systems into which the ideas were fitted. Thus, taking as an example those systems to which Schmithals has appealed for parallels, we can say that the beliefs of Cerinthus were Gnostic, but only in the particular way in which he formulated the individual elements into a comprehensive system. The elements themselves were not necessarily 'Gnostic'. It is at this point that the alleged bridge between the second-century Gnostic systems and ideas current in the first century breaks down.

77 Log. 53. *Thomas*, of course, may not be Gnostic at all. According to B. Gärtner, *The Theology of the Gospel of Thomas*, Eng. trans. (London, 1961), this gospel represents a Valentinian Gnosis, while E. Haenchen considers it to be completely Gnostic, representing a Gnosticism at least as old as Christianity: cf. *Die Botschaft des Thomas-Evangeliums* (Berlin, 1961), p. 70. R. M. Grant thinks that *Thomas* is a reinterpretation of the canonical gospels along the lines of Naassene Gnosis (cf. R. M. Grant and D. N. Freedman, *The Secret Sayings of Jesus* (London, 1960), pp. 105–11). K. Grobel, on the other hand, considers that 'some portions of it testify to a radical encratitism that may be of Gnostic origin but may, rather, belong to some other eccentric Christian group of the second century' ('How Gnostic is the Gospel of Thomas?' in *NTS* 8, 1961/62, p. 373). G. Quispel supports him in 'Gnosticism and the New Testament', in *The Bible in Modern Scholarship*, ed. J. P. Hyatt (London, 1966), p. 257, as also does W. H. C. Frend in 'The Gospel of Thomas: Is Rehabilitation Possible?', in *JTS* ns. 18 (1967), pp. 13–26. But it seems likely that *Thomas* has at least some Gnostic affiliations, and so our point here can still be valid.

78 Though *eti* is omitted in some MSS, it is best to include it, since it is the more difficult reading. It also adds extra force if in fact Paul is drawing a contrast between his pre-conversion days and his Christian experience.

79 In the light of 6.12, it seems better to take the verse this way. The use of the technical term *kērussō* suggests that Paul was referring to his 'official' message. Burton disagrees, on the basis that Paul was not persecuted in his pre-Christian days for preaching circumcision (*Galatians*, pp. 286ff.). But if there is here a contrast rather than a parallel, this would not apply. F. F. Bruce suggests that there may have been some foundation for the charge in Paul's attitude to *Jewish* Christians (cf. Acts 21.21): see his 'Galatian Problems: 3. The "Other" Gospel', pp. 262ff.

80 The term appears in connection with Simon Magus only in a reference to the transmigration of Helen from one body to another (Irenaeus, *Adv. Haer.* I.23.2), though the Valentinians evidently used other terms (*hulikos* and *choikos*) to describe the same thing (cf. *Adv. Haer.* I.5, 6.1, 7.5, 8.3). See E. Schweizer, '*sarx* in Gnosticism', in *TDNT* VII. The Gnostic view comes out in the *Gospel of Philip* (log. 62) and *Thomas* (cf. R. McL. Wilson, *Studies in the*

Gospel of Thomas (London, 1960), pp. 36ff., B. Gärtner, *The Theology of the Gospel of Thomas*, pp. 194ff.).

81 Cf. 1QS 11.7–12, 1QM 4.3. It is also in contrast to Philo's estimate of the body as being of a corrupting nature in itself. Because of this, he concluded that fellowship with God was a matter for the soul only (*De Migr. Abr.* 7–9). Doubtless Paul was aware of the Philonic view, and of others current in the Hellenistic world, and perhaps he had an eye on this in writing as he does here. But we can go no further than the conclusion of W. L. Knox: 'The wisdom of the world might indeed be foolishness, but [Paul] was quite ready to use it to glorify Jesus, just as Judaism was ready to use it to glorify the Torah' (*Gentiles*, p. 90).

82 This is made very clear in v. 16, by the use of *ou mē* plus the aorist subjunctive. For parallels to the lists of sins in vv. 19–21, cf. Romans 1.29ff., 13.13, 1 Corinthians 5.10, and outside the New Testament, especially in Stoic literature. Cf. W. K. L. Clarke, *New Testament Problems* (London, 1929), pp. 157–60.

83 *Paul and Rabbinic Judaism* (London, 1948), p. 129. Though it is clear (cf. 6.6) that such instruction played a part in the service of the early church, it is not certain that this section of Galatians is a paraenesis taken over by Paul from some other context and inserted here. In any case, it is clear from a comparison with the paraenetical passages in other epistles that this passage is lacking in specific instructions, and almost everything Paul says is expressed in terms of broad principles rather than detailed instructions.

84 Op. cit., p. 131. Davies traces three possible sources of Pauline ethics: the *Pirke Aboth*, the rules of certain parties in Judaism (e.g. the Zadokite Document), and the *derek 'eretz* literature. But questions of dating and origin make him unable to produce anything more than vague speculations.

85 Even 5.14 is not certainly from gospel traditions, and may well be from Leviticus 19.18. The way Paul has repeatedly used the Torah itself to prove his own points here supports this.

86 J. Oman, *Grace and Personality* (Cambridge, 1917), p. 238. For a useful treatment of some of the other problems associated with the use of Christ as an ethical example, cf. W. Lillie, *Studies in New Testament Ethics* (London/Edinburgh, 1961), pp. 24–33.

87 Even Davies recognizes this: 'At no point in the Pauline epistles is the recognition of Jesus as a New Torah made explicit in so many words' (*Paul and Rabbinic Judaism*, p. 148). Nor is Jesus ever regarded as a 'latter-day Moses'; cf. C. K. Barrett, *From First Adam to Last* (London, 1962), p. 60.

88 Guthrie comments that the Law of Christ 'involves submission to a person rather than to a code . . . All that Christ has become to the believer incurs a new kind of obligation upon him' (*Galatians*, p. 153).

89 We should emphasize that this is our main disagreement with the work of these two scholars. We are not here making assertions about the whole of New Testament ethics, for moral rules of some kind quite clearly do come into the Christian ethic. But the fact remains that there is no trace of them in Galatians, whatever may be said of other parts of the New Testament. Davies and Longenecker have, probably unconsciously, fallen into the snare which is laid for any systematic treatment of the theme, viz. the danger of overemphasizing certain parts of the evidence in order to fit them into an overall picture. But in a historical investigation we must take note of the distinctive nature of each part of the evidence, as well as the similarities.

90 W. Lillie, *The Law of Christ* (Edinburgh, 1966), 2nd edn, p. 20.

91 *St. Paul and the Church of Jerusalem* (Cambridge, 1925), p. 318, n.3. Knox says it is also inconsistent with his theology in Romans, but this statement needs to be modified.

CHAPTER 3

1 F. F. Bruce, *1 and 2 Corinthians* (London, 1971) (*NCB*), p. 138.

2 A. Robertson and A. Plummer, *A Critical and Exegetical Commentary on the First Epistle of St. Paul to the Corinthians* (Edinburgh, 1911) (*ICC*), p. 228.

3 Cf. L. Morris, *The First Epistle of Paul to the Corinthians* (London, 1958), Tyndale Commentary: 'They were not Paul's own. The teachings had been handed down to Paul, and he passed them on to the converts. The term stresses the derivative nature of the gospel. It does not originate in the fertile mind of the teacher' (p. 151). Also T. C. Edwards, *A Commentary on the First Epistle to the Corinthians* (London, 1885), p. 268, for a similar view. This is preferable to the idea expressed by F. F. Bruce, *1 and 2 Corinthians*, p. 103, that this piece of tradition goes no further back than Paul himself. There were, of course, other 'traditions' which Paul himself seems to have originated. 1 Corinthians 15 is the most striking example of this, where Paul outlines what he has received, and then (vv. 8ff.) adds his own testimony to it, a testimony which then became a regular part of the tradition itself.

4 H. L. Goudge, *The First Epistle to the Corinthians* (London, 1911), 3rd edn *WC*, p. 35.

5 It is important also to note that this is the only lesson that Paul ever draws directly from the example of Christ Himself. In 1 Corinthians 11.1, Paul takes the same statement as he makes here a stage further: 'Be imitators of me, as I am of Christ.' We may well ask why Paul does not refer directly to the example of Christ. It is not a sufficient explanation to point out that 'there is no reason to think that the

Corinthians knew much about the life and behaviour of Christ, whereas Paul had lived for months under their eyes' (C. K. Barrett, *A Commentary on the First Epistle to the Corinthians* (London, 1968) (*BNTC*), p. 116), for in the only contexts where Paul does refer to Christ as an example he makes it quite clear that it is not in the details of his earthly life that the Lord could be a viable example for Christians to follow. One way out of the problem is to take Michaelis's suggestion that the idea of obedience to authoritative teaching is predominant here, so that 'the thought of an example is quite overshadowed' (*TDNT* IV, p. 672). Or we can suppose that Paul has changed the whole emphasis of his moral teaching, to lay emphasis not on broad principles, such as could be learned directly from the example of Christ, but on specific types of behaviour, which were to be learned from Paul as an authoritative moral teacher. In either case, the element of an authoritative interpretation of Christian moral principles has come in, the outcome of which must clearly have been some kind of moral code.

6 Cf. J. Héring, *The First Epistle of St. Paul to the Corinthians*, Eng. trans. (London, 1962), p. 32.

7 *1 Corinthians*, p. 117 (my emphasis). There follows the statement, 'as I teach them everywhere in every church', which makes it most unlikely that the 'ways' of which Paul speaks would refer to his style of life, since such could hardly have been a suitable subject for instruction. According to Michaelis, the word *hodos* here can be traced to a usage found in the Old Testament, and so becomes equivalent to *entolē*, i.e. 'commanded ways', or 'rules' (*TDNT* V, p. 88). Moffat describes Paul's ways as 'authoritative instructions . . . belonging to the Christian Torah of the Gospel' (*The First Epistle of Paul to the Corinthians* (London 1938) (*MC*), p. 51).

8 Cf. H. L. Goudge, *1 Corinthians*, p. 58; F. F. Bruce, *1 and 2 Corinthians*, p. 71. Also G. Schrenk, on *entolē* in *TDNT* II, p. 552. There is, in fact, an interesting distinction to be noted, for in Galatians 5.14 Paul implies, though he does not say, that love of one's neighbour amounts to keeping the commandments of God. In Romans 13.9, on the other hand, when he refers to the same 'law of love', he explicitly says that to observe this is to keep God's commandments – which supports our suggestion that in Romans we have a synthesis of his earlier Galatians and 1 Corinthians teaching.

9 Edwards, *1 Corinthians*, p. 180. The general meaning of the term *entolē* for Paul is clear: it is 'both the concrete Mosaic Law and the characteristic mark of the Law, i.e. its character as command' (Schrenk, *TDNT* II, p. 552). In Galatians, Paul emphasizes that Abraham, and those who would be like him, could not be justified by any works of the Law, but by faith (3.6ff.). Here in 1 Corinthians, keeping 'the commandments of God' is the all-important thing. Presumably Paul does not mean this to refer to the Mosaic Law here, though it can hardly be denied that, taken at face value, he

clearly refers to a law-principle of some sort. In the epistle to the Romans, on the other hand, he declares that all the commandments of God are fulfilled by 'love', which is nothing other than the indwelling Christ (Rom. 13.9ff.). So within the overall theological framework of his thought Paul is able to bring together the indwelling Christ, on the one hand, and the idea of moral rules, on the other. Indeed, he can even speak of the 'obedience of faith' (Rom. 1.5), something that he could hardly have accepted in the writing of Galatians, while in 1 Corinthians the emphasis is all on the obedience without very much stress being laid on the faith which through the power of the indwelling Christ would have produced a Christian morality.

10 According to J. C. Hurd, *The Origin of 1 Corinthians* (London, 1965), pp. 184ff., Paul had at first opposed the idea that women should be veiled when taking part in church services, but by the time he wrote 1 Corinthians he had changed his mind. Whatever may be said for or against this suggestion, it is certainly the case, as Moffatt observed, that throughout the whole of this confused discussion, Paul was 'half conscious that his own principle of Christian equality for the sexes did not exactly square with the dress regulation which he felt bound to enforce . . . '(*1 Corinthians*, p. 155).

11 Cf. C. K. Barrett, *1 Corinthians*, pp. 331ff., for a useful summary of the possibilities. Barrett prefers the idea that 14.34 was originally a marginal note that has been incorporated into the text. Schmithals overcomes the contradiction between 11 and 14 by saying that 1 Corinthians 11 is from an earlier epistle than 1 Corinthians 14. At first Paul did not realize that the Gnostics, whom Schmithals believes to have been in control in Corinth, were encouraging women to take a part in public worship, and so he allowed it. But later, when he realized that by allowing it he was pandering to Gnostic views, he took up the Jewish position, which is also reflected in the Pastoral Epistles (*Gnosticism in Corinth*, pp. 237ff.). Schmithals supports this by arguing that the original statement in Galatians 3.26–8 is 'a liturgical piece of Gnostic origin which, already employed in pre-Pauline Hellenistic communities, was taken over by Paul and by him was demythologized by means of the catchword *dia tēs pisteōs* . . . Without this phrase the passage offers purest Gnosticism' (op. cit., p. 239, n. 162). But the fact that Paul and the Gnostics agreed on *some* things does not necessarily mean that Paul was himself some kind of Gnostic, as Schmithals appears to believe. It is far better to conclude simply that St Paul was in a quandary here, and in the effort to impose both liberty and legality on the Christian women of Corinth, he quite consciously left us with a problem that has plagued every generation of Christians since his time. For a particularly lucid and helpful exposition of the general principles of Pauline teaching in relation to the sexes, see G. B. Caird, 'Paul and Women's Liberty', in *BJRL* 54 (1971/72), pp. 268–81.

12 One of the major problems in understanding the passage in 1 Corinthians 14 is that Paul specifically says he is referring to 'the Law', though it is impossible to find any passage in the Old Testament which agrees with the prohibition implied here. 'The Law did not prohibit prayer and praise by a woman in public worship either at the tabernacle or in the temple or in the synagogue' (L. Birney, *The Role of Women in the N.T. Church* (Pinner, 1971) (C.B.R.F. Occasional Paper no. 4), p. 15). In any case, the only Old Testament passage that can be adduced here would be something like Genesis 3.16, which lays down a much broader principle than the one Paul evidently had in mind. Because of this, a recent author has argued that Paul was actually quoting not the Old Testament, but a rabbinic tradition also found in the Babylonian Talmud, to the effect that 'It is a shame for a woman to let her voice be heard among men.' (Cf. especially J. Harper, *Women and the Gospel*, no date and privately circulated, pp. 15ff.). Whatever view we take, the point we have made is clearly established, that Paul here introduced a legalistic principle which was not only absent from Galatians, but ran totally against everything said in that epistle.

13 Cf. the comment of H. Chadwick: 'The apostle manages to combine an ability to retreat so far as to seem to surrender almost everything in principle to the opposition with an ability to make practical recommendations not easily reconciled with the theory he virtually accepts' ('All Things to All Men', in *NTS* 1, 1954/55, p. 264).

14 F. W. Grosheide, *Commentary on the First Epistle to the Corinthians* (Grand Rapids, 1953) (*NIC*), pp. 145ff., makes an important point about Paul's original teaching. Paul had made it perfectly clear in Galatians that all things are lawful to him only as he stands beneath the authority of his Lord. Because of this, certain things should self-evidently be undesirable. It was this aspect of Pauline teaching that the Corinthians had forgotten: 'They forgot that although all things belong to believers, the believers themselves belong to Christ so that they must be subject to him.' Longenecker expresses it succinctly: 'Christian liberty finds its basis in Christ and must be considered both a gift and a demand' (*Paul, Apostle of Liberty*, p.181). Cf. the whole of Longenecker's chapter 8, 'The Exercise of Liberty', for a valuable discussion of the problems raised here.

15 Galatians itself is indeed full of Old Testament allusions and quotations, but the distinction between this and 1 Corinthians is that in Galatians, Paul is using the Old Testament simply as a convenient source of information acceptable to both sides in the debate. Most, though not all, of the examples drawn from it are brought in only so that Paul could score a point against his opponents on their own ground. In 1 Corinthians, however, Paul has adopted a slightly different moral and theological stance towards the Old Testament, and we now find that he can apply Old Testament concepts for the benefit of his Christian faith, even in its ethical aspect. C. K. Barrett

draws attention to an interesting variation between the ways Moses is depicted in 1 Corinthians 10 and 2 Corinthians 3 respectively. In 1 Corinthians 'Moses' is placed on a level with 'Christ', while in 2 Corinthians Paul uses similar terminology to make only a 'paradoxical glorification' of Moses (*From First Adam to Last*, p. 53).

16 *Orthodoxy and Heresy in Earliest Christianity*, Eng. trans. edited by R. A. Kraft and G. Krodel (Philadelphia, 1971), p. 104. On the importance of *entolē* in the fight against the Gnostics, see G. Schrenk in *TDNT* II, pp. 553–6, and cf. the movement in the same direction in 1 John 2.2ff.; 1 Timothy 6.14. On the importance of the sayings of Jesus, cf. P. Fannon, 'The Influence of Tradition in St. Paul', in *Studia Evangelica IV*, pp. 304ff. It is noteworthy that Fannon can find only one such allusion in Galatians (6.1), and even here it is widely recognized that the gospel saying on which this is supposedly based (Matt. 18.15) owes more to the experiences of the early church than it does to the direct teaching of Jesus Himself.

17 The fact that we have drawn all our examples from 2 Corinthians 1–9 makes no real difference to our argument here. Even if, as is often supposed, 10–13 are to be separated from 1–9 the statement in 10.8 ('even if I boast a little too much of our authority . . .') indicates a later stage than 1 Corinthians, for Paul had emphasized there his authority as both moral teacher and moral exemplar. The rhetorical questions of 11.22 seem to suggest that those whom Paul was opposing had claimed to be better Jews than he was, which would fit in with our suggestion that the ethics of 2 Corinthians 1–9 are better suited to a Judaizing opposition than to a Gnosticizing one. This kind of opposition would also be a logical thing, coming after Paul's attempts at 'legal liberty' in 1 Corinthians. If 10–13 here are to be separated from 1–9, we can only do so by assigning 10–13 to a slightly *later* date, though the evidence for any kind of separation is slight. The form of Paul's teaching here excludes the position advocated by Schmithals, that 11.22 proves Paul's opponents in 2 Corinthians to have been Jewish Christians-cum-Gnostics (*Gnosticism in Corinth*, pp. 115ff.).

18 It is better here to take *pneuma* as a reference to the Holy Spirit rather than simply to the spirit of the gospel over against the sense of death which the old legal relationship had produced, especially in view of the contact here with Galatians 3.21. On the antithesis of spirit/flesh and spirit/letter, and their uses in Galatians, 2 Corinthians and Romans, cf. F. F. Bruce's comments in 'Galatian Problems: 4. The Date of the Epistle', in *BJRL* 54 (1971/72), pp. 259ff.

19 A. Plummer, *A Critical and Exegetical Commentary on the Second Epistle of St. Paul to the Corinthians* (Edinburgh, 1915) (*ICC*), p. 87. Romans 7.5–12 is an especially close parallel here.

20 P. E. Hughes, *Paul's Second Epistle to the Corinthians* (Grand Rapids, 1962) (*NIC*), p. 100.

21 Probably to be translated, 'the love of Christ leaves us no option' (cf. F. F. Bruce, *1 and 2 Corinthians*, in loc.). This does not affect our point, for *the love of Christ* is still the controlling factor.

22 It is widely supposed that 6.14—7.1 is an interpolation here, and that it may in fact be a fragment of a 'previous letter' referred to in 1 Corinthians 5.9, which seems to have been concerned with the same subject. See J. C. Hurd, *The Origin of 1 Corinthians*, pp. 45, 215, 235ff. for a comprehensive summary of those holding this view. Hurd himself contends that these verses were in fact part of the 'previous letter', a document which was 'well in the direction of an extreme cautiousness in matters of conduct. The Christian was directed to observe what amounted to taboos concerning his diet and his relationship to the world' (p. 273). If our analysis of the ethical implications of this passage is correct, however, it would hardly fit into the context of such a letter. In addition, in 1 Corinthians 5.9ff. Paul explicitly and emphatically declares that the previous directions to which he refers had nothing to do with relations between Christians and pagans, but only with the internal affairs of the church. In any case, it is far from certain that Hurd's hypothesis of a reactionary 'previous letter', countered by an extremely liberal reply from the Corinthians, which ultimately resulted in 1 Corinthians as a compromise document, can be sustained. Our own study shows that the characteristics which Hurd presupposes in the 'previous letter' would actually be more applicable to 1 Corinthians itself.

CHAPTER 4

1 For a useful summary treatment of some of the more important of the earlier interpreters, see F. F. Bruce, 'Galatian Problems: 3. The "Other" Gospel', pp. 254ff.

2 K. Lake, *The Earlier Epistles of St. Paul: Their Motive and Origin*, (London, 1911), p. 253. Lake himself later changed his view, and argued that since there is in the epistle no clear indication that the false teachers came from Jerusalem, they may have been local Galatian Jews, and not Jewish Christians at all. Cf. *Beginnings* V, p. 215. But there appears to have been a Judaizing party in the Jerusalem church (cf. Acts 15.5), and there are also indications that the opposition came from outside.

3 The most significant contributions are the following: J. H. Ropes, *The Singular Problem of the Epistle to the Galatians* (Cambridge, Mass., 1929), Harvard Theological Studies XIV, which in turn is a development of W. Lütgert, *Gesetz und Geist* (Gütersloh, 1919). F. R. Crownfield has further developed this theory in his article, 'The Singular Problem of the Dual Galatians', in *JBL* 64 (1945), pp. 491–500. R. Jewett has recently concluded that 'the congregation seems to have had an enthusiastic self-consciousness based on possession of the Spirit', a view similar in many ways to that of

Ropes and Crownfield (cf. 'The Agitators and the Galatian Congregation', in *NTS* 17, 1970/71, pp. 198–212). The theory of W. Schmithals in *Paul and the Gnostics*, already noted, is of some importance. J. Munck should also be mentioned for the sake of completeness (cf. his *Paul and the Salvation of Mankind*, Eng. trans. (London, 1959), pp. 87ff.).

4 Cf. R. McL. Wilson, 'Gnostics in Galatia?' in *Studia Evangelica IV*, p. 360: 'It is not beyond the bounds of possibility that a conservative emissary, sent for some totally different purpose, might have been so taken aback at what he found that he took it upon himself to lodge a protest which for a time had the effect of making even Peter withdraw.'

5 Most scholars would agree with R. McL. Wilson that, 'In the broad and comprehensive sense of the term Gnosis, it is perfectly correct to speak of Gnosis at Corinth, but this is not really helpful unless we can determine the relation between this Gnosis and the later developed Gnosticism' (*Gnosis and the New Testament* (Oxford, 1968), p. 52). This is not to say, of course, that Paul was dealing only with Gnosticizing tendencies here. Probably he was fighting a battle on two fronts.

6 It can hardly be a coincidence that Marcion deleted the reference in Corinthians 15.3 to the reception of the tradition. Cf. H. E. W. Turner, *The Pattern of Christian Truth* (London, 1954), p. 171.

7 If a late date for Galatians is preferred, this difference would be even more striking, for Paul would be more or less engaged in the Corinthians' problems by now. C. H. Buck, following suggestions made by J. B. Lightfoot, wants to place Galatians *after* 2 Corinthians ('The Date of Galatians', in *JBL* 70, 1951, pp. 113–22). See Appendix B.

8 Proselytes never had this title anyway: see above, p. 28.

9 To argue that Paul's statements are somewhat vague here because he himself was confused as to the exact nature of the heresy is question-begging, for the only evidence we have for the heretical teaching is what Paul says about it. To assume that he did not know what he was writing about is to open the door for any kind of heresy we care to read into the situation.

10 If, as Acts suggests was Paul's custom, much of his teaching had originally been given in the local synagogues, this would have been a natural starting-point for any sermon.

11 Some qualification of the term 'Judaizer' is in place here. In using the term, we mean to distinguish those who, unlike the Jerusalem apostles (if we are to believe Paul, Galatians 2.7ff.), could not accept the validity of the Gentile mission even in principle, but who believed that it was essential to become a Jew first in order to be a proper Christian.

12 Cf. Philippians 3.2ff. In both instances mentioned here, Paul appears to be taking up a line emanating from Jeremiah, a prophet with

whom he seems to have found himself in considerable sympathy (cf. 1.15). Paul's teaching on circumcision can find its antecedent in Jeremiah 4.4, 6.40, and 9.25, while his insistence on obedience as the formative characteristic of the true people of God is at least foreshadowed in Jeremiah 31. Cf. R. Meyer, on *peritemnō* in *TDNT* VI.

13 Cf. W. Lütgert, *Freiheitspredigt und Schwarmgeister in Korinth* (Gütersloh, 1908).

14 The same kind of argument also refutes Munck's contention that, though only Judaizers were in view here, they were in fact Paul's own Gentile converts (*Paul and the Salvation of Mankind*, pp. 87ff.). Cf. also F. F. Bruce, 'Galatian Problems: 3. The "Other" Gospel', pp. 259ff.

15 An idea also propounded by E. R. Goodenough, *By Light, Light* (New Haven, 1935).

16 Wilson's comment is a fair one: 'One might ask what grounds there are for the assumption that this group rejected a Gentile mission which would bring the converts into Judaism, particularly in view of the evidence from Jewish missionary propaganda' ('Gnostics—in Galatia?', p. 360, n. 1). We might go further, and ask if there is any reason why they should not bring such converts into the Christian church via Judaism?

17 *Paul*, p. 78. According to W. M. Ramsay, it was information to this effect that led Paul to write Galatians in the first place: 'At this time arrived a letter or message from Galatia, mentioning among other serious facts that Paul's converts were observing the Sabbatic year 48 (*Gal.* 4.10)' (*St. Paul the Traveller and the Roman Citizen* (London, 1920), 14th edn, p. xxxi).

18 W. Lütgert, *Freiheitspredigt und Schwarmgeister in Korinth*. Baur's viewpoint still has its representatives, though they are in a definite minority. Cf. Schoeps, *Paul*, pp. 74ff.

19 On the 'parties' in Corinth, see Appendix D. By seeing an allusion to the 'Christ party' in 2 Corinthians 10.7, it was also assumed that Paul faced the same kind of Gnosticizing opposition in both 1 and 2 Corinthians. The same assumption had previously led Baur to see Judaizers in both epistles, particularly connected, again, with the 'Christ party'. But, as C. K. Barrett points out ('Christianity at Corinth', in *BJRL* 46, 1963/64, pp. 269–97), while 1 Corinthians 11.2 deals with natives of Corinth, 2 Corinthians 10—13 quite clearly concerns people coming in from outside (especially 10.12–18; 11.4ff., 12–15, 22; and 12.11ff.). Cf. also D. Georgi, *Die Gegner des Paulus im 2. Korintherbrief* (Neukirchen, 1964) (*WMANT* 11), pp. 303ff.

20 Cf. A. Schlatter, *Die Korinthische Theologie* (Gütersloh, 1914), in which he postulated a Palestinian background for the Corinthians' beliefs.

21 R. Reitzenstein, *Die hellenistischen Mysterienreligionen* (Leipzig, 1910), pp. 75ff., 333–93.

22 Bultmann, *Theology* I, p. 175. Cf. Haenchen in *RGG*³, II, cols. 1,652ff.

23 For a succinct account of the history of this view, see Georgi, *Gegner*, pp. 7–16.

24 Op. cit., pp. 87–113. These letters were as follows:

(i) From Ephesus after Stephanas's information (2 Cor. 6.14–7.1; 1 Cor. 6.12–20; 9.24–10.22; 11.2–34; 15; 16.13–24). Paul's information, however, was inadequate, and so he could not give a satisfactory analysis of the situation in Corinth.

(ii) A reply to a letter brought by members of Chloe's household, asking various questions on matters of discipline and belief (1 Cor. 1.1–6.11; 7.1–9.23; 10.23–11.1; 12.1–14.40; 16.1–12).

(iii) A letter taken by Titus, conciliatory in tone, after Paul's unexpected visit to Corinth (2 Cor. 2.14–6.13; 7.2–4).

(iv) The 'severe letter' (1 Cor. 16.15ff.; 2 Cor. 10.1–13.13).

(v) A more cheerful letter, written to recommend Titus and his companions to the Corinthian church (2 Cor. 9.1–15).

(vi) A letter expressing Paul's relief at the change in the Corinthian situation following Titus's arrival there (2 Cor. 1.1—2.13; 7.5—8.24).

Such a division of the letters is, however, extremely unlikely, and should be rejected. Cf. Kümmel, *Introduction*, pp. 203ff.

25 Also connected with this was the substitution of a *logos sophias* or *logos gnōseōs* for the Christian gospel. Cf. Schmithals, op. cit., pp. 171–5. But see Barrett, 'Christianity at Corinth', pp. 276ff., on the uses of *sophia* and *gnōsis*.

26 Op. cit., pp. 124–30. A viewpoint accepted also by Wilckens, *Weisheit und Torheit*, p. 121, n.1.

27 Op cit., pp. 293ff. One wonders what Schmithals would make of Paul's statement in 1 Corinthians 6.20, which seems far removed from this kind of dualism: 'Glorify God in your body.'

28 Cf. Schmithals's article, 'Das Verhältnis von Gnosis und Neuem Testament als methodisches Problem', in *NTS* 16 (1970), pp. 373–83, especially pp. 377ff. On the Eucharist in general, cf. *Gnosticism in Corinth*, pp. 250ff.

29 F. F. Bruce, *1 and 2 Corinthians*, p. 194. A typical example of such curiosity is the question of Gnostic cursing of Jesus, as reflected, according to Schmithals, in 1 Corinthians 12.3. The article by B. A. Pearson, 'Did the Gnostics Curse Jesus?', in *JBL* 86 (1967), pp. 301–5, reveals the shallow methodology of Schmithals, and suggests that, contrary to his assertions, 'the Gnostics themselves did not curse Jesus; by identifying him with their venerated Serpent they were honoring him as highly as possible!' (p. 304). The reply by N. Brox ('*Anathema Iēsous* (1 Kor. 12,3)'), in *Biblische Zeitschrift* 12 (1968), pp. 103–11 attempts to reinstate Schmithals's case merely by

a restatement of the same evidence, and Schmithals accepts this effort as a valid approach to the subject (*Gnosticism in Corinth*, p. 350). It is this kind of exegesis that led J. Munck to say of Schmithals's work: 'The author of this book lacks historical training. He forces his *a priori* opinions upon the texts with offensive boldness . . . Schmithals's book is a striking proof of the decline of exegetic research since the 1930s' ('The N.T. and Gnosticism', in *Current Issues in N.T. Interpretation*, p. 230).

30 Hurd argues that Paul's Corinthian ministry preceded the Apostolic Decree, basing his chronology on the Pauline letters, not on Acts (the method of J. Knox, *Chapters in a Life of Paul* (New York, 1950), pp. 13–88). On this, see Hurd's article, 'Pauline Chronology and Pauline Theology', in *Christian History and Interpretation*, pp. 225–48.

31 If, on the other hand, he had accepted it only as a part of his policy of being 'all things to all men', or if he had considered it to apply only to a limited situation, it is easy to see why he should have omitted mention of it here. According to T. W. Manson, *Studies in the Gospels and Epistles*, p. 200, the question was raised by the Cephas party, and Paul deals with it in this way to oppose them: 'He takes it as a matter of purely domestic concern within the Gentile-Christian community, the implication being that the Jerusalem compromise is doubtless suitable for Churches like that of Antioch with a mixed membership, but that in predominantly Gentile-Christian communities Jewish taboos do not count . . .' Barrett ('Things Sacrificed to Idols', in *NTS* 11, 1964/65, pp. 138–53) suggests there may have been an earlier attempt to impose the Decree on the Corinthians, and this is why Paul starts out from first principles. However we try to explain the fact, it is still a complete mystery why Paul should not have referred to the Decree, if only to support his own view over against its requirements.

32 Barrett, *1 Corinthians*, pp. 7ff. Cf. also the observations on Hurd's theory made by J. C. K. Freeborn, 'The Development of Doctrine at Corinth', in *Studia Evangelica* IV, pp. 404–10.

33 This is, of course, exactly the charge which Paul's opponents in 2 Corinthians appear to have made against him, though he would have none of it.

34 Cf. A. Schlatter, *Paulus, der Bote Jesu* (Stuttgart, 1934). According to Manson, *Studies in the Gospels and Epistles*, p. 199, this asceticism was being criticized by the (Jewish) Cephas party, which at least suggests it was not of Jewish origin. Barrett ('Christianity at Corinth') sees it as the view of the Paul party, because Paul comes close to accepting this view in 1 Corinthians 7.7. G. Quispel, on the other hand, traces the Corinthian asceticism to Jewish Encratites: cf. his article, 'Gnosticism and the New Testament', in *The Bible in Modern Scholarship*, ed. J. P. Hyatt (London, 1966), pp. 254ff.

35 The expression of H. J. Cadbury, 'Overconversion in Paul's Churches', in *The Joy of Study* (Essays presented to F. C. Grant), ed. S. E. Johnson (New York, 1951), p. 48.

36 J. M. Robinson, 'Basic Shifts in German Theology', in *Interpretation* 16 (1962), pp. 82–6. F. F. Bruce says of Q that it 'cannot . . . be called a Gospel, if only because it lacks a passion narrative' ('When is a Gospel not a Gospel?', in *BJRL* 45, 1962/63, p. 323). This, as Bruce goes on to show, would be as good a qualification as any for a Gnostic 'gospel'.

37 Cf. C. K. Barrett, 'Christianity at Corinth', p. 276, and 'Things Sacrificed to Idols', p. 151.

38 Barrett, 'Christianity at Corinth', p. 280.

39 In 1 Corinthians 2.10, Paul declares himself to be a *pneumatikos* who has pierced the mysteries of the *bathē tou Theou* (for him, the 'word of the cross'). In 2.14ff. and 15.44 the dualism of *Psychikos pneumatikos* emerges, which perhaps indicates its importance to certain people in the Corinthian church. According to B. A. Pearson, the usage of this terminology here can be traced back to a Hellenistic-Jewish exegesis of Genesis 2.7 (LXX), a passage which assumed considerable importance in later Gnostic speculation, though the Gnostics differed from Paul in separating the pneumatic nature of man from God's creative activity, and regarding his psychical nature as the product of a fallen Demiurge working in ignorance of the true Deity (cf. his work, *The Pneumatikos-psychikos Terminology of 1 Corinthians*, (Missoula, 1974), SBL Dissertation series no. 12). Also J. Dupont, *Gnosis* (Louvain/Paris, 1949), pp. 151–80. Despite similarities between Pauline and Gnostic expressions, Paul was completely different from his opponents, and the ethical and communal aspects of his argument in 1 Corinthians mark him off completely from any form of Gnosis. Cf. S. Laeuchli, *The Language of Faith* (London, 1965), pp. 47ff.

40 Cf. Laeuchli, op. cit., pp. 15–93, for a valuable introductory study of the linguistic problems involved.

41 Cf. H. von Soden, 'Sakrament und Ethik bei Paulus', in *Urchristentum und Geschichte* I (Tübingen, 1951), pp. 239–75. The designation of charismatic gifts as *pneumatika* in 1 Corinthians (12.1, 14.1, and possibly 2.13) is probably significant in this connection, and may suggest that the excesses of miracle and ecstasy mentioned in 12–14 were also traced back to a false view of the sacraments. Cf. E. Käsemann, *Essays on New Testament Themes* (London, 1963), pp. 66ff. (Referred to below as *ENTT*).

42 This is the most natural implication of the reference to 'our fathers' in v. 1. Cf. H. Conzelmann, *Der erste Brief an die Korinther* (Göttingen, 1969, *KEK*), p. 194. If W. D. Davies is right, there may also be here an intention on Paul's part to criticize the Corinthians' attitude to *sophia*, dealt with in 1 Corinthians 1–4, if the apostle was

adopting a common convention of exegesis to show Christ ('the rock', v. 4) as the true divine wisdom (*Paul and Rabbinic Judaism*, p. 153). On the midrashic background of all this, cf. C. K. Barrett, *From First Adam to Last*, pp. 48ff.

43 This point also disposes of the suggestion of J. H. Wilson, 'The Corinthians who say there is no resurrection of the dead', in *ZNW* 59 (1968), pp. 90–107, who argues that the Corinthians had misunderstood Paul's original teaching in the sense of a heavenly exaltation and not a bodily resurrection. But this would be difficult to understand if this very materialistic reference to burial had been a part of Paul's teaching, as he explicitly says it was.

44 M. L. Peel has shown that in certain Gnostic circles there was just this kind of tension between a present and a future resurrection, though it is likely that the views to which he draws attention may have taken Paul's statements here as their starting-point, and they cannot therefore provide any real parallel to the Corinthians' views ('Gnostic Eschatology and the New Testament', in *Nov. Test.* 12 (1970), pp. 141–65).

45 According to R. Bultmann, *Theology* I, p. 169, Paul at first misunderstood the Corinthians, but by the time he wrote 2 Corinthians 5, his mistaken impression had been corrected, and he was able to oppose the real error of which the Corinthians were guilty. Cf. also Schmithals, *Gnosticism in Corinth*, p. 156. But if we are correct in seeing more Jewish opponents in 2 Corinthians, the changed circumstances would be sufficient to explain the varying emphasis (cf. Georgi, *Gegner*, pp. 301–5). The question of 1 Corinthians 15 and 2 Corinthians 5 is of course a highly contentious issue in itself. Whiteley, *Theology of St. Paul*, pp. 248–60 has a concise summary of the most important viewpoints. For a recent re-examination of some of the problems, cf. F. F. Bruce, 'Paul on Immortality', in *SJT* 24 (1971), pp. 457–72.

46 For a history of this view, cf. J. H. Wilson, 'The Corinthians who say there is no resurrection of the dead', pp. 95ff.

47 Bauer, *Orthodoxy and Heresy*, pp. 99ff. Even if we do not accept Bauer's impression of 'the strong', he has still shown that the Gnostics opposed in *1 Clement* had their predecessors at a much earlier period.

48 Georgi, *Gegner*. Cf. also H. Köster, 'Häretiker im Urchristentum', in *RGG*[3] III, cols. 17–21; F. F. Bruce, *1 and 2 Corinthians*, pp. 172–4; C. K. Barrett, 'Christianity at Corinth', and 'Paul's Opponents in 2 Corinthians', in *NTS* 17 (1970/71), pp. 233–54.

49 On Cephas's connection with Corinth, see Barrett's article, 'Cephas and Corinth', in *Abraham unser Vater: Festschrift für O. Michel*, O. Betz, etc., eds. (Leiden/Köln, 1963), pp. 1–12.

50 Cf. H. J. Schoeps, *Paul*, p. 80, n. 4. Käsemann has shown that the main issue between Paul and his opponents was not the possession

of special powers *per se*, but the fact of his apostolic authority. Cf. his article, 'Die Legitimität des Apostels', in *ZNW* 41 (1942), pp. 33–71.

51 *Exegetische Probleme des Zweiten Korintherbriefes* (Uppsala, 1947), pp. 20ff. (in reply to Käsemann, art. cit. in previous note).

52 Schmithals makes a valuable observation on the ways Paul defends his own authority in Galatians and 2 Corinthians: 'In general he places no special value on the possibility . . . of being able as an apostle to make the claim to be a direct recipient of revelation. Only in Galatians does he expressly appeal to this aspect of the apostolic self-understanding, and this in fact is obviously because the stout contesting of his gospel provoked such an appeal. When some time later, he has to defend himself in II Cor. against no less vigorous attacks on his message and his apostleship, he does not again seize upon this argument used in Galatians but defends himself differently, one might conclude that *it is not the direct imparting of the revelation to the apostle as such but the appeal to it in order to defend the truth of his words that has in the meantime become suspect for him*' (*The Office of Apostle*, p.32; my emphasis). The reason for Paul's suspicion of this method of justifying his own position in 2 Corinthians becomes clear only if the thesis put forward here is accepted.

53 It is probably best to view 2 Corinthians as a unity, despite the unevenness that is evident between 1–9 and 10–13. Cf. Kümmel, *Introduction*, pp. 211ff. But this question is not material to our own theory, since it is plain that 10–13 cannot have come before 1–9 (cf. Bruce, *1 and 2 Corinthians*, pp. 170ff., who, with Barrett, 'Christianity at Corinth', separates 10–13 as a letter written later than 1–9). Schmithals, of course, sees 10–13 as the central part of Paul's argument with the Corinthians. But he still recognizes that they must come later than the polemic of 1–9: 'I regard it as an assured result of New Testament research that these chapters do not belong with II Cor. 1–9, but are the torso of a separate epistle which is later than the polemical parts of II Cor. 1–9' (*The Office of Apostle*, p. 39, n. 75).

54 Though these people doubtless laid claim to the authority of the 'superlative apostles' in Jerusalem, there is no guarantee that they actually had such authority, nor any indication of what character it may have had. Barrett finds an interesting parallel in the men sent 'from James' in Galatians 2.12 ('Christianity at Corinth', p. 294).

55 W. Lütgert, op. cit., pp. 70ff. drew out a series of contrasts between the accusations made against the Judaizers in Galatians and the accusations made against Paul by his opponents in 2 Corinthians. But it gives a more likely picture to think of Judaizers at Corinth making such accusations with tongue in cheek, than to suppose with Lütgert that Gnostics of some kind would have made the same accusations.

56 Cf. the valuable article by G. W. MacRae, 'Anti-Dualist Polemic in 2 Cor. 4,6?', in *Studia Evangelica* IV, pp. 420–31. If MacRac is right (and our own study suggests that he probably is), this must dispose once and for all of the idea that Paul himself was some sort of Gnostic dualist.

CHAPTER 5

1 Clement of Alexandria, *Strom.* VII. 106.4. Basilides also made such claims, and had a particular regard for Romans and 1 Corinthians.

2 Cf. Th. Zahn, *Geschichte des Neutestamentlichen Kanons* (Erlangen, 1888), Bd. I, p. 758: 'The teaching of Valentinus is just as inconceivable without the letters of Paul as without the Prologue to the Fourth Gospel, and it is no accident that Paul is preferred by all Valentinians as the preacher of the hidden wisdom who speaks out most clearly.'

3 G. L. Story, *The Valentinian (Gnostic) Use of the Letters of Paul*, unpublished PhD dissertation (Northwestern University (USA), 1968).

4 Cf. W. Bauer, *Orthodoxy and Heresy*, p. 222: 'It is certain that it was from Galatians and not, say, from Romans with its concise explanation that Christ was the end of the Law (10:4), that Marcion got the idea that he could break the back of the Old Testament . . .'

5 Cf. H. E. W. Turner, *The Pattern of Christian Truth*, pp. 232ff.; J. Doresse, *The Secret Books of the Egyptian Gnostics*, Eng. trans. (London, 1960), pp. 306ff; R. McL. Wilson, *Gnosis and the New Testament*, pp. 60–84, and the literature cited there. C. K. Barrett, *The Signs of an Apostle*, pp. 100ff. is also useful.

6 H. E. W. Turner, *Pattern of Christian Truth*, p. 186. Cf. the comment of Wilson (*Gnosis and the New Testament*, p. 76): 'The essential point is that it is the Gnostic theories which are dominant, and not the plain meaning of the Biblical text.'

7 Cf. also the points made by Wilson in 'Gnostics—in Galatia?', p. 363.

8 This dichotomy is, of course, the basis for most of the other difficulties which exegetes find in this passage. Cf. Haenchen, *Acts*, pp. 455–72. But in view of the fact that, as we have already seen, Paul showed a singular ineptitude in some statements that he made in Galatians, there seems to be no reason to suppose that, dealing as he thought with the purely practical issue of table fellowship between Jews and Gentiles, and being particularly anxious to avoid confrontation with the original apostles, he could not have agreed to such an arrangement without fully working out the theological consequences that could, or, as we have suggested, did, follow in some Gentile congregations. Many of the alleged problems over Paul's action here are the result of too mechanical an approach to the operations of the human mentality. Paul was no automaton, guaranteed to work in

precisely the same way on every occasion. He was an impulsive man, as some of his extreme statements in Galatians show when compared with, say, Romans, and it is psychologically more likely that he made an unthinking blunder than that Luke fabricated the whole event.

9 The title of an article on this subject in *American Journal of Theology* XI (1907), pp. 454–74: 'Acts versus Galatians: the Crux of Apostolic History'.

10 W. M. Ramsay, *St. Paul the Traveller and the Roman Citizen.* Ramsay was not actually the first to propose the South Galatian theory, though he, along with Th. Zahn, was one of its most influential advocates. It was first put forward by a little-known German schoolmaster, J. J. Schmidt, in two works: *Prolusio de Galatis, ad quos Paulus literas misit* (1748), and *Prolusionem suam de Galatis—ab objectionibus doctissimorum virorum vindicare conatur* (1754).

11 According to W. D. Davies (*Paul and Rabbinic Judaism*), the basic problem dealt with at the Apostolic Council was not the practical one of table fellowship between circumcised Jews and uncircumcised Gentiles, but was in itself a legal problem, connected with the so-called Noachic commandments that Jews expected even uncircumcised Gentiles to observe. 'There were certain requirements . . . that James and every Rabbi would have no hesitation in demanding from all men, moral requirements the rejection of which, *ipso facto*, kept one outside the pale of salvation' (pp. 112ff.). Cf. also H. J. Schoeps, *Theologie und Geschichte des Judenchristentums*, pp. 259ff. The fact that the Apostolic Decree does seem to have had some connection with this Noachic law may explain Paul's unusual readiness to accept it as an obligation for Gentile Christians, though it is doubtful whether we can go so far as Davies in supposing that the theological position of Gentiles *vis-à-vis* these commandments was the main reason for the Council. In any case, the connection with the Noachic commandments is not certain: cf. Lake, *Earlier Epistles*, pp. 55ff.

12 The fact that James quotes Amos 9 from the LXX, which has an entirely different implication from the MT, can only be noted and not discussed here. In the LXX text, '*adām*, 'man', has taken the place of '*edōm*, 'Edom', and *yidreshu* from *dārash*, 'to seek', comes in instead of *yireshu* from *yārash*, 'to possess'. But this may not be so great a problem as at first appears to be the case. Cf. F. F. Bruce, *The Book of the Acts* (London, 1954, *NIC*), p. 310.

13 Cf. Leviticus 3.17; 5.2; 17.10–16. That these OT passages lie behind the Decree here is plain from the order of Acts 15.29, which closely follows Leviticus 17–18. 17.1–9 deals with idolatry, in not offering animals to Yahweh (cf. especially v. 7); in 17.10–16 the eating of blood is forbidden; and in 18.1–23 immorality is the main topic, with special emphasis on marriage within the permitted degrees. See further Schoeps, *Paul*, pp. 66ff.

It is hard to see how James's compromise here can be differentiated from the original demand of the Judaizers. Though James admittedly rejected circumcision, yet to the believers of the Gentile churches familiar with Paul's teaching in Galatians, he would have appeared to be adopting the same legalistic principles, though unwilling to carry them through to their logical outcome. An additional complicating factor here is the reading of the Western text, which omits the reference to 'what is strangled', and adds *pheromenoi en tō Hagiō* (v. 29). Other ancient MSS and versions also have *kai hosa mē thelete heautois ginesthai heterō mē poiein.* Though this latter addition is probably not original, the omission of 'what is strangled' has, according to many interpreters, a strong claim to originality. If this text was the original reading, the character of the Decree changes from a ritual requirement to a purely moral regulation. But whatever reading is adopted, our own hypothesis is unaffected, for in Galatians Paul seems to do away with the law-principle of the OT not only in respect of religious ritual, but also for ethics. For full consideration of the D text, see K. Lake, *Earlier Epistles*, pp. 48–60; J. G. Machen, *The Origin of Paul's Religion* (London, 1921), pp. 87ff; A. C. Clark, *The Acts of the Apostles* (Oxford, 1933), pp. 359ff. Cf. also E. J. Epp, *The Theological Tendency of Codex Cantabrigiensis in Acts* (Cambridge, 1966), pp. 97ff.

14 See the evidence adduced by E. Molland, 'La circoncision, le baptême et l'autorité du décret apostolique (Actes XV, 28sq.) dans les milieux judéo-chrétiens des Pseudo-Clémentines', in *Studia Theologica* IX (1955), pp. 1–39. Molland has argued that in particular the Jewish-Christian traditions behind the *Preaching of Peter* kept very rigidly to the terms of the Apostolic Decree. The fact that certain other writers, standing more within the tradition of the catholic church, also take a similar attitude (cf. *Did.* 6.3, Justin, *Dial.* 34, Tertullian, *Apol.* 9, Eusebius, *H.E.* V.1.26, etc.) does not discount our argument here.

15 Cf. Haenchen, *Acts*, pp. 479ff. Haenchen is right to say that no compilation of sources need lie behind this passage, though his assertion that Luke has been the unwitting victim of an unreliable tradition does not convince all interpreters. See also J. C. O'Neill, *The Theology of Acts in its Historical Setting* (London, 1970), pp. 126ff. According to A. S. Geyser, the Apostolic Decree was originally intended only for the churches of Syria and Cilicia, and Acts 16.4 is a later addition, influenced by 15.41, inserted at the end of the first century when the issue of eating *eidōlothuta* had come to play a major role as the touchstone of Christian orthodoxy. This would also explain why Paul never mentioned the Decree at Corinth, for he never felt that the Gentile churches were envisaged under its terms ('Paul, the Apostolic Decree and the Liberals in Corinth', in *Studia Paulina in honorem Johannis de Zwaan*, eds. J. N. Sevenster and W. C. van Unnik (Haarlem, 1953), pp. 136ff.).

16 *St. Paul the Traveller*, p. 173. See the whole section here, pp. 171–4. Such a distinction between 'higher' and 'lower' orders of believers would be familiar to Jewish Christians from their experiences in Judaism itself, where there was a similar division between the true-born Jew and the proselyte, on the one hand, and the 'Godfearer' on the other. Whereas the former group could observe the whole Law, the latter was expected only to observe the seven Noachic 'commandments' (i.e. the prohibition of idolatry, blasphemy, unchastity, blood-shedding, robbery, enjoying the flesh of living animals, and the positive command to act justly). H. J. Schoeps (*Paul*, p. 251) is right in characterizing these 'Godfearers' as 'an inferior level' of Jewish believer. This being the case, it could be that a clue may be found here for the intrusion of Gnosticizing elements into Judaism quite independently of its incursion into the church, though traceable to similar circumstances, viz. the creation of a spiritual élite, able to keep the entire Law, over against a lower class who were bound only to specific principles. Cf. Jonas's comment that Gnosticism may have originated '*in close vicinity* and in partial reaction to Judaism' ('Delimitation of the Gnostic Phenomenon', in *Le Origini dello Gnosticismo*, p. 102. His emphasis).

17 To consider the historicity of Acts is quite outside our terms of reference here. For a judicious survey of the problems in connection with this particular episode, cf. O. Cullmann, *Peter: Disciple, Apostle, Martyr*, Eng. trans. (London, 1953), pp. 42ff. Cullmann wants to separate the Apostolic Decree from the meeting with which Acts associates it, arguing that the Decree had no original connection with Paul, but came at a later stage. See also M. Dibelius and W. G. Kümmel, *Paul*, pp. 129ff. For a succinct summary of the wider historical problems involved, cf. W. W. Gasque, 'The Historical Value of the Book of Acts', in *EQ* XLI (1969), pp. 68–88.

18 *Luke and the Gnostics* (Nashville/New York, 1966), pp. 94ff.

19 In Mani's system, 'perpetual abstinence' from certain foods was 'for the sake of destroying and contemning and abominating the works of the creator' (Jerome, *Adv. Jovinian*, II.16). The Ebionites, whose 'attitude towards the Lord is like that of Cerinthus and Carpocrates' (Irenaeus, *Adv. Haer.* I.26.2), also fall into this category, as also, according to Epiphanius *Pan.* 30, does the kind of Jewish Christianity represented by the Clementine *Homilies* and *Recognitions*.

20 According to H. J. Schoeps, *Theologie und Geschichte des Judenchristentums*, Ebionite Christianity survived in strength for some time even after A.D. 70. But the evidence for this is not convincing.

21 Cf. R. M. Grant, *Gnosticism and Early Christianity*, pp. 39–69. H. Jonas has emphasized the perversion of such Jewish elements in Gnostic thought, though he argues that this does not necessarily indicate that some Gnostics were also Jews. Judaism would have been familiar enough for the average Gentile to have had as clear an

idea of its contents as most Gnostics seem to have had. (Cf. 'Delimitation of the Gnostic Phenomenon', in *Le Origini dello Gnosticismo*, p. 102, n. 1).

22 The main difficulties in this theory are:
(i) It is not true to the facts, for Jewish apocalyptic did not end in A.D. 70 (*Baruch* and *IV Ezra* both came later), nor was the faith of the Jews broken by the events of that year. They were led not to despair, but to another revolution in A.D. 132.
(ii) It is unlikely that Jews would have used the OT in the way that some Gnostics did, and since Gnostic knowledge of the OT is generally limited to the first few chapters of Genesis, it is more likely that OT elements entered Gnosticism by some indirect route.
(iii) On this theory, it is hard to see why the events of A.D. 70 found no place in Gnostic teaching. The Gnostics were eager to devalue the God of the OT, and his evident defeat by the Romans would at least have supported their case.

23 The fact that even James himself could be given honourable mention in certain Gnostic circles also suggests there must have been a change of outlook from the very earliest days. Eusebius, *H.E.* II.1.4–5 tells how after the resurrection Christ revealed himself to James, 'who was one of those who are regarded as brothers of the Lord'. After this, Jesus 'passed on Gnosis to James the Just, to John, and to Peter, who themselves [passed it on] to the other apostles, the other apostles to the Seven . . .' The so-called *Apocryphon of James*, preserved in the Jung Codex, is ascribed to James, who is stated to be both the brother of the Lord and also the disciple of that name. According to H. C. Puech (*NTA* I, p. 338), it is Valentinian. The (second) *Apocalypse of James*, which consists of some twenty tattered pages of Coptic text in Nag Hammadi codex V, is again reputedly a speech of James the Lord's brother, given in Jerusalem and recorded by one Mareim, a priest. The work ends with an account of James's death, reminiscent of the martyrdom of Stephen in Acts 7, and presumably therefore bearing some relation to Hegessipus's account of the same incident (in Eusebius, *H.E.* II.23). A saying which clearly holds James in great respect is also found in the *Gospel of Thomas*, log. 12, where heaven and earth are said to have been created for his benefit.

24 Cf. the argument of A. Ehrhardt, *The Apostolic Succession* (London, 1953).

25 *ENTT* and *NTQ*. Cf. also E. Haenchen in *RGG*³ II, cols. 1,652ff.

26 For a convenient summary and evaluation of some of these, cf. J. H. Elliot, 'A Catholic Gospel: Reflections on "Early Catholicism" in the N.T.', in *CBQ* xxxi (1969), pp. 213–23.

27 J. W. Drane, 'Eschatology, Ecclesiology and Catholicity in the N.T.', in *ExpT* LXXXIII (1972), pp. 180–84.

28 *NTQ* p. 237, n. 1. The generally subjective nature of all such distinctions becomes clear when we compare C. H. Dodd's conclusions on the same matter, i.e. that the original gospel proclaimed a realized eschatology, which was perverted by Judaizing influences to produce a futuristic eschatology. Cf. his *Parables of the Kingdom* (London, 1935).

29 *NTQ* p. 237, n. 1. This seems to represent a change of mind from Käsemann's earlier essay in *ENTT* pp. 169–95 (originally in German in 1952), where he appears to argue that the view of the early church was that the *eschaton* had already dawned with the coming of Jesus, a view which was discarded in 'early catholicism' so that the 'last days' could become a definite phase following the coming of Jesus and the apostolic preaching. On this basis, Käsemann could see as little to commend the 'early catholics' as the Gnostics themselves: 'Both adversaries have destroyed that tension between present and future salvation which was peculiar to primitive Christianity' (*ENTT* p. 185). The mention of a *tension* here in primitive eschatology is more valid than the monochrome distinctions which Käsemann has depicted in his later essays.

30 See Romans 8.23; Ephesians 1.14; and compare 1 Corinthians 6.9 with Romans 14.17.

31 Romans 1.2–4; Philippians 1.5ff., cf. Colossians 1.15ff., Ephesians 5.14. See A. M. Hunter, *Paul and His Predecessors* (London, 1940); P. Carrington, *The Primitive Christian Catechism* (Cambridge, 1940).

32 Cf. my article, 'Simon the Samaritan and the Lucan Concept of Salvation History', in *EQ* XLVII (1975), pp. 131ff.

33 Cf. his essay, 'The Canon of the N.T. and the Unity of the Church', in *ENTT* pp. 95–107, originally in *Evan. Theol.* 11 (1951/52), pp. 13–21. For different opinions on various aspects of the subject, see also the symposium edited by Käsemann, *Das Neue Testament als Kanon* (Göttingen, 1970).

34 See above, especially pp. 63–9.

35 Cf. especially the article by C. E. B. Cranfield, 'St Paul and the Law', referred to above. Galatians 3.24 may be taken to support this meaning here, though it is certainly not as specific as what Paul says in Romans about the Law's positive function.

36 Cf. C. K. Barrett, *A Commentary on the Epistle to the Romans* (London, 1957, *BNTC*), pp. 197ff.: 'Christ is the end of the law, with a view not to anarchy but righteousness. He puts an end to the law, not by destroying all that the law stood for but by realizing it.'

37 According to C. A. Anderson Scott, *New Testament Ethics* (Cambridge, 1930), pp. 80ff., Paul's dual attitude to the Law could also be derived from the teaching of Jesus. The gospel could not destroy the Law (Rom. 7.12, 14, etc., cf. Matt. 5.17), but at the same time it did have a passing and relative value (Gal. 3.19, etc., cf. Lk. 16.16). But in this case it is more likely that the tension ultimately accepted

by Paul was a result of his own experiences rather than of close acquaintance with the gospel traditions. In any case, the *provenance* of Matthew 5.17 is quite uncertain.

APPENDIX B

1 Cf. D. Guthrie, *NT Introduction: the Pauline Epistles*, 2nd edn (London, 1963), pp. 79–87 for a comprehensive summary of the various arguments.

2 Cf. J. B. Lightfoot, *Galatians* (London, 1865), pp. 35–55. The possibility of actually dating Paul's epistles solely by reference to internal characteristics must remain a doubtful one, and we employ it here only because it can be seen to fit into the picture drawn by advocates of the early date on directly historical grounds. Though the 'historical' approach through Acts has been seriously challenged by J. C. Hurd (*The Origin of 1 Corinthians*, pp. 3–42), we can hardly accept that it should be abandoned. For all the problems involved in the historicity and chronology of Acts, it does at least give some kind of 'historical' evidence, which can be judged by scholars on historical grounds. But if we move the debate away from this and carry it on exclusively on the basis of the theology of Paul's epistles, we open the door for a completely subjective criticism. Subjective assessment of Pauline doctrine has its place, but it cannot rank in the first line of evidence when we come to date the Pauline correspondence.

3 The following are typical examples:

Galatians		= 2 Corinthians	
3.13	(Christ the Curse)	=	5.21
6.7	('sowing/reaping')	=	9.6
1.6	('another gospel')	=	11.4
6.15	('new creation')	=	5.17
4.17	(zealously affect)	=	11.2
1.10	('persuade men')	=	5.11

4 C. H. Buck, 'The Date of Galatians', in *JBL* 70 (1951), pp. 113–22. Cf. also C. E. Faw, 'The Anomaly of Galatians', in *Biblical Research* IV (1960), pp. 25ff., who, as Bruce comments, simply 'dotted the i's and crossed the t's of the case made by Bishop Lightfoot and Dr Buck' ('Galatian Problems, 4: the Date of the Epistle', in *BJRL* 54, (1971/72), p. 261). Buck's *magnum opus* (with G. Taylor), *Saint Paul: a Study in the Development of His Thought* (New York, 1969), does not materially carry the argument any further.

5 Art. cit., p. 117.

6 W. L. Knox, noting the more Jewish tone of argument in 1 Corinthians, stated that Galatians 'possesses . . . a claim to consideration . . . as being logically prior to the development of Paul's thought in the Corinthian epistles', though, illogically, he still held that 1 Corinthians and 2 Corinthians were of earlier date! (*St. Paul and the Church of the Gentiles*, p. 96).

7 Op. cit., p. 44.

8 Cf. Galatians 5.10/Romans 4.15, Galatians 5.11/Romans 3.21, Galatians 5.15–18/Romans 4.13, 14, 16.

9 Op. cit., p. 48.

10 It is true that no radical development in Paul's theology can be traced in his epistles (cf. J. Lowe, 'An Examination of Attempts to Detect Development in St. Paul's Theology', in *JTS* 42 (1941), pp. 129–42), and indeed, when we consider that the time from his earliest to his latest epistle was no more than fifteen years at the most, in comparison with almost twenty years of meditation on the gospel before he began his ministry, we would expect him to have been fairly sure about his basic beliefs from the start. But this does not rule out a development of emphasis such as we have suggested here. Quite the opposite is more likely, for when a theology worked out in the study is put to the test of practical performance, alterations to its expression, if not its essence, are almost inevitable.

11 See above, pp. 29ff.

12 See above, pp. 55ff.

13 Cf. 1 Corinthians 7.10ff., Romans 12.14ff. In both contexts, of course, Paul emphasizes that though this kind of ruling moves in a 'law direction', he is not imposing a legalistic norm, for he brings in such precepts on a new and different basis of morality, the indwelling of Christ, which forms the one common denominator of his moral teaching in both Galatians and 1 Corinthians/Romans.

14 Cf. 1 Corinthians 8.9ff., Romans 14.13ff.

Bibliography

Albright, W. F., *History, Archaeology and Christian Humanism*. New York, 1964.

Bacon, B. W., 'Acts versus Galatians: the crux of apostolic history' (*American Journal of Theology* XI, 1907), pp. 454–74.

Baeck, L., *Aus drei Jahrtausenden*. Tübingen, 1958.

Baird, W., 'What is the Kerygma?' (*JBL* 76, 1957), pp. 181–91.

Bandstra, A. J., *The Law and the Elements of the World*. Kampen, 1964.

Barrett, C. K., *From First Adam to Last*. London, 1962.

—, 'Cephas and Corinth' in *Abraham unser Vater: Festschrift für O. Michel*, ed. O. Betz *et al.* (Leiden/Köln, 1963), pp. 1–12.

—, 'Christianity at Corinth' (*BJRL* 46, 1963/64), pp. 269–97.

—, 'Things sacrificed to idols' (*NTS* 11, 1964/65), pp. 138–53.

—, *A Commentary on the First Epistle to the Corinthians*. London, 1968 (*BNTC*).

—, *A Commentary on the Second Epistle to the Corinthians*. London, 1973 (*BNTC*).

—, *The Signs of an Apostle*. London, 1970.

—, 'Paul's opponents in II Corinthians' (*NTS* 17, 1970/71), pp. 233–54.

—, 'Pauline controversies in the post-Pauline period' (*NTS* 20, 1973/74), pp. 229–45.

Bartsch, H. W., (ed.), *Kerygma and Myth*. English translation, New York/London, 1953.

Bauer, W., *Johannesevangelium*. Tübingen, 1925.

—, *Orthodoxy and Heresy in Earliest Christianity*. English translation ed. Kraft, R. A. and Krodel, G., Philadelphia, 1971.

Baur, F. C., *Die christliche Gnosis*. Tübingen, 1835.

—, *Paul*. English translation, London/Edinburgh, 1875 (vol. II) and 1876 (vol. I, 2nd edn).

—, *The Church History of the First Three Centuries*. English translation, London, 1878 (3rd edn).

Betz, H. D., 'Orthodoxy and heresy in primitive Christianity' (*Interpretation* 19, 1965), pp. 299–311.

Bianchi, U. (ed.), *Le Origini dello Gnosticismo*. Leiden, 1967 (Studies in the History of Religions, vol. XII).

Bornkamm, G., *Paul*. English translation, London, 1971.

Bousset, W. *Hauptprobleme der Gnosis*. Göttingen, 1907 (FRLANT 10).

—, *Kyrios Christos*. English translation of fifth German edition (1964), with introductory essay by R. Bultmann, Nashville/New York, 1970.

Brox, N. 'Anathema Iēsous (1 Kor. 12, 3)' (*Biblische Zeitschrift* 12, 1968), pp. 103–11.

Bruce, F. F., *The Acts of the Apostles*. London, 1951.

—, *The Book of the Acts*. London, 1954 (*NIC*).

—, 'When is a gospel not a gospel?' (*BJRL* 45, 1962/63), pp. 319–39.

—, 'Galatian Problems: 3. The "other" Gospel' (*BJRL* 53, 1970/71), pp. 253–71.

—, *1 and 2 Corinthians*. London, 1971 (*NCB*).

—, 'Galatian Problems: 4. The date of the Epistle' (*BJRL* 54, 1971/72), pp. 250–67).

—, 'Galatian Problems: 5. Galatians and Christian Origins' (*BJRL* 55, 1972/73), pp. 264–84.

Buck, C. H., 'The Date of Galatians' (*JBL* 70, 1951), pp. 113–22.

— and Taylor, G., *Saint Paul: a Study of the Development of his Thought*. New York, 1969.

Bultmann, R., *Exegetische Probleme des Zweiten Korintherbriefes*. Uppsala, 1947.

—, *Theology of the New Testament*. English translation, London, 1952 (vol. 1) and 1955 (vol. 2).

—, *Primitive Christianity in its Contemporary Setting*. English translation, London, 1960.

Burton, E. D., *A Critical and Exegetical Commentary on the Epistle to the Galatians*. Edinburgh, 1921 (*ICC*).

Cadbury, H. J., 'Overconversion in Paul's churches' in *The Joy of Study* (Essays presented to F. C. Grant), ed. S. E. Johnson (New York, 1951), pp. 43–50.

Caird, G. B., 'Paul and women's liberty' (*BJRL* 54, 1971/72), pp. 268–81.

Campenhausen, H. von, *Ecclesiastical Authority and Spiritual Power in the Church of the First Three Centuries*. English translation, London, 1969.

Casey, R. P., 'Gnosis, Gnosticism and the New Testament' in *The Background of the New Testament and its Eschatology* (*Festschrift* for C. H. Dodd), ed. W. D. Davies and D. Daube (Cambridge, 1956), pp. 52–80.

Chadwick, H., 'All things to all men' (*NTS* 1, 1954/55), pp. 261–75.

Conzelmann, H., *Der erste Brief an die Korinther*. (*KEK*), Göttingen, 1969.

Conzelmann, H., *An Outline of the Theology of the New Testament*. English translation, London, 1969.

—, *History of Primitive Christianity*, English translation, Nashville/New York, 1973.

Cranfield, C. E. B., 'St Paul and the law' (*SJT* 17, 1964), pp. 43–68.

Crownfield, F. R., 'The singular problem of the dual Galatians' (*JBL* 64, 1945), pp. 491–500.

Cullmann, O., *Le Problème littéraire et historique du roman pseudo-clémentin*. Paris, 1930.

—, *Peter: Disciple, Apostle, Martyr*. English translation, London, 1953.

Dahl, N. A., 'Paul and the church at Corinth in 1 Cor 1:10–4:21' in *Christian History and Interpretation: studies presented to John Knox*, ed. W. R. Farmer *et al.* (Cambridge, 1967), pp. 313–35.

Daniélou, J. *Theology of Jewish Christianity*. English translation, London, 1964.

Davies, W. D., *Paul and Rabbinic Judaism*. London, 1970 (3rd edn).

—, 'Paul and the Dead Sea Scrolls' in *The Scrolls and the New Testament*, ed. K. Stendahl (London, 1958), pp. 157–82.

Dibelius, M. and Kümmel, W. G., *Paul*. English translation, London, 1953.

Dodd, C. H., 'A problem of interpretation' (*Studiorum Novi Testamenti Societas Bulletin* II, 1951), pp. 7–18.

—, *Gospel and Law*. Cambridge, 1951.

Doresse, J., *The Secret Books of the Egyptian Gnostics*. English translation, London, 1960.

Duncan, G. S., *The Epistle of Paul to the Galatians*. London, 1934 (*MC*).

Dungan, D. L., *The Sayings of Jesus in the Churches of Paul*. Oxford, 1971.

Dupont, J., *Gnosis*. Louvain/Paris, 1949.

Ehrhardt, A. A. T., *The Apostolic Succession*. London, 1953.

—, *The Framework of the New Testament Stories*. Manchester, 1964.

Elliott, J. H., 'A Catholic Gospel: reflections on "early catholicism" in the New Testament' (*CBQ* xxxi, 1969), pp. 213–23.

Ellis, E. E., *Paul's Use of the Old Testament*. Edinburgh/London, 1957.

Eltester, W. (ed.), *Christentum und Gnosis*. Berlin, 1969.

Fannon, P., 'The influence of tradition in St. Paul' in *Studia Evangelica IV*, ed. F. L. Cross (Berlin, 1968), pp. 292–307.

Filson, F. V., 'The central problem concerning Christian origins' in *The Study of the Bible Today and Tomorrow*, ed. H. R. Willoughby (Chicago, 1947).

—, *The New Testament against Its Environment*. London, 1950 (Studies in Biblical Theology, no. 3).

Foerster, W., *Gnosis*. English translation, Oxford, 1972 (vol. I) and 1974 (vol. II).

Freeborn, J. C. K., 'The development of doctrine at Corinth' in *Studia Evangelica IV*, pp. 404–10.

Frend, W. H. C., 'The Gospel of Thomas: is rehabilitation possible?' (*JTS* ns. 18, 1967), pp. 13–26.

Friedrich, G., 'Die Gegner des Paulus im 2. Korintherbrief' in *Abraham unser Vater*, pp. 181–215.

Gärtner, B., *The Theology of the Gospel of Thomas*. English translation, London, 1961.

Gasque, W. W., 'The historical value of the book of Acts' (*EQ* XLI, 1969), pp. 68–88.

Georgi, D., *Die Gegner des Paulus im 2. Korintherbrief*. Neukirchen, 1964 (WMANT 11).

Geyser, A. S., 'Paul, the Apostolic Decree and the liberals in Corinth' in *Studia Paulina in honorem Johannis de Zwaan*, ed. J. N. Sevenster and W. C. van Unnik (Haarlem, 1953), pp. 124–38.

Giversen, S., *Apocryphon Johannis*. Copenhagen, 1963 (Acta Theologica Danica V).

Goodenough, E. R., *By Light, Light*. New Haven, 1935.

Grant, R. M. and Freedman, D. N., *The Secret Sayings of Jesus*. London, 1960.

Grant, R. M., *Gnosticism: an anthology*. London, 1961.

—, *Gnosticism and Early Christianity*. New York, 1966 (2nd edn.)

Grobel, K., 'How Gnostic is the Gospel of Thomas?' (*NTS* 8, 1961/62), pp. 367–73.

Grosheide, F. W., *Commentary on the First Epistle to the Corinthians*. Grand Rapids, 1953 (*NIC*).

Gunther, J. J., *St. Paul's Opponents and Their Background*. Leiden, 1973.

Guthrie, D., *Galatians*. London, 1969 (*NCB*).

Haardt, R., 'Erlösung durch Erkenntnis: Probleme und Ergebnisse der Gnosis-Forschung' (*Wort und Wahrheit* 16, 1961), pp. 848–52.

—, *Gnosis: Character and Testimony*. English translation, Leiden, 1971.

Haenchen, E., *Die Botschaft des Thomas-Evangeliums*. Berlin, 1961.

—, *The Acts of the Apostles*. English translation, Oxford, 1971.

Hanson, A. T., *Jesus Christ in the Old Testament*. London, 1965.

—, *Studies in Paul's Technique and Theology*. London, 1974.

Harrington, W. J., 'St. Paul and the status of women' (*Australasian Catholic Record* 50, 1973), pp. 39–50.

Harvey, A. E., 'The opposition to Paul' in *Studia Evangelica IV*, pp. 319–32.

Hawkins, R. M., 'The Galatian Gospel' (*JBL* 59, 1940), pp. 141–6.

Héring, J., *The First Epistle of St. Paul to the Corinthians*. English translation, London, 1962.

—, *The Second Epistle of St. Paul to the Corinthians*. English translation, London, 1967.

Hughes, P. E., *Paul's Second Epistle to the Corinthians*. Grand Rapids, 1962 (*NIC*).

Hurd, J. C., 'Pauline chronology and Pauline theology' in *Christian History and Interpretation*, pp. 225–48.

—, *The Origin of 1 Corinthians*. London, 1965.

Jewett, R., 'The agitators and the Galatian congregation' (*NTS* 17, 1970/71), pp. 198–212.

Jonas, H., *The Gnostic Religion*. Boston, 1963 (2nd edn).

Käsemann, E., *Leib und Leib Christi*. Tübingen, 1933 (Beiträge zur historischen Theologie 9).

—, 'Die Legitimität des Apostels' (*ZNW* 41, 1942), pp. 33–71.

—, *Essays on New Testament Themes*. English translation, London, 1963 (Studies in Biblical Theology 41).

—, *New Testament Questions of Today*. English translation, London, 1969.

—, (ed), *Das Neue Testament als Kanon*. Göttingen, 1970.

Kirk, J. A., 'Apostleship since Rengstorf: towards a synthesis' (*NTS* 21, 1974/75), pp. 249–64.

Knox, W. L., *St. Paul and the Church of Jerusalem*. Cambridge, 1925.

—, *St. Paul and the Church of the Gentiles*. Cambridge, 1939.

Ladd, G. E., 'Revelation and tradition in Paul' in *Apostolic History and the Gospel* (*Festschrift* for F. F. Bruce), ed. W. W. Gasque and R. P. Martin (Exeter, 1970), pp. 223–30.

Laeuchli, S., *The Language of Faith*. London, 1965.

Lake, K., *The Earlier Epistles of St. Paul: their motive and origin*. London, 1911.

Lemaire, A., 'The ministries in the New Testament' (*Biblical Theology Bulletin* III, 1973), pp. 133–66.

Lightfoot, J. B., *St. Paul's Epistle to the Galatians*. London, 1865.

Longenecker, R. N., *Paul, Apostle of Liberty*. New York, 1964.

Lowe, J., 'An examination of attempts to detect development in St. Paul's theology' (*JTS* 42, 1941), pp. 129–42.

Lütgert, W., *Freiheitspredigt und Schwarmgeister in Korinth*. Gütersloh, 1908.

—, *Gesetz und Geist*. Gütersloh, 1919.

MacRae, G. W., 'Anti-Dualist polemic in 2 Cor. 4, 6?' in *Studia Evangelica IV*, pp. 420-31.

—, 'The Jewish background of the Gnostic Sophia myth' (*Nov. Test.* 12, 1970), pp. 86–101.

Manson, T. W., *Studies in the Gospel and Epistles*. Manchester, 1962.

Moffatt, J., *The First Epistle of Paul to the Corinthians*. London, 1938 (*MC*).

Molland, E., 'La circoncision, le baptême, et l'autorité du décret apostolique (Actes xv, 28sq.) dans les milieux judéo-chrétiens des Pseudo-Clémentines' in *Studia Theologica* IX (1955), pp. 1–39.

Munck, J., 'Israel and the Gentiles in the New Testament' (*JTS* ns. 2, 1951), pp. 3–16.

—, *Paul and the Salvation of Mankind*. English translation, London, 1959.

—, 'The New Testament and Gnosticism' in *Current Issues in New Testament Interpretation* (*Festschrift* for O. A. Piper), ed. W. Klassen and G. F. Snyder (London, 1962), pp. 224–38.

Oepke, A., *Der Brief des Paulus an die Galater*. Berlin, 1964 (2nd edn), *THNT* 9.

Oman, J., *Grace and Personality*. Cambridge, 1917.

O'Neill, J. C., *The Recovery of Paul's Letter to the Galatians*. London, 1972.

—, *Paul's Letter to the Romans*. London, 1975.

Pagels, E. H., ' "The mystery of the Resurrection": A Gnostic reading of 1 Corinthians 15' (*JBL* 93, (1974), pp. 276–88.

Pearson, B. A., 'Did the Gnostics curse Jesus?' (*JBL* 86, (1967), pp. 301–5.

—, *The Pneumatikos-Psychikos Terminology in 1 Corinthians: A Study in the Theology of the Corinthian opponents of Paul and its relation to Gnosticism*. Missoula, Montana, 1974 (SBL Dissertation Series no. 12).

Peel, M. L., 'Gnostic eschatology and the New Testament' (*Nov. Test.* 12, 1970), pp. 141–65.

Plummer, A., *A Critical and Exegetical Commentary on the Second Epistle of St. Paul to the Corinthians*. Edinburgh, 1915 (*ICC*).

Prümm, K., *Gnosis an der Werzl des Christentums?*. Salzburg, 1972.

Quispel, G., 'Christliche Gnosis und Judische Heterodoxie' (*Evan. Theol.* 14, 1954), pp. 1–11.

—, 'Gnosticism and the New Testament' in *The Bible in Modern Scholarship*, ed. J. P. Hyatt (London, 1966) pp. 252–71.

Ramsay, W. M., *A Historical Commentary on St. Paul's Epistle to the Galatians*. London, 1899.

—, *St. Paul the Traveller and the Roman Citizen*. London, 1920 (14th edn.).

Reicke, B., 'The Law and this world according to Paul' (*JBL* 70, 1951), pp. 259–76.

Ridderbos, H. N., *The Epistle of Paul to the Churches of Galatia*, Grand Rapids, 1953 (*NIC*).

Robertson, A. and Plummer, A., *A Critical and Exegetical Commentary on the First Epistle of St. Paul to the Corinthians*. Edinburgh, 1911 (*ICC*).

Robinson, J. M., 'Basic shifts in German theology' (*Interpretation* 16, 1962), pp. 76–97.

— and Koester, H., *Trajectories through Early Christianity*. Philadelphia, 1971.

Ropes, J. H., *The Singular Problem of the Epistle to the Galatians*. Cambridge, Mass., 1929 (Harvard Theological Studies XIV).

Schlatter, A., *Die Korinthische Theologie*. Gütersloh, 1914.

—, *Paulus, der Bote Jesu*. Stuttgart, 1934.

Schlier, H., *Der Brief an die Galater*. Göttingen, 1965 (*KEK* 13th edn).

—, *Der Brief an die Epheser*. Düsseldorf, 1968 (6th edn).

Schmithals, W., *Gnosticism in Corinth*. English translation, Nashville/New York, 1971.

—, *Paul and the Gnostics*. English translation, Nashville/New York, 1972.

—, 'Das Verhältnis von Gnosis und Neuen Testament als methodisches Problem' (*NTS* 16, 1970), pp. 373–83.

—, *The Office of Apostle in the Early Church*. English translation, London, 1971.

Schnackenburg, R., 'Apostles before and during Paul's time' in *Apostolic History and the Gospel*, pp. 287–303.

Schoedel, W. R., 'The Rediscovery of Gnosis' (*Interpretation* 16, 1962), pp. 385–401.

Schoeps, H. J., *Theologie und Geschichte des Judenchristentums*. Tübingen, 1949.

—, *Paul*. English translation, London, 1961.

Scholer, D. M., *Nag Hammadi Bibliography, 1948–1969*. Leiden, 1971 (Nag Hammadi Studies, vol. I).

—, 'Bibliographica Gnostica, Supplement I' (*Nov. Test.* 13, 1971), pp. 322–36.

—, 'Bibliographica Gnostica, Supplement II' (*Nov. Test.* 14, 1972), pp. 312–31.

—, 'Bibliographica Gnostica, Supplement III' (*Nov. Test.* 15, 1973), pp. 327–45.

—, 'Bibliographica Gnostica, Supplement IV' (*Nov. Test.* 16, 1974), pp. 316–36.

Soden, H. von, 'Sakrament und Ethik bei Paulus' in *Urchristentum und Geschichte* I (Tübingen, 1951), pp. 239–75.

Story, G. L., *The Valentinian (Gnostic) Use of the Letters of Paul*. Unpublished Ph.D. dissertation, Northwestern University (U.S.A.), 1968.

Talbert, C. H., *Luke and the Gnostics*. Nashville/New York, 1966.
Turner, H. E. W., *The Pattern of Christian Truth*. London, 1954.
Tyson, J. B., '"Works of Law" in Galatians' (*JBL* 92, 1973), pp. 423–31.
Whiteley, D. E. H., *The Theology of St. Paul*. Oxford, 1964.
Wilckens, U., *Weisheit und Torheit*. Tübingen, 1959.
Wilson, J. H., 'The Corinthians who say there is no resurrection of the dead' (*ZNW* 59, 1968), pp. 90–107.
Wilson, R. McL., *The Gnostic Problem*. London, 1958.
—, *Gnosis and the New Testament*. Oxford, 1968.
'Gnostics—in Galatia?' in *Studia Evangelica IV*, pp. 358–67.
Wintermute, O., 'A study of Gnostic exegesis of the Old Testament' in *The Use of the Old Testament in the New and Other Essays* (Essays in honour of W. F. Stinespring), ed. J. M. Efird (Durham, N.C., 1972), pp. 241–70.
Yamauchi, E. M., *Pre-Christian Gnosticism*. London, 1973.

Index of Names and Subjects

Index of References

5 *Early Christian Writings*